T0393988

THE ASTROLOGICAL WORLD OF JUNG'S *LIBER NOVUS*

C.G. Jung's *The Red Book: Liber Novus*, published posthumously in 2009, explores Jung's own journey from an inner state of alienation and depression to the restoration of his soul, as well as offering a prophetic narrative of the collective human psyche as it journeys from unconsciousness to a greater awareness of its own inner dichotomy of good and evil. Jung utilised astrological symbols throughout to help him comprehend the personal as well as universal meanings of his visions.

In *The Astrological World of Jung's* Liber Novus, Liz Greene explores the planetary journey Jung portrayed in this remarkable work and investigates the ways in which he used astrological images and themes as an interpretive lens to help him understand the nature of his visions and the deeper psychological meaning behind them. Greene's analysis includes a number of mythic and archetypal elements, including the stories of Salome, Siegfried and Elijah, and demonstrates that astrology, as Jung understood and worked with it, is unquestionably one of the most important foundation stones of analytical psychology, and an essential part of understanding his legacy.

This unique study will appeal to analytical psychologists and Jungian psychotherapists, students and academics of Jungian and post-Jungian theory, the history of psychology, archetypal thought, mythology and folklore, the history of New Age movements, esotericism and psychological astrology.

Liz Greene is a Jungian analyst and professional astrologer who received her Diploma in Analytical Psychology from the Association of Jungian Analysts in London in 1980. She holds doctorates in both Psychology and History, and worked for a number of years as a tutor in the MA in Cultural Astronomy and Astrology at the University of Wales, Lampeter. She is the author of a number of books, some scholarly and some interpretive, on the relationships between psychology and astrology, Tarot, Kabbalah, and myth, and of *Jung's Studies in Astrology* (Routledge).

And as I was ascending the fourth step, I saw, to the east, one approaching, holding a sword in his hand. And another [came] behind him, bringing one adorned round about with signs, clad in white and comely to see, who was named the Meridian of the Sun. And as they drew near to the place of punishments, he who held the sword in his hand [said]: 'Cut off his head, immolate his body, and cut his flesh into pieces, that it may first be boiled according to the method, and then delivered to the place of punishments'. Thereupon I awoke and said: 'I have well understood, this concerns the liquids in the art of the metals'. And he who bore the sword in his hand said again: 'You have completed the descent of the seven steps'.[1]

—Zosimos

Astrologically . . . this process [alchemy] corresponds to an ascent through the planets from the dark, cold, distant Saturn to the sun . . . The ascent through the planetary spheres therefore meant something like a shedding of the characterological qualities indicated by the horoscope . . . The journey through the planetary houses, like the crossing of the great halls of the Egyptian underworld, therefore signifies the overcoming of a psychic obstacle, or of an autonomous complex, suitably represented by a planetary god or demon. Anyone who has passed through all the spheres is free from compulsion; he has won the crown of victory and become like a god.[2]

—C. G. Jung

Notes

1 Zosimos, *The Visions of Zosimos*, III.v, trans. A.S.B. Glover, from the French translation by C.E. Ruelle in Marcellin Berthelot, *Collection des anciens alchimistes grecs*, 3 volumes (Paris: G. Steinheil, 1887–88), pp. 117–42. This translation appears in the English translation of Jung, CW13, ¶85–87. For the German version of CW13, Jung translated Ruelle's French into German himself.

2 Jung, CW14, ¶308.

THE ASTROLOGICAL WORLD OF JUNG'S *LIBER NOVUS*

Daimons, Gods, and the Planetary Journey

Liz Greene

Routledge
Taylor & Francis Group

LONDON AND NEW YORK

First published 2018
by Routledge
2 Park Square, Milton Park, Abingdon, Oxon OX14 4RN

and by Routledge
711 Third Avenue, New York, NY 10017

Routledge is an imprint of the Taylor & Francis Group, an informa business

British Library Cataloguing-in-Publication Data
A catalogue record for this book is available from the British Library

Library of Congress Cataloging-in-Publication Data
Names: Greene, Liz, author.
Title: The astrological world of Jung's *Liber Novus*: daimons, gods, and
    the planetary journey / Liz Greene.
Description: Abingdon, Oxon ; New York, NY : Routledge, 2018. |
    Includes bibliographical references.
Identifiers: LCCN 2017041506 (print) | LCCN 2017049778 (ebook) |
    ISBN 9781315267333 (Master e-book) | ISBN 9781138289161
    (hardback) | ISBN 9781138289178 (pbk.)
Subjects: LCSH: Jung, C. G. (Carl Gustav), 1875–1961. *Liber novus.* |
    Astrology and psychology.
Classification: LCC BF109.J8 (ebook) | LCC BF109.J8 G74 2018 (print) |
    DDC 150.19/54—dc23
LC record available at https://lccn.loc.gov/2017041506

ISBN: 978-1-138-28916-1 (hbk)
ISBN: 978-1-138-28917-8 (pbk)
ISBN: 978-1-315-26733-3 (ebk)

Typeset in Bembo
by Apex CoVantage, LLC

CONTENTS

IMAGES

Figures

Plates

A NOTE ON REFERENCES

The works of C.G. Jung cited in the text are referenced in the endnotes by the number of the volume in *The Collected Works of C.G. Jung*, followed by the paragraph number. For example: Jung, CW13, ¶82–84. Full publishing information is given in the Bibliography. Cited works by Jung not included in the *Collected Works* are referenced in the endnotes by the main title, volume if applicable, and page number, with full publication details given in the Bibliography. For example: Jung, *Visions Seminars* I:23. Jung's autobiography, *Memories, Dreams, Reflections*, is referenced in the endnotes as *MDR*, with full publication details given in the Bibliography.

The works of Plato and other ancient authors cited in the text in an English translation are given in the endnotes according to the title of the work and its standard paragraph reference, with full references including translation and publication information given in the Bibliography. For example, Plato, *Symposium*, 52a–56c; Iamblichus, *De mysteriis*, I.21.

When a cited work has a lengthy subtitle, only the main title is given in the endnotes along with publication details and page reference, but the full title is given in the Bibliography.

ACKNOWLEDGEMENTS

I would like to offer my grateful thanks to Professor Sonu Shamdasani for his careful perusal of the manuscript, and the support and helpful suggestions he offered throughout. I would also like to thank Andreas Jung and his wife Vreni for giving me their kind permission to examine the material in Jung's private archives and files of personal papers, and for their interest in and support of the writing of this book.

INTRODUCTION

Close encounters of the daimonic kind

> They [the daimons] are the envoys and interpreters that ply between heaven and earth, flying upward with our worship and our prayers, and descending with the heavenly answers and commandments ... They form the medium of the prophetic arts, of the priestly rites of sacrifice, initiation, and incantation, of divination and of sorcery, for the divine will not mingle directly with the human, and it is only through the mediation of the spirit world that man can have any intercourse, whether waking or sleeping, with the gods. And the man who is versed in such matters is said to have spiritual powers.[1]
>
> —Plato

> What I call coming to terms with the unconscious the alchemists called 'meditation'. Ruland says of this: 'Meditation: The name of an Internal Talk of one person with another who is invisible, as in the invocation of the Deity, or communion with one's self, or with one's good angel'. This somewhat optimistic definition must immediately be qualified by a reference to the adept's relations with his *spiritus familiaris*, who we can only hope was a good one.[2]
>
> —C.G. Jung

In the autumn of 2009, a new work by C.G. Jung, titled *The Red Book: Liber Novus*, was posthumously published in a beautiful hardback edition, with the original calligraphic text and paintings impeccably reproduced along with a translation, appendices, and voluminous notes.[3] Close to the time of his death in 1961, Jung emphasised the crucial importance of the period of his life when he was engaged in creating *Liber Novus*:

> The years when I was pursuing my inner images were the most important in my life – in them everything essential was decided. It all began then; the

later details are only supplements and clarifications of the material that burst forth from the unconscious, and at first swamped me. It was the *prima materia* for a lifetime's work.[4]

Liber Novus, known as *The Red Book* because of its red leather binding, was Jung's careful revision of a series of private diaries, known as the *Black Books*. He worked continuously on the material from 1913 – the time of his public break with Freud – to 1932. Virtually every page of the work contains a meticulously executed painted image, and the calligraphic writing, mimicking a medieval manuscript complete with illuminated letters at the start of each section, is itself a remarkable piece of craftsmanship. The dominant narrative of *Liber Novus* is Jung's journey from an inner state of alienation and depression to the restoration of his soul, through the long and painful process of integrating a seemingly irreconcilable conflict within his own nature: the dichotomy between reason and revelation, outer and inner worlds, facts and prophecies, and between the scientist and the visionary, both of whom he experienced as authentic, demanding, and mutually exclusive dimensions of his own being. But the resolution of Jung's personal conflict is only one dimension of the work. *Liber Novus* is also a prophetic narrative of the collective human psyche as it journeys from unconsciousness to a greater awareness of its own inner dichotomy of good and evil, on the eve of the passage from one great astrological Aion, that of Pisces, into the next, that of Aquarius.

During the period of his life when Jung was creating this extraordinary visionary work, he was deeply engaged in the study of a number of religious currents from antiquity. The extant literature generated by these currents – Gnostic, Hermetic, Platonic and Neoplatonic, Jewish, Orphic, Stoic, Mithraic – hint at or directly describe a cosmos symbolised by, and infused with, celestial patterns reflecting what was understood as *Heimarmene*: the astral compulsions that constitute fate. Jung referred to this ancient concept of fate frequently in his work, and he was also thoroughly immersed in the study of astrology, although this crucial dimension of his work is rarely discussed in the existing biographical literature.[5] Inspired in part by the ritual practices described in late antique religious texts as a means of individual transformation, Jung began to formulate a psychotherapeutic technique that he later called 'active imagination'. This approach to the unconscious, which Jung preferred to articulate in psychological rather than religious language, appropriated methods systematically developed and described by the Neoplatonic philosopher-magicians of late antiquity, who were themselves well-versed in astrological lore. Although psychological terminology may be more appropriate for modernity, active imagination is virtually indistinguishable from what these older authors referred to as theurgy: 'god-work', or ritual practices facilitating a transformative encounter between the human soul and the realm of the divine through the medium of the imagination.

The visions of the *Black Books* were the concrete fruits of Jung's experiments in this liminal magico-psychological realm. His introduction to, and immersion in, astrological studies, as well as his development of the technique of active imagination, are discussed in depth in my book *Jung's Studies in Astrology*. His involvement with astrology and its concomitant philosophical, religious, and theurgic currents appears to have helped him to contain, understand, and integrate the 'teeming chaos' of the visions he experienced and transcribed, first in the *Black Books* and then in the final, polished form he called *Liber Novus*.[6] Jung's astrology was utilised in a number of ways: as a tool to ascertain innate psychological structures or 'complexes' and their archetypal roots within the individual and the collective; as a method of shedding light on other symbolic systems such as alchemy and Tarot; and as a form of hermeneutics to help him interpret his visions and relate them to both his own horoscope and the imminent psychological and religious changes in the collective psyche that he continued to anticipate with trepidation from the first decades of the twentieth century to the time of his death in 1961. Astrology also seems to have contributed inestimably to the formulation of his most important psychological theories: the archetypes, the psychological types, the complexes, and the process of individuation, which he believed could lead to an eventual integration of the whole personality.

Jung attributed the ideas behind all his later work to the period during which he worked on *Liber Novus*. Given the importance that astrology held for him, then and throughout his life, it is vital that some understanding of Jung's immersion in this liminal sphere of study and practice is included in any assessment of his life and work. The sources from which Jung drew his astrological knowledge, the religious and philosophical texts that he absorbed and cited in his letters, papers, and early publications as well as in the *Collected Works*, and the evidence of the depth of his involvement provided by the large collection of astrological works in his library and the astrological documents and horoscopes in his private archives, are covered in detail in *Jung's Studies in Astrology*. *Liber Novus* provides another and equally illuminating route into the ways in which Jung used his knowledge of astrology – particularly the mythic and symbolic dimensions – to structure, understand, and articulate the chaotic visionary material he recorded in the *Black Books*. *The Astrological World of Jung's* Liber Novus is an exploration of the planetary journey Jung portrayed in his remarkable work, and an investigation into the ways in which he utilised astrological images, many of them reflecting ancient theurgic and religious contexts, as an interpretive lens that could provide a symbolic framework within which the final polishing, honing, and illustrating of *Liber Novus* could be achieved.

Liber Novus is not an astrological textbook. There are no overt delineations of zodiacal signs, no direct references to planetary configurations, and no recognisable horoscopic interpretations. These, I have argued throughout this book, are all amply present in *Liber Novus*, but not in the 'cookbook' form that astrological students so often rely on as they learn to interpret horoscopes. Nor is *Liber Novus* an intellectually constructed, thinly disguised portrayal of the archetypal planetary journey of the soul that interested Jung so deeply in the Gnostic, Neoplatonic, and Hermetic literature of antiquity and the alchemical and literary works of the medieval and early modern periods, and which he equated with the individuation process. There *is* a planetary journey in *Liber Novus*, but it is intensely personal and follows no recognisable order of steps or stages. It more closely resembles a Wagnerian opera with dashes of Mozart's *Magic Flute* thrown in, using an enormous range of musical instruments and a repetitive current of specific *leitmotifs* that weave a complex work impossible to reduce to any single tune. It is unlikely that Jung set about intending to create any kind of deliberate planetary structure in *Liber Novus*; rather, it seems, from his own descriptions, that the planetary daimons relevant to his natal horoscope pursued him, clothed in the garments of the inner conflicts of his personal life.

Despite the deeply personal nature of *Liber Novus*, Jung also recognised the universality as well as the intensely individual dimension of his visions, associating them with the kind of creative outpouring he believed to emerge from the artist when primordial experiences 'rend from top to bottom the curtain upon which is painted the picture of an ordered world'.[7] *Liber Novus* presents a celestial soul-journey enacted through a cast of characters who are both celestial and earthy, and it describes encounters with what, in the late antique world, would have been understood as planetary daimons or planetary gods. *Liber Novus* reflects Jung's own journey from fragmentation – 'my soul having flown away from me'[8] – to unity, and from the strictures of a determined and lopsided scientific rationality to what he understood as a rediscovery of the completeness of his full nature. It is a work full of pain, crises, despair, and hopeful vision, reflecting in different ways and on different levels the profound internal suffering of a man who was both a clear and rational thinker and a poetic visionary, and who could not, for many decades, find a way of reconciling these opposites within himself.

Liber Novus is also a magical work. I have described this dimension of the book in detail in *Jung's Studies in Astrology*. Rachel Elior, a scholar of late antique Jewish esoteric literature, describes magic as those ritual practices specifically concerned with developing and maintaining 'the system of bonds and relationships between the revealed and concealed worlds'.[9] By Jung's own admission, this development and maintenance of bonds and relationships between revealed consciousness and the unrevealed unconscious was his primary concern, although for obvious reasons he preferred to use psychological language to describe it. Suggesting that active imagination is a theurgic ritual is not likely to appeal to today's more scientifically inclined segments of the psychological community, and not even within the apparently more open-minded world of analytical psychology; and it would hardly have won Jung applause in the psychiatric milieu in which he worked in the early decades of the twentieth century. It was through friends such as the Theosophist G.R.S. Mead and the astrologer John M. Thorburn, whom I have discussed at length in *Jung's Studies in Astrology*, that he found the kind of intellectual support he needed for his forays into the liminal world.

Jung was willing to explore any approach to the human psyche that yielded knowledge and helpful results, including the apparently disreputable worlds of astrology, magic, spiritualism, Theosophy, and ancient mystery cults. He drew on a large number of late antique and medieval works of magic and theurgy, and utilised ritual and its attendant symbols to invoke and explore his visions, always understanding these approaches as tools or techniques, and always pursuing that psychological goal of wholeness or integration that he defined as the Self. The text and paintings of *Liber Novus* are replete with what the Neoplatonists referred to as *sunthemata*: those symbols that were believed to be the 'tokens' of a divine essence that the planetary gods themselves had embedded in manifest reality, and through which, utilising the instrument of the imagination as a bridge between human and divine, the individual could safely approach the eternal realm of what Jung understood as the archetypes. These *sunthemata* are not only magical; they are also astrological, in keeping with the ancient idea of cosmic sympathies that Jung later defined as 'synchronicity'.

Jung was also not averse to learning whatever he could about the deeper levels of the psyche from the increasing interest in ritual magic that was burgeoning in the world around him in the early decades of the twentieth century, particularly those currents connected with the British 'occult revival' and its practitioners. G.R.S. Mead wrote extensively, not only about older ritual practices in Gnostic, Orphic, Hermetic, and Mithraic contexts, but also about the magical work emerging in his own Theosophical milieu. Various works by members of occult societies such as the Hermetic Order of the Golden Dawn provided further insights into the use of ritual for the generation of altered states of consciousness. The writings of the more notorious British magicians of the late nineteenth and early twentieth centuries – Samuel Liddell MacGregor Mathers, Aleister Crowley, Dion Fortune – do not appear in Jung's library, although this does not necessarily mean he was unfamiliar with them, particularly since he acquired the works of other members of the Golden Dawn and its offshoots, such as Arthur Machen, A.E. Waite, and Algernon Blackwood. But Dion Fortune, who was herself strongly influenced by Jung's early publications in English, expressed ideas about the purposes of ritual magic that might have come, with only slight alterations in a more neutral terminology, from the pen of Jung himself:

> The racial past lives on in the subconscious mind of each of us . . . but it can be evoked to visible appearance in a manner which no orthodox psychologist is acquainted with. It is this evocation of the racial past which is the key to certain forms of ceremonial magic which have as their aim the evocation of Principalities and Powers.[10]

Jung did not believe, as many sociologists do today, that symbols are social constructs. Like the Neoplatonists and, closer to his own time, the German Romantic writers, he perceived symbols as 'encountered' or 'discovered', rather than generated by human activity to provide a form of social cohesion. For Jung, symbols were pregnant with an intrinsic ontological meaning, independent of culture or historical epoch; and astrological images, like those of alchemy, could therefore serve as imaginal intermediaries between consciousness and the unconscious as effectively today as they did in antiquity. Astrological images abound in *Liber Novus*, not only in the characters themselves, but also in the landscapes in which Jung encounters them. It seems that, like his Neoplatonic predecessors, Jung also understood the evocative application of symbols in the service of enlarging consciousness as a viable tool to facilitate the breaking the chains of astral fate:

> To the same degree . . . that individuation implies autonomy, this 'compulsion' of the complexes and the stars falls away.[11]

Jung did not pursue this 'autonomy', for himself or for his patients, solely in order to achieve personal power, success, and worldly happiness, although, being human, no doubt such motives helped to fuel his efforts. But he viewed the process of individuation as a way of working with the unconscious compulsions symbolised by the natal horoscope in order to live more creatively its innate patterns and the complete individual it portrays. In order to achieve this, he seems to have placed great emphasis on developing the maximum possible cooperation with what the Neoplatonists understood as the personal daimon or 'Master of the House', whom Jung, in *Liber Novus*, called his 'psychagogue', Philemon.

The raw material for the three parts of *Liber Novus* was written between 1913 and 1916, and this 'enigmatic stream' was then revised and reshaped over a period of nearly twenty years.[12] The initial outpouring was genuinely spontaneous, although it was clearly impregnated, albeit unintentionally, with themes and images from the many mythological, philosophical, and astrological texts Jung had been reading. However, although the visions were spontaneous, the practical procedure of 'exercises in the emptying of consciousness', to allow the images to constellate and develop, was intentional.[13] The first spontaneous 'layer' of *Liber Novus* seems to have lacked any deliberate inclusion of specific astrological symbolism or, for that matter, any intellectual reflection on the psychological meaning of the visions.[14] They were simply recorded as they emerged. The more self-conscious aspects of the work, forming a kind of second 'layer', developed from 1916 onward, and it is here that specific astrological themes and *sunthemata* began to appear in a more constructed fashion, along with reflections on the psychological dimension of the visions.

Astrologically meaningful allusions involving Sun and Moon, as well as zodiacally significant creatures such as the lion, can be discerned in the primary, spontaneous 'layer' of *Liber Novus*. But Sun, Moon, and animals such as lions and bulls are not limited to zodiacal associations; viewed as symbols, they reflect a vast repository of meanings and connections to which astrology provides only one, albeit extremely rich and dynamic, point of entry. Although Jung was convinced that astrological cycles provided the basis for the earliest myths, and that astrology was 'indispensable for a proper understanding of mythology',[15] it is unhelpful, and contrary to Jung's own way of thinking, to assume that the only valid method of approaching myth's manifold meanings is through astrological symbolism. Moreover, as Jung was already steeped in astrology from 1911 onward, the appearance of astrologically relevant material in the spontaneous layer of *Liber Novus* is no more surprising or contrived than if an astrological motif had appeared in a dream, since the basic analytic approach to dreams – and Jung understood his visions as 'waking dreams' – assumes that they use the stuff of the individual's everyday personal life, including his or her spheres of intellectual interest, to clothe their deeper meaning.

The deliberate inclusion of precise astrological symbols surrounding particular characters seems to be related to Jung's use of astrology as a form of hermeneutics in the second 'layer' of *Liber Novus*. Jung understood hermeneutics as a method of

> Adding more analogies to that already given by the symbol . . . The initial symbol is much enlarged and enriched by this procedure, the result being a highly complex and many-sided picture.[16]

Astrological symbols, used as a means of 'adding more analogies' to his visions, helped Jung to make psychological sense of them and connect them, not only to the patterns of his birth horoscope, but also to the larger cycles of the collective, such as the astrological Aions and their concomitant changes in religious representations. In fact, *Liber Novus* begins with a painting depicting the movement of the equinoctial point from the constellation of Pisces into that of Aquarius, the symbolic celestial reflection of an imminent changing of the Aions;[17] Jung seems to have perceived his personal journey within the context of a greater collective journey that was about to arrive at what he understood as a dangerous crisis point. That Jung utilised astrological *sunthemata* in a form of theurgic work with the figures in *Liber Novus* is not mutually exclusive with his use of astrology as a hermeneutic tool to help him comprehend the personal as well as universal meanings of his visions, or, at the same time, as a method of understanding his own as well as his patients' psychic compulsions through the patterns of the birth horoscope. It is a reflection of the depth and extent of his astrological understanding that he was able to encompass the magical, symbolic, technical, psychological, and characterological dimensions of astrological symbolism without needing to restrict astrology to one 'right' or 'true' approach.

Although many of the figures in *Liber Novus* are identified by a name or appellation related to a mythic narrative, they were, at least by the time Jung began developing the second 'layer', understood by him to be aspects of his own psyche as well as archetypal dominants. When he wished to refer to his ego-consciousness or everyday self in the text, he referred to this self as 'I'. Some of the figures are minor supporting actors in the drama, while others play more dominant roles. Not all are given a visual description or illustrated by an image. Following is a list of the major *dramatis personae*, in the order of their appearance:[18]

1 Jung's Soul	12 The Librarian
2 The Spirit of the Depths	13 The Cook
3 Siegfried the Hero	14 Ezechiel the Anabaptist
4 Elijah	15 The Professor
5 Salome	16 The Superintendent
6 The Red One	17 The Fool
7 The Old Scholar	18 Phanes
8 The Scholar's Daughter	19 Philemon
9 The Tramp	20 The Serpent
10 The Anchorite Ammonius	21 The Hunchback
11 Izdubar/the Sun	22 Satan

Although this specific number of figures may seem peculiarly relevant to scholars of Kabbalah or practitioners of the Tarot – there are twenty-two letters in the Hebrew alphabet, and twenty-two Major Arcana in the Tarot deck – the list of figures can easily be expanded, as there are other characters who appear briefly and then vanish without any direct encounter. In Book One of *Liber Novus*, for example, there is mention of a Scarab as well as a Youth, a Killed Man, and the Spirit of the Time. These figures are noted as part of a particular vision, but Jung engages in no dialogue with them. However, the relative brevity of the appearances of many of the figures is not necessarily a measure of their importance to Jung himself. Parallels between the figures, the painted images, and various symbolic systems apart from astrology, such as the Tarot and the Kabbalah, can be found in *Liber Novus*. Jung's painting of the unmistakably lunar 'veiled woman', for example, bears many similarities to A.E. Waite's image of the High Priestess of the Major Arcana of the Tarot, as well as to the Kabbalistic *Shekhinah*, who mirrors all the divine potencies – the ten *sefirot* – through the manifestations of Nature.[19]

These recognisable resonances with a number of symbolic systems are unlikely to be coincidental, as most belong to the second 'layer' of the work. Sonu Shamdasani has commented that the impact of Jung's mythological studies is clearly evident in *Liber Novus*, and many of the images and ideas expressed in the work 'derive directly from his readings'.[20] The same may be said of the astrological, Kabbalistic, and Tarot motifs that appear in relation to the figures. From Jung's own perspective, these parallels were relevant because the mythic human soul-journey – portrayed in different ways by the Major Arcana of the Tarot, the 'paths' of the twenty-two Hebrew letters connecting the ten *sefirot* of the Kabbalistic Tree, the stages of the alchemical *opus*, and the soul's ascent through the planetary spheres – is an imaginal expression of that archetypal interior process of development that Jung later called individuation, clothed in forms appropriate for particular cultural contexts at particular epochs of history.

In a review of *Liber Novus* written soon after its publication in October 2009, the American analytical psychologist Murray Stein suggested that an '*Agon*' (from the Greek αγων, a 'contest') forms the core of *Liber Novus*: 'Jung is wrestling with angels, light and dark', and each figure 'represents an aspect of Jung's psyche'.[21] The interior, subjective dimension of these figures is inarguable – they are, after all, imaginal expressions of the psyche of one individual. But the more universal aspects of these beings are equally relevant, particularly in the context of Jung's deep involvement with late antique Gnostic, Hermetic, Orphic, Jewish, Mithraic, and Neoplatonic sources during the period he worked on *Liber Novus*. Jung understood these figures to be cosmological as well as personal, although he tended to use the term 'archetypal' to describe them. This apparent paradox of a simultaneously deeply individual yet universal pattern lies at the basis of Jung's understanding of the archetypes.

There is no reason to question the fact that the characters of *Liber Novus* were initially spontaneous or deliberately invoked fantasies that were allowed to develop in their own way, rather than beginning their lives as calculated conscious constructions.[22] Between 1913 and 1916, it seems that Jung was, in the language of the Neoplatonists, in the grip of a powerful daimon who demanded both images and words to make its voice heard. Jung's deeply disturbing experience of writing *Septem sermones ad mortuos* – Book Three of *Liber Novus*, which he later titled 'Scrutinies' – is testimony to just how ferocious a grip that daimon exercised.[23] But he continued to refine and shape the images until 1932, as well as honing the text and presenting it in calligraphic form for the final product he called *Liber Novus*. The care and detail with which he adorned his paintings with meaningful symbols created a fertile marriage between revelatory states and the deliberate conscious insertion of motifs significant not only to Jung personally, but also to those familiar with the lineage of these symbols through their historical unfoldment. Jung seems to have been fully aware of what he was trying to achieve with *Liber Novus*. In 1922, while he was still working on the text and images, he gave a lecture to the Society for German Language and Literature in Zürich on the subject of analytical psychology and its relation to poetry, and offered his views on the creative process:[24]

> The creative process, so far as we are able to follow it at all, consists in the unconscious activation of an archetypal image, and in elaborating and shaping this image into the finished work. By giving it shape, the artist translates it into the language of the present, and so makes it possible for us to find our way back to the deepest springs of life.[25]

The images may be interpreted in many ways and through a number of symbolic and psychological frameworks, and it appears that Jung used these various frameworks himself to bring clarity to the material. The following chapters are an exploration of Jung's use of astrology to amplify the raw images of *Liber Novus*. But they are not meant to demonstrate that only astrological symbolism is relevant to the work; Jung's understanding of astrology was inclusive rather than exclusive, and embraced many related mythic and mantic approaches. Like dreams or the subtleties of Kabbalistic texts, *Liber Novus* will undoubtedly continue to be an inspiration for a variety of hermeneutical approaches by analytical psychologists, historians, astrologers, and magicians. But the astrological attributes of many of the figures are recognisable to anyone acquainted with astrology's history, language, and symbolism, and it seems that Jung deliberately inserted these attributes as he slowly refined his work. He 'recognised' the planetary figures when they emerged, and later gave them traditional symbolic attributes in keeping with their nature.

Jung was entirely capable of producing the kind of characterological descriptions found in the astrological textbooks of his time, and many of the figures in *Liber Novus* display temperamental qualities immediately recognisable in works by astrologers such as Alan Leo, whose books were of immense importance for Jung's study of astrology. The figure of The Red One, for example, is portrayed by Jung as cynical, critical, provocative, and inclined to argue about religious matters, and this is precisely what Alan Leo had to say about the planet Mars placed in the zodiacal sign of Sagittarius, as it was in Jung's natal horoscope.[26] But beyond this kind of characterological analysis, Jung's method of amplifying symbols through other symbols, which he regularly applied to the dream material of his patients,[27] is also evident in his astrological interpretations. By relating a planet or zodiacal sign to mythic images and stories, he transformed the astrological significator into a dynamic narrative revealing the core of an archetypal potency, with its intrinsic teleology and its multiple possibilities of expression.

It would appear that Jung deliberately avoided presenting the cast of characters in *Liber Novus* through direct astrological statements about the planets and their meanings. He was inclined to conceal explicit astrological references beneath a cloak of related symbols that revealed the same meaning but linked astrology to a broader mythic framework. This allowed his paintings greater aesthetic fluency and, perhaps equally important to him, provided some protection against the criticism of his colleagues. In the cosmological map he called *Systema Munditotius*, for example, discussed in greater detail below in Chapter 7, the seven 'star-gods', designated by their traditional astrological glyphs in his original drawing in the *Black Books*, were represented as a group in the polished final painting by the *menorah* or seven-armed candelabrum, which the Alexandrian Jewish Platonic philosopher Philo explicitly described in the first century CE as a symbol of the planetary system:

> And from this candlestick there proceeded six branches, three on each side, projecting from the candlestick in the centre, so as altogether to complete the number of seven . . . being symbols of those seven stars which are called planets by those men who are versed in natural philosophy.[28]

Jung was familiar with Philo's writings and knew precisely what he was doing when he inserted the menorah into his painting. He was also familiar with the work of the astrologer Max Heindel, who explicitly equated the 'Seven Spirits before the Throne' with the 'Seven-Branched Candlestick' of the Jewish Tabernacle and the 'seven lightgivers or planets'.[29] For those unfamiliar with the planetary relevance of these celestial 'Spirits', however, the seven-armed candelabrum bears no astrological significance, and is either a traditional symbol of Judaism or simply something that provides light.

In *Liber Novus*, some of the planets do not seem to be clearly represented by a single character, but display their traditional attributes through several different figures; other planets do not appear to be present at all. Some of the characters combine the symbolism of more than one planet; some, such as the Hunchback – 'a plain, ugly man with a contorted face' who has poisoned his parents and his wife 'to honor God'[30] – do not have any recognisable astrological connections at all, but appear to have a greater affinity with one or another of the Major Arcana of the Tarot. Jung's Hunchback is 'a hanged man' who may be in Hell but has not encountered the devil. He could have a relationship to the Major Arcana card of the Hanged Man – Jung's interest in the Tarot is amply supported by his perception of the cards as a portrayal of the archetypal soul-journey[31] – despite the fact that A.E. Waite, whose Tarot deck Jung seems to have favoured, declared that the card of the Hanged Man is concerned with 'the sacred Mystery of Death' and the 'glorious Mystery of Resurrection', a far loftier description than Jung's portrayal of a foolish and well-meaning but unintentionally destructive and self-destructive individual.[32] The names of the seven traditional planets are never mentioned in *Liber Novus*, with the exception of Sun and Moon. However, the visual attributes, personalities, and landscape settings of figures such as The Red One, Salome, Izdubar, and Philemon reveal specific astrological associations that can be found in the modern astrological texts Jung was reading at the time, as well as in older works such as Ptolemy's *Tetrabiblos*, with which Jung was familiar. Any effort at interpreting the astrology of *Liber Novus* requires a multifaceted approach, rather than a search for obvious parallels.[33]

Astrologers hoping that the order of the figures whom Jung met will prove to reflect the traditional order of the planets in terms of their distance from the Earth — Moon, Mercury, Venus, Sun, Mars, Jupiter, Saturn — will be disappointed to find that Jung's imaginal encounters do not adhere to any conventional astrological scheme. The order of his meetings with these figures seems to reflect a highly individual and spontaneous process of psychological confrontation moving toward an eventual goal of integration, later amplified through the hermeneutics of a symbolic planetary journey unique to the individual experiencing it, rather than a constructed sequence of universal stages or processes. The context is not that of technical horoscopic analysis, unless the horoscope is seen — as Jung himself saw it — as the symbolic map of a dynamic process beginning with the qualities of time reflected in the moment of birth, and unfolding its meaning in a labyrinthine pattern over the course of a lifetime. But if Jung's gradual refining of *Liber Novus* reflects the intentional interpolation of astrological symbols representing his own highly individual planetary soul-journey, his disregard for the traditional planetary order has earlier precedents, especially the celestial ascent narratives of the Gnostics and the Mithraic initiates, with which he became deeply familiar during the time of writing *Liber Novus*. The highly subjective nature of these late antique narratives reflects not only specific cultural elements, but also the particular predisposition of the individual or group of individuals producing the narrative.[34] Henry Corbin (1903–1978), a renowned scholar of Islamic esotericism whose work was strongly influenced by Jung, commented that the cosmic 'dramaturgy' of the celestial ascent as portrayed in late antique and medieval texts is completely unrelated to any 'prescientific' astronomical explanation of the cosmos; it is a mode of comprehension that both transcends and precedes such external perceptions.[35] This might also be said of the soul-journey of *Liber Novus*. Because there is no recognised planetary or zodiacal order in which the figures in *Liber Novus* emerge, and because single planetary themes are often developed through more than one figure, the explorations in the following chapters of this book are also not arranged in any traditional order, but focus on particular characters and their relationships to other characters, and to Jung himself, in terms of the importance they seem to hold in the overall narrative.

The figures of *Liber Novus* are incorrigibly mutable, as befits living psychic entities. Some of them enjoy a series of incarnations in various guises, and they cross and recross each other's paths and, at certain moments in the narrative, become virtually indistinguishable from one another. Although there are many more figures in *Liber Novus* than there are planets, some are not as different from each other as they might seem. The figure of Elijah, for example, who appears early in Book One of *Liber Novus*, eventually emerges as Philemon, as Jung himself later noted,[36] and absorbs and transforms elements of the figures of the Old Scholar, the Librarian, and the solitary Anchorite, Ammonius, *en route*. All these *personae* present multiple aspects, dark and light, of the *senex* or 'old man', who, as Jung acknowledged, is invariably identified in alchemical iconography with the planetary god Saturn.[37] The giant Izdubar, who initially appears to Jung as a solar hero modelled after the Babylonian hero Gilgamesh, transforms into the Sun-god and then reappears as the Orphic deity Phanes; and in Jung's first encounter with Izdubar, the giant bears the bull's horns that Jung first described in *Memories, Dreams, Reflections*, and initially painted in 1914, as an attribute of Philemon.[38]

These figures do not embody a fixed astral fate. Astral fate, for Jung, was experienced as psychological compulsion, and to the extent that the figures in *Liber Novus* embody Jung's own unconscious compulsions, their transformations reflect a gradual process of consciousness and integration. The figures seem to be images of archetypal principles specifically relevant to Jung's life and, not coincidentally, to his horoscope. They bear mythic attributes as well as personal ones because they are archetypal:

> The primordial image, or archetype, is a figure – be it a daemon, a human being, or a process – that constantly recurs in the course of history and appears wherever creative fantasy is freely expressed. Essentially, therefore, it is a mythological figure.[39]

Jung's figures are never static; they relate to each other in constantly changing ways, and exhibit many faces. And Jung himself, throughout *Liber Novus*, achieves new insights and experiences transformations through his encounters with them. Yet through Jung's use of astrological hermeneutics, the figures become linked with his own birth chart, sometimes very specifically, and reflect his reliance on what Ptolemy referred to as the 'seed' moment, anchored in the unique qualities of time inherent in the moment of birth and bearing within it the 'final cause' of its existence: to become that which it has always potentially been.

> For to the seed is given once and for all at the beginning such and such qualities by the endowment of the ambient [the heavens]; and even though it may change as the body subsequently grows, since by natural process it mingles with itself in the process of growth only matter which is akin to itself, thus it resembles even more closely the type of its initial quality.[40]

Bearing planetary *sunthemata* in the details and colours of their clothing, physiognomy, and landscape settings, the figures of *Liber Novus* are daimons rather than personality traits, and their actions in Jung's narrative depend on the nature of his reactions to them. This seems to reflect Jung's belief that, the more conscious the individual becomes, the greater the free will he or she is able to exercise over the compulsions of *Heimarmene*:

> The journey through the planetary houses boils down to becoming conscious of the good and the bad qualities in our character, and the apotheosis means no more than maximum consciousness, which amounts to maximal freedom of the will.[41]

It would seem that Jung's paintings are also hieratic, in the sense that the Neoplatonist Iamblichus described such images: composites of various *sumbola* or *sunthemata* that form part of a particular chain of correspondences, all of which, combined together, create a ritual object of sufficient resonance with the god or daimon to attract the divinity's approach and permit a process of conscious participation in its creative life.[42] The paintings might thus be understood as magical talismans that invoke and serve as gateways, and they are aspects of an ongoing theurgic ritual aimed at integration into, and of, the Self. This kind of magic might also be understood as art, in the sense that Jung defined it:

> The primordial experience is the source of his [the poet's] creativeness, but it is so dark and amorphous that it requires the related mythological imagery to give it form . . . Since the expression can never match the richness of the vision and can never exhaust its possibilities, the poet must have at his disposal a huge store of material if he is to communicate even a fraction of what he has glimpsed, and must make use of difficult and contradictory images in order to express the strange paradoxes of his vision.[43]

Jung's various dimensions as the artist, the magician, the astrologer, and the psychologist have merged in the pages of *Liber Novus*. This may be one of the reasons why efforts to define this profoundly liminal work in any fixed way according to any discrete scholarly categories – is it art, science, psychology, esotericism, psychotic hallucination, religious vision? – will always be doomed to failure.

Notes

1   Plato, *Symposium*, 203, trans. Michael Joyce, in Edith Hamilton and Huntington Cairns (eds.), *The Collected Dialogues of Plato* (Princeton, NJ: Princeton University Press, 1961), pp. 526–74.
2   Jung, CW14, ¶707.
3   For the history of the publication of *Liber Novus,* see Sonu Shamdasani's Introduction in Jung, *Liber Novus*, pp. viii–xii. For Jung's own description of the genesis of *Liber Novus,* see Jung, *MDR*, pp. 194–225.
4   Jung, *MDR*, p. 225.
5   An exception is the recently published compilation of Jung's comments on astrology: C.G. Jung, *Jung on Astrology*, selected and introduced by Keiron le Grice and Safron Rossi (Abingdon: Routledge, 2017).

6 For the 'teeming chaos' of the artist's visions, see Jung, CW15, ¶146.

7 Jung CW15, ¶141.

8 Jung, *MDR*, p. 216.

9 Rachel Elior, 'Mysticism, Magic, and Angelology', *Jewish Quarterly Review* 1 (1993), pp. 3–53, on p. 19.

10 Dion Fortune, *Aspects of Occultism* (Wellingborough: Aquarian Press, 1962), p. 5.

11 Jung, Letter to Erich Neumann, 24 March 1935, in Jung, *Analytical Psychology in Exile*, p. 95.

12 Jung used this phrase in 1957; see Jung, *Liber Novus*, p. vii.

13 See Shamdasani, 'Introduction', in Jung, *Liber Novus*, p. 200, n. 69.

14 For the idea of 'layers', see Shamdasani, 'Introduction', in Jung, *Liber Novus*, p. 203.

15 See Jung, Letter to Sigmund Freud, 8 May 1911, in *The Freud-Jung Letters*, p. 412.

16 Jung, 'The Conception of the Unconscious', in Jung, *Collected Papers on Analytical Psychology*, p. 469.

17 For Jung's preoccupation with the imminent astrological aion of Aquarius, see Liz Greene, *Jung's Studies in Astrology* (Abingdon: Routledge, 2018), chapter 6.

18 This very useful list is taken from Murray Stein, 'Critical Notice: *The Red Book*', *Journal of Analytical Psychology* 55 (2010), pp. 423–25.

19 The veiled woman appears in Book Two of *Liber Novus*, p. 155. For more on these similarities, see Chapter 3.

20 Sonu Shamdasani, *C. G. Jung: A Biography in Books* (New York: W.W. Norton, 2012), p. 68.

21 Stein, 'Critical Notice', p. 423.

22 According to Shamdasani in *C. G. Jung: A Biography in Books*, p. 68, from December 1913 onward 'Jung carried on with the same procedure: deliberately evoking a fantasy in a waking state and then entering into it as into a drama'.

23 For Jung's description of the phenomena preceding the writing of *Septem sermones*, see Jung, *MDR*, pp. 215–16. Jung's description was corroborated by his daughter Gret Baumann in a personal discussion with me in 1985. She was seven years old at the time the phenomena occurred.

24 Jung, 'Über die Beziehungen der analytischen Psychologie zum dichterischen Kunstwerk', first published in *Wissen und Leben* XV (1922), pp. 19–20, later published in Jung, CW15, ¶¶97–132.

25 Jung, CW15, ¶130.

26 See Chapter 1.

27 For 'amplification', see Jung, CW8, ¶¶403–4; Jung, CW10, ¶¶618, 646, 733, 771; Jung, CW18, ¶¶173–74.

28 Philo, *On Moses*, in *Philo, Vol. VI: On Abraham. On Joseph. On Moses*, trans. F.H. Colson (Cambridge, MA: Harvard University Press, 1935), II:103–104.

29 Max Heindel, *Ancient and Modern Initiation* (Oceanside, CA: Rosicrucian Fellowship, 1931), p. 31. The Seven Spirits appear in Revelation 4:5.

30 Jung, *Liber Novus*, p. 322.

31 See Jung, *Visions*, p. 923.

32 A.E. Waite, *The Pictorial Key to the Tarot* (London: William Rider & Son, 1910), p. 119.

33 See Greene, *Jung's Studies in Astrology*, chapters 1 and 2.

34 For the Mithraic planetary ascent, see Roger Beck, *Planetary Gods and Planetary Orders in the Mysteries of Mithras* (Leiden: Brill, 1988), pp. 8–11. For the Gnostic planetary journey, see Roelof van den Broek, 'The Creation of Adam's Psychic Body in the *Apocryphon of John*', in Roelof Van den Broek and M.J. Vermaseren (eds.), *Studies in Gnosticism and Hellenistic Religions* (Leiden: Brill, 1981), pp. 38–57, esp. pp. 41–42. For the alchemical order, see Origen, *Contra Celsum*, trans. Henry Chadwick (Cambridge: Cambridge University Press, 1953), 6:22.

35 Henry Corbin, *Avicenna and the Visionary Recital* (Princeton, NJ: Princeton University Press, 1960), p. 17.

36 Jung, *MDR*, p. 207.

37 For the alchemical Saturn as *senex*, see Jung, CW14, ¶298.

38 Jung, *MDR*, p. 207. For other painted versions of Philemon, see Chapter 5.

39 Jung, CW15, ¶127.
40 Ptolemy, *Tetrabiblos*, ed. and trans. F.E. Robbins (Cambridge, MA: Harvard University Press, 1971), III.1.
41 Jung, CW14, ¶309.
42 See Greene, *Jung's Studies in Astrology*, chapter 4.
43 Jung, CW15, ¶151.

1

MARTIAL MATTERS

It [Ares] is the giver of seed, the occult dispenser of Nature in the three prime principles, and the bond of their union. It distributes to all things whatsoever its peculiar form, species, and substance, so that it may put on its proper and specific nature, and no other.[1]

—Martin Ruland

Ares [Mars] . . . is the 'assigner, who extends the peculiar nature to each species, and gives individual form'. It can therefore be taken as the principle of individuation in the strict sense . . . Ares, accordingly, is an intuitive concept for a preconscious, creative, and formative principle which is capable of giving life to individual creatures.[2]

—C.G. Jung

The red horseman

One of the most readily identifiable planetary *personae* whom Jung describes in detail in *Liber Novus* is called 'The Red One'. This entity makes his entrance at the beginning of Book Two of *Liber Novus*, at a moment when Jung finds himself in a state of apathy, indecision, and depression:

I feel that my will is paralyzed and that the spirit of the depths possesses me. I know nothing about a way: I can therefore neither want this nor that, since nothing indicates to me whether I want this or that. I wait, without knowing what I'm waiting for.[3]

The appearance of this figure heralds a threatening change. The threat is reflected in the defensive position Jung holds as 'the tower guard' standing on 'the highest tower of a castle', and in the *frisson* he experiences when he sees the figure approaching:

> I look out into the distance. I see a red point out there . . . It is a horseman in a red coat, the red horseman . . . I hear steps on the stairway, the steps creak, he knocks: a strange fear comes over me: there stands the Red One, his long shape wholly shrouded in red, even his hair is red. I think: in the end he will turn out to be the devil.[4]

The Red One has not come by chance; as he informs Jung, 'Your waiting has called me'.[5]

If Jung created a pictorial representation of this entity, it was either destroyed or has not yet surfaced. But he provided enough descriptive material to allow the reader to recognise which astral potency had arrived to counteract his listless apathy and breach his defences. The epithet, 'The Red One', might have been entirely Jung's invention, but it was more likely to have been directly inspired by mythic sources. The Egyptians referred to the planet Mars as *Har décher*, which means 'The Red One'.[6] The horned warrior-god Cocidius, known from archaeological evidence around Hadrian's Wall and equated by the Romans with their battle-god Mars, and the Gaulish Rudiobus, likewise identified by the Romans with Mars, were both called 'The Red One'.[7] A powerful Celtic deity called the Dagda was also known as Ruadh Rofessa, the 'Red One of Great Knowledge'.[8] As Jung's familiarity with the myths of various cultures was encyclopaedic, it is unlikely that he had failed to encounter this epithet for Mars in the course of his studies. And even if the name was spontaneous, the planet itself, when viewed from the Earth, appears to be red.

In his later explorations into alchemy, Jung discovered and quoted many descriptions of the dangerous Martial spirit and its potential transformation.[9] But at the time Jung was working on Book Two of *Liber Novus*, alchemical texts had not assumed the psychological significance they held for him later, and it is likely that he relied more on Alan Leo's various descriptions of Mars, as well as on Wilhelm Roscher's *Detailed Lexicon of Greek and Roman Mythology*.[10] Leo published the following description of the astrological Mars in 1912:

> All the animal propensities, sensations, passions, desires, and appetites come under the vibration of Mars . . . Mars is the ruler over the animal nature in man; and the task set for humanity is not only that of subjecting, ruling and controlling the animal nature, but also *its transmutation into a higher force than that which ministers to the animal soul*.[11]

Leo implied a purposive or teleological element in the Martial force that closely resembles the more succinct, alchemically orientated description Jung articulated many decades later:

> Astrologically, Mars characterizes the instinctual and affective nature of man. *The subjugation and transformation of this nature seems to be the theme of the alchemical opus*.[12]

In 1918, Max Heindel declared that Mars presides over the 'holy function of generation' and imparts fertility.[13] Heindel's interpretation accords with that of the alchemist Martin Ruland, who stated in the seventeenth century that Mars is 'the giver of seed';[14] Jung in turn cited Ruland's statement when he noted that Mars is 'the formative principle which is capable of giving life to individual creatures'.[15] According to Heindel, 'the brusque' Mars arouses 'the passion that has caused sorrow, sin and death', and is thus 'a Lucifer spirit'.[16] This demonic quality mirrors Jung's initial perception of The Red One as the devil. In a seminar on children's dreams given in 1936, Jung, exploring the historical transformation of the figure of the devil, noted:

> When he appears red, he is of a fiery, that is, passionate nature, and causes wantonness, hate, or unruly love.[17]

Heindel, like Leo, emphasised the creative face of Mars when its ferocious instinctual energy is directed toward loftier goals. Mars, in Heindel's view, provides 'a strong constitution and physical endurance, a positive, independent and self-reliant nature, determined and proud, generous and energetic, resourceful and quick to learn'.[18] It may be significant that, in Jung's natal horoscope, the planet Mars, as he himself was fully aware, was placed in the zodiacal sign of Sagittarius.[19] This sign, and the constellation with which it is connected, have been portrayed in astrological iconography from the Babylonian world to the present day as a centaur – half human and half horse – carrying a bow.[20] When The Red One first appears in *Liber Novus*, he is on horseback. In Jung's view, the horse itself, like Mars, is a symbol of the instinctual side of the human being, and can even personify the devil.[21] In the text accompanying the horoscope that the Freudian analyst Johan van Ophuijsen prepared for Jung in 1911, citing interpretive paragraphs in Alan Leo's *The Key to Your Own Nativity*,[22] Jung was offered a description of Mars in Sagittarius that resembles The Red One, and an important aspect of Jung himself, with disturbing accuracy:

> You have the courage of your ideas and opinions, which are not always those of the people around . . . In religion, this position makes one who is either a little unorthodox or who is very active, devoted, and perhaps a little militant in manner . . . It favours travel, and change of opinion, occupation, and abode . . . Quarrels and disputes are probable.[23]

In an earlier work, Alan Leo offered a similar character portrait of Mars in Sagittarius, emphasising the quality of aggressive religious scepticism:

> An active mind seldom in agreement with others, fixed and positive in its own ideas, and frequently at variance with accepted opinions. In religion militant, aggressive, unorthodox or sceptical . . . He is mentally and morally brave, daring and fearless of the opinions of others. The position makes him somewhat of a traveller, walker, rider, sailor or athlete.[24]

Heindel's description of Mars in the zodiacal sign of Sagittarius may also be relevant. This placement 'gives an argumentative disposition and fondness of debating on subjects of serious nature such as law, philosophy and religion'. Moreover, Mars in Sagittarius 'gives a sharp tongue and a quarrelsome disposition'.[25] The Red One's personality echoes these astrological descriptions precisely: he is aggressive, argumentative, unorthodox, sceptical, and irritatingly un-Christian, and his dialogue with Jung is focused specifically on 'philosophy and religion'. Jung, offended by The Red One's 'cool and sneering' attitude, asks him: 'Have you never broken your heart over the holiest mysteries of our Christian religion?' The Red One replies: 'You take literally what the scriptures say, otherwise you could not judge me so hard'.[26]

In the *Collected Works*, and particularly in his three volumes on alchemy,[27] Jung had quite a lot to say about Mars, although these descriptions were written long after *Liber Novus* was completed. This quarrelsome planetary god, according to Jung, is equated with the metal iron, the colour red (which Jung called 'a masculine colour' representing the 'material, physical side'),[28] the astrological element of fire, the fiery sulphur personified as the *vir rubaeus* ('red man') of the alchemical opus, and the wolf as an image of hunger and appetite.[29] The Red One is red-haired and wearing a red coat, mirroring Ptolemy's description of the 'fiery colour' of Mars.[30] His garments 'shine like glowing iron', once again linking him to the planetary potency traditionally associated with that metal, as described in Firmicus Maternus' *Matheseos*, an astrological work from late antiquity which Jung had already acquired by 1912.[31] A malefic aspect from Mars to another planet, according to Jung, 'injures' the receiving planet by 'martial violence'.[32]

Yet despite its dangerous nature, this planet as a psychic potency can, as Jung pointed out, be 'taken as the principle of individuation in the strict sense'.[33] The alchemical *opus* should begin 'in the month of Aries, whose ruler is Mars'.[34] The incapacity to exercise individual will or experience individual desire – in effect, a state of depression, which is Jung's psychic condition when The Red One first appears – suggests what astrologers inclined toward psychological approaches recognise as a 'Mars problem': a psychic drive or potency split off from consciousness and rendered dangerous, psychologically and physically, because the instinctual life-giving energies the planet symbolises have, through cultural and personal repression, been lost to consciousness. The American astrologer Howard Sasportas described this problem succinctly:

> If we deny Mars because we are afraid of its more negative side, then we are in danger of losing touch with that bit of us that wants to grow into what we are. And when the desire to grow is blocked (either by other people, external events, or other parts of our own selves) then that energy turns to anger.[35]

The high tower in which Jung's 'I' – his ego-consciousness – stands guard before his encounter with The Red One suggests a defended position: reliance on a safe and stable structure, guarded against invasion through its elevation above the chaos of the emotional and instinctual aspects of life. Jung made clear his understanding of the general symbolism of the tower in *Psychological Types*:

> The tower undoubtedly has the meaning of something solid and secure, as in Psalm 61:4:'For thou hast been a shelter for me, and a strong tower from the enemy' . . . The tower is also the Church.[36]

'The Tower' is also one of the cards in the Major Arcana of the Tarot. In A.E. Waite's 1910 work on the symbolism of the Major Arcana, one of several books by Waite that Jung acquired, The Tower is described as 'a card of confusion':

> It is the rending of a House of Doctrine . . . The Tower has been spoken of as the chastisement of pride and the intellect . . . It may signify also the end of a dispensation.[37]

Jung himself offered a succinct 'keyword' definition of the Tarot card of The Tower:

> Burning tower. Hospital, prison, struck by lightning. Sacrifice.[38]

The Red One, whose anarchic attributes are so fittingly described by Leo's and Heindel's descriptions of Mars in Sagittarius, is like the lightning bolt that destroys the Tower in the great cycle of the Tarot. He arrives to challenge and transform an entrenched, safe, and stable 'House of Doctrine', rooted in traditional Christian values and intellectual defensiveness, yet painfully vulnerable to the intrusion of a vitally important yet previously neglected unconscious potency necessary for the fulfilment of Jung's personality.

The devil in the detail

The Red One's passion, ferocity, and mocking cynicism initially convince Jung that he is demonic rather than daimonic – an assumption which prompts The Red One to observe:

> Who am I? You think I am the devil. Do not pass judgment . . . What sort of a superstitious fellow are you, that immediately you think of the devil?[39]

The equation of the devil with Mars, whom Heindel called 'a Lucifer spirit', is not merely a predictable Swiss Protestant's response to The Red One's lack of proper Christian inhibitions. It is an ancient symbolic association that derives from both astrological and early esoteric Jewish cosmological frameworks, and Jung was familiar with both. In Babylonian astral cosmology, the planet Mars was equated with the fiery, destructive Nergal, chthonic god of war and pestilence.[40] Mars is described as 'maleficent' in Ptolemy's *Tetrabiblos*,[41] and this perception of the planet as dangerous and potentially destructive continued over the centuries.[42] In Jewish lore, the angelic being associated with the war-god's planet is Samael, lord of the demonic realm:

> His height was so great, it would have taken five hundred years to cover a distance equal to it, and from the crown of his head to the soles of his feet he was studded with glaring eyes ...'This one', said Metatron, addressing Moses, 'is Samael, who takes the soul away from man'.... Thereupon Moses prayed to God in these words, 'O may it be Thy will, my God and the God of my fathers, not to let me fall into the hands of this angel'.[43]

In the Gnostic *Apocryphon of John*, Samael is 'impious in his madness'.[44] The relationship between this dangerous angel and his red planet is stated explicitly in the eleventh-century Arab grimoire known as the *Picatrix*, which provided the basis for many later Christian grimoires.[45] Samael appears as the angel presiding over Tuesday, the day of Mars, in the medieval Jewish magical compilation known as *Sefer ha-Raziel*, another work with which Jung was familiar.[46] A sixteenth-century English redaction of the thirteenth-century grimoire known as *Liber iuratus* presents the reader with representational images of the various planetary angels, wearing helmets and arranged in military formation as befits their Hebrew title of *sar*: 'prince' or 'captain'.[47] Their planetary associations are designated not only by the text, but by the colours of their robes and wings, and by the planetary glyphs below the images (see Plate 1).

The angels of Mars bear red wings and are entirely clothed in red, like The Red One in *Liber Novus*. They 'cause war, murder, destruction, and mortality of people and of all earthly things'. First of the four Martial angels, on the far left of the image, is Samael. Below on the right is the astrological glyph for Mars, familiar to many today because, when tilted with its arrow pointing slightly upward, it is commonly used as the symbol of masculinity. Samael must be invoked on a Tuesday, the traditional day of Mars.[48] Grimoires replete with recipes for invoking the astral angels were well known to Jung during the time he worked on *Liber Novus*; the *Sixth and Seventh Books of Moses*, for example, presents the angel Samael as prince of the Fifth Heaven (Mars is the fifth planet from the Earth in the ancient geocentric cosmos), who 'stands continually before God' and brings wrath, hate, lies, and war.[49] The association of the angel and the planet continued into the occult revival of the late nineteenth century, primarily through the work of the French magus Éliphas Lévi, who declared that, among the Seven Spirits before the Throne of God, Samael was the 'Spirit of Mars'.[50]

The transformation of the Red One

In the course of Jung's encounter with him, The Red One alters, as does Jung's 'I'. This mutual transformation highlights Jung's unique understanding of planetary symbols as psychic dimensions of life: subjective dynamisms as well as archetypal patterns that, although universal, can nevertheless undergo change through the intervention of human consciousness, which is itself changed in the process. This is a perspective radically different from the more fatalistic astrologies of the medieval and early modern periods. Such transformations do not rely on sheer force of will, nor on the kind of sublimation apparently practiced by Theosophically inclined astrologers such as Alan Leo, who, according to the testimony of his wife, dealt with the problem of a potentially unruly Mars by maintaining celibacy throughout his marriage.[51] Jung's perspective is closer to Neoplatonic and Hermetic ideas about the mutuality and consubstantiality of human and divine, and to Iamblichus' insistence that the gods themselves, of their own volition, achieve the divinisation of the theurgist. The Red One transforms Jung's green clothing into living foliage – in other words, awakening his instincts and uniting him with the life of nature – and reveals his own secret identity, informing Jung: 'Here, my dear fellow, I doff my mask'.[52]

> The red of the rider transforms itself into a tender reddish flesh color. And behold – Oh miracle – my green garments burst into leaf.[53]

Jung describes the nature of the joy he experiences as 'red-coloured, red-scented, warm bright red joy'.[54] The Red One is 'my devil', and embodies 'that strange joy of the world that comes unsuspected like a warm southerly wind with swelling fragrant blossoms and the ease of living'. This joy belongs to spring, marked by the vernal equinox when the Sun enters the zodiacal sign of Mars-ruled Aries:

> You know it from the poets, this seriousness, when they expectantly look toward what happens in the depths, sought out first of all by the devil because of their springlike joy . . . Whoever tastes this joy forgets himself.[55]

This remarkable mutual transformation can only occur through a direct emotional engagement with the imaginal figure, conducted 'in all seriousness', as Jung insists a few paragraphs later. 'Coming to an understanding' allows him to 'accept your other standpoint'.[56] The 'other standpoint' here seems to be a figure personifying a planetary daimon whom Jung initially perceived as demonic because the daimon's values were in direct contradiction to Jung's own consciously held religious and moral standpoint. The Red One is close to Ruland's alchemical description of Mars as 'the giver of seed'; he does not merely represent simple character traits such as anger or aggression, or concrete events such as violence or war, as one might expect from descriptions of Mars in most of the astrological sources available to Jung at the time. The Red One is an autonomous entity with a distinct individuality, a daimon or a god who, prior to their encounter, appears to have been what Jung understood as an unconscious and thus potentially dangerous dimension of his own personality. The astrological *sunthemata* associated with this figure seem to have provided the dominant metaphors through which Jung perceived The Red One's qualities. Astrological symbols, for Jung, were dynamic potencies of an archetypal nature, accessible to the human being through imaginal encounters:

> This I learned in the Mysterium: to take seriously every unknown wanderer who personally inhabits the inner world, since they are real because they are effectual.[57]

Later in *Liber Novus*, Jung encounters The Red One again. At this second meeting, the 'Lucifer spirit' has changed radically, and his transformation this time initially seems negative:

> He has grown old, his red hair has become grey, his fiery red clothes are worn out, shabby, poor.[58]

The Red One has taken up with the Saturnine and intellectually rigid Christian Anchorite called Ammonius,[59] and appears to have been bludgeoned into that same repressive Christian dogmatism of which he had earlier accused Jung. He seems frightened by Jung's approach and makes 'the sign of the cross', apparently because Jung is now a 'pagan', still covered in the green leaves that The Red One originally caused to spring from Jung's body. The Red One informs Jung that he has become 'serious, so serious that I went into the monastery, prayed, fasted, and converted myself'. But then he admits that he 'developed a deep aversion against the whole Christian religion since my experience in the monastery', and reveals that he is, in effect, in disguise, accompanying the Anchorite not because he enjoys the old man's company or has altered his essential nature, but because 'I need to come to an arrangement with the clergy, or else I will lose my clientele'.[60]

This brief episode reveals a new and far more devious facet of The Red One. No longer repressed or repudiated by Jung, he still cannot fully unleash his fiery nature without devastating consequences to his profession, which is that of an *agent provocateur*. But he has now learned to move within the established system in ways that allow him to achieve his ends without discovery. He is no friend of Ammonius, but has decided to stick close to the Anchorite in order to continue his 'devilish' work. The Red One no longer operates within Jung as an unconscious and potentially destructive force, but exercises his talents within the larger world in which Jung worked and pursued his goals. It is perhaps not coincidental that Mars, in Jung's birth chart, forms a benign aspect to Saturn, which Alan Leo described as having 'much subtlety'; the individual is 'subtle to scheme, and quick to execute'.[61] This useful planetary partnership, along with Leo's textual description, was noted in the horoscope that Johan van Ophuijsen prepared for Jung in 1911, and describes a character attribute that seems to mirror Jung's ability to remain a respected figure within the conventional 'system' despite the profoundly unconventional nature of his views and personal life. After The Red One offers his quiet but nevertheless important revelation, he makes one further brief and unhelpful appearance in *Liber Novus*: he runs off into the fields 'with horrified cries' when he sees Jung carrying the wounded giant Izdubar to the place of the giant's resurrection.[62] The Red One and the Anchorite are now 'relics of the past, which one still often encounters in the Western lands. They used to be very important'.[63] The Red One is no longer threatening because many of his dynamic attributes have been integrated into consciousness.[64] In Jung's terminology, the complex is less emotionally charged and therefore no longer compulsive.[65] In astrological terminology, Jung has 'owned' his natal Mars.

Siegfried the Hero

There are no other figures in *Liber Novus* who so clearly display the qualities of the astrological Mars. Siegfried the Hero might be interpreted as a Martial figure because, in Teutonic legend, he was a warrior and therefore could be associated with the ancient war-god; but Jung's understanding of Siegfried was more complex. In December 1913, Jung recorded a vision of a dead hero, and then experienced a dream of the slaying of Siegfried. He described the dream later as one in which Siegfried 'was killed by myself'.[66] The section of *Liber Novus* titled 'Murder of the Hero', which amalgamates the dream with the vision, occurs in Book One, long before Jung's encounter with The Red One.[67]

In the narrative, Jung is in high mountains, accompanied by a 'little brown man'.[68] He hears Siegfried's horn sounding in the distance and, armed with guns – a modern form of destruction of which the ancient hero can have no foreknowledge – Jung and the brown man hide beside a narrow, rocky path until Siegfried appears in a chariot made of the bones of the dead. Jung and his companion then fire simultaneously and kill the hero. A small painting of Jung and the brown man shooting Siegfried appears within the text. In this painting, Siegfried bears a red shield, while Jung himself is dressed in red.[69] The colour red, when it appears in association with Siegfried in the twelfth-century German epic, the *Niebelunglied*, is used to describe his 'fine horn'; but the horn is 'of reddish gold' and suggests solar rather than Martial attributes, as gold is the traditional metal of the Sun.[70] Jung may have intended a blend of the two planetary principles in Siegfried since, according to Roscher, who was one of Jung's main sources for myths, Apollo the Sun-god and Mars the war-god were originally both solar deities.[71]

Jung's perception of Mars, based on both his portrayal of The Red One and his comments about the astrological symbol in various published works, was not typical of the Martial warrior of conventional astrological texts. But even allowing for a more individual image of Mars, Jung's interpretation of the vision of Siegfried's death, written in 1925, focused on psychological typology rather than on myth. Not every figure in *Liber Novus* carries clear astrological symbolism, and it may be unhelpful to attempt to categorise Siegfried too quickly as exclusively either a Martial or a solar planetary daimon.

> It was a case of destroying the hero ideal of my efficiency. This has to be sacrificed in order that a new adaptation can be made, in short, it is connected with the sacrifice of the superior function in order to get at the libido necessary to activate the inferior functions.[72]

According to a letter Jung wrote to the German astrologer Oskar Schmitz in 1923, his 'superior function' was the thinking function.[73] Jung understood the murder of Siegfried as a symbol of the collapse of his rational intellect:

> I had killed my intellect, helped on to the deed by a personification of the collective unconscious, the little brown man with me. In other words, I deposed my superior function.[74]

Jung understood this sacrifice as the necessary preliminary to a descent into the deeper levels of the unconscious, since the 'superior function' in any individual serves conscious adaptation and acts as a bulwark against the threatening forces of the unknown depths. Jung viewed the death of Siegfried as a symbol of the sacrifice of his habitual mode of adaptation to life, so that he could 'get at' the unconscious and undeveloped dimensions of his personality.

However, astrological symbolism may still be relevant to Siegfried. Jung's earlier understanding of the archetypal image of the hero seems to have been as much solar as Martial. According to his description in *Psychology of the Unconscious*, Siegfried symbolises the libido striving to break free of the grip of the devouring maternal unconscious, and the hero's sword 'has the significance of the phallic sun power'.[75] Jung's portrayal of the physical attributes of Siegfried in *Liber Novus* is likewise as solar as it is Martial, and the hero's death is compared to the dying and resurrected god of Christianity:

> Oh that Siegfried, blond and blue-eyed, the German hero, had to fall by my hand, the most loyal and courageous! He had everything in himself that I treasured as the greater and more beautiful; he was my power, my boldness, my pride . . . Think of the blond savage of the German forests, who had to betray the hammer-brandishing thunder to the pale Near-Eastern God who was nailed to the wood like a chicken marten.[76]

Siegfried is thus also related to what Jung perceived as a historical shift in the God-image of the German collective psyche, from the 'hammer-brandishing thunder' of Wotan, the Teutonic ruler of the gods, to the 'pale, Near-Eastern God' of Christianity. This shift was in turn reflected in the astrological symbolism of the precessional movement from the Aion of Aries to the Aion of Pisces, suggesting that Siegfried — although he bears distinctly solar attributes — also belongs, like 'hammer-brandishing' Wotan, to the Aion of Aries.

This hero's death, in Jung's view, was therefore a necessary sacrifice on both personal and collective levels. But for Jung, as for many nineteenth-century anthropologists and historians of religion, the symbol of the dying and resurrected god lay beyond the specific imagery of any particular astrological Aion. Jung related the myth of cyclical death and rebirth to the Sun in its annual round through the zodiac, reflecting the constantly changing cycle of the libido that bursts forth each spring as the Sun enters the Mars-ruled zodiacal sign of Aries. Siegfried might thus be understood as a solar daimon clothed in Martial garb, or a Martial daimon who serves and is ultimately an emanation of the solar source of life. The death of Siegfried at the beginning of *Liber Novus* heralds a long succession of images and encounters dealing with the changing forms of that 'flame-curled, entwined, crucified and revived' deity who eventually emerges in Part Three of *Liber Novus* bearing his classical name:[77]

> We call God *HELIOS* or sun.[78]

Notes

1 Martin Ruland, *A Lexicon of Alchemy or Alchemical Dictionary,* trans. A.E. Waite (London: privately printed, 1892), p. 38. Jung possessed an original edition of this work: Martin Ruland, *Lexicon alchemiae sive Dictionarium alchemisticum* (Frankfurt: Zachariah Palthenus, 1612). However, he usually cited Waite's translation.
2 Jung, CW13, ¶176, n. 39.
3 Jung, *Liber Novus*, p. 259.
4 Jung, *Liber Novus*, p. 259.
5 Jung, *Liber Novus*, p. 259.
6 Markus Hotakainen, *Mars: From Myth and Mystery to Recent Discoveries* (New York: Springer, 2008), p. 13. Mars was known to the Babylonians as the 'Red Star'; see Erica Reiner and David Pingree, *Babylonian Planetary Omens* (Groningen: Styx, 1998), p. 49.
7 For these deities and others with the same epithet see <http://faculty.indwes.edu/bcupp/solarsys/Names.htm>; <http:planetarynames.wr.usgs.gov>; <www.celtnet.org.uk/gods_c/cocidius.html>.
8 For the Dagda, see <www.tairis.co.uk/index.php?option=com_content&view=article&id=125:the-dagda-part-1&catid=45:gods&Itemid=8>.
9 See Jung's comments on the Mars principle in Jung, CW13, ¶¶176–78.
10 Wilhelm Heinrich Roscher, *Ausführliches Lexikon der griechisches und römisches Muythologie* (Leipzig: Teubner, 1884–1937). Jung relied heavily on this work; see below, and see also Shamdasani, *C. G. Jung: A Biography in Books*, p. 90.
11 Alan Leo, *How to Judge a Nativity* (London: Modern Astrology, 1912), pp. 30–31. Italics mine.
12 Jung, CW13, ¶177 n. 39. Italics mine. See also Jung, CW9ii, ¶130.
13 Max Heindel, *The Message of the Stars* (Oceanside, CA: Rosicrucian Fellowship, 1918), p. 303.
14 See the quote cited at the beginning of this chapter.
15 Jung, CW13, ¶176 and n. 39, citing Ruland, *A Lexicon of Alchemy*, p. 38.
16 Heindel, *The Message of the Stars*, pp. 304, 31.
17 Jung, *Children's Dreams*, p. 174. See also Shamdasani's comment in Jung, *Liber Novus*, p. 260, n. 12.
18 Heindel, *The Message of the Stars*, pp. 303–7.
19 For Jung's familiarity with his own horoscope, see Greene, *Jung's Studies in Astrology*, chapter 2.
20 See, for example, Sagittarius portrayed as a centaur in the Dendera Zodiac of the Roman period.
21 Jung, CW5, ¶421; Jung, CW16, ¶347.
22 Alan Leo, *The Key to Your Own Nativity* (London: Modern Astrology Office, 1910). For this horoscope, see Greene, *Jung's Studies in Astrology*, chapter 2.
23 Leo, *The Key to Your Own Nativity*, p. 43.
24 Alan Leo, *Astrology for All* (London: Modern Astrology, 1910), pp. 221–22.
25 Heindel, *The Message of the Stars*, pp. 323–24.
26 Jung, *Liber Novus*, pp. 259–60.
27 Jung, CW12, CW13, and CW14.
28 Jung, CW10, ¶790; Jung, *The Visions Seminars*, II.332.
29 Jung, CW13, ¶176, n. 39; Jung, CW14, ¶6 n. 26; Jung, CW10, ¶790; Jung, CW12, ¶440 n. 50. For Jung's familiarity with the mythic associations of Mars with the wolf, see Jung, *The Visions Seminars*, II.342.
30 Ptolemy, *Tetrabiblos,* I.4.
31 Firmicus Maternus, *Ancient Astrology, Theory and Practice*, p. 140, where those whom Mars rules 'have red hair' and whose 'occupations have to do with iron and fire'.
32 Jung, CW9ii, ¶151 n. 2.
33 Jung, CW13, ¶176.
34 Jung, CW13, ¶193.

35 Howard Sasportas, 'The Astrology and Psychology of Aggression', in Liz Greene and Howard Sasportas, *Dynamics of the Unconscious* (York Beach, ME: Samuel Weiser, 1988), pp. 1–74, on p. 24. Jung recognised rage as a compensation for feelings of impotence; see Jung, CW17, ¶¶213–14.
36 Jung, CW6, ¶¶390–91.
37 Waite, *The Pictorial Key to the Tarot*, pp. 132–35.
38 Description from Hanni Binder's notes of a conversation with Jung, at <http://mary greer.wordpress.com/2008/04/18/carl-jung-on-the-major-arcana/>.
39 Jung, *Liber Novus*, p. 259.
40 For Mars and Nergal, see Ev Cochrane, *Martian Metamorphosis* (Ames, IA: Aeon Press, 1997), pp. 30–35.
41 Ptolemy, *Tetrabiblos*, I.5.
42 See Alan Leo's more hopeful portrayal in Leo, *How to Judge a Nativity*, p. 31.
43 *The Ascension of Moses*, in Louis Ginzberg, *The Legends of the Jews*, 2 volumes, trans. Henriette Szold (Philadelphia, PA: Jewish Publication Society of America, 1913), II.304–308.
44 *Apocryphon of John*, II.1, trans. Frederik Wisse, *Nag Hammadi Library*, p. 105.
45 *Picatrix*, ed. H. Ritter (1933), 226.
46 *Sefer ha-Raziel* 34b. Jung cited this important Jewish magical text in CW14, ¶572.
47 For *Liber iuratus*, see Gösta Hedegård, *Liber Iuratus Honorii* (Stockholm: Almqvist and Wiksell, 2002); Richard Kieckhefer, 'The Devil's Contemplatives', in Fanger (ed.), *Conjuring Spirits*, pp. 250–65. For a list of extant MS versions and a modern English translation, see <http://lucite.org/lucite/archive/abdiel/liber_juratus.pdf>.
48 Samuel Liddell MacGregor Mathers (ed. and trans.), *Grimoire of Armadel* (posthumously published, London: Routledge & Kegan Paul, 1980; repr. San Francisco, CA: Red Wheel/Weiser, 2001), p. 41.
49 Joseph Peterson (ed. and trans.), *The Sixth and Seventh Books of Moses* (Lake Worth, FL: Ibis Press, 2008), p. 165. For Jung's involvement with this and other grimoires, see Greene, *Jung's Studies in Astrology*, chapter 4.
50 Éliphas Lévi, *The Magical Ritual of the Sanctum Regnum*, trans. William Wynn Westcott (private publication, 1896), p. 8.
51 For Alan Leo's celibate marriage, see Bessie Leo, *The Life and Work of Alan Leo, Theosophist – Astrologer – Mason* (London: Modern Astrology Office/N.L. Fowler, 1919), p. 65.
52 Jung, *Liber Novus*, p. 260.
53 Jung, *Liber Novus*, p. 260.
54 Jung, *Liber Novus*, p. 260.
55 Jung, *Liber Novus*, p. 260.
56 Jung, *Liber Novus*, p. 261.
57 Jung, *Liber Novus*, p. 260.
58 Jung, *Liber Novus*, p. 275.
59 See Chapter 4.
60 Jung, *Liber Novus*, p. 276.
61 Leo, *How to Judge a Nativity*, p. 248.
62 Jung, *Liber Novus*, p. 282.
63 Jung, *Liber Novus*, p. 282.
64 For Izdubar, see Chapter 2.
65 For Jung's idea of 'feeling-toned' complexes, see Jung, CW3, ¶77–106; Jung, CW8, ¶¶194–219.
66 See Jung, *Liber Novus*, p. 202.
67 Jung, *Liber Novus*, pp. 241–42.
68 For mountains and rocks as symbols of Saturn, see Chapter 4.
69 Jung, *Liber Novus*, 1:5. The image is reproduced in Shamdasani, *C. G. Jung: A Biography in Books*, p. 67.
70 *Niebelunglied*, trans. A. Hatto (London: Penguin, 2004), p. 129.
71 For this identification in early myth, see Cochrane, *Martian Metamorphoses*, p. 59; Michael G. Theodorakis, 'Apollo of the Wolf, the Mouse and the Serpent', *Kronos* 9:3 (1984),

pp. 12–19. For ancient associations of the colour red with solar power, see Liz Greene, 'The God in the Stone: Gemstone Talismans in Western Magical Traditions', *Culture and Cosmos* 19:1–2 (Autumn–Winter 2015), pp. 47–85.

72 Jung, *Analytical Psychology*, p. 48.
73 Jung, Letter to Oskar Schmitz, 26 May 1923, in 'Letters to Oskar Schmitz', p. 82.
74 Jung, *Analytical Psychology*, pp. 56–57. See Shamdasani's n. 115 in Jung, *Liber Novus*, p. 242.
75 Jung, *Psychology of the Unconscious*, p. 218.
76 Jung, *Liber Novus*, p. 242.
77 Jung, *Liber Novus*, p. 271.
78 Jung, *Liber Novus*, p. 349.

2

THE 'CENTRAL SPIRITUAL SUN'

Draw nigh, O Lord!

Upon this utterance His Rays shall be turned on thee, and thou shalt be in midst of them. When, then, thou hast done this, thou shalt behold a God, in flower of age, of fairest beauty, [and] with Locks of Flame, in a white Tunic and a scarlet Mantle, wearing a Crown of Fire. Straightway salute Him with the Salutation of the Fire:

Hail Lord! O Thou of mighty Power; O King of mighty Sway; Greatest of Gods; O Sun; Thou Lord of Heaven and Earth; O God of Gods! Strong is Thy Breath; strong is Thy Might!' [1]

—*Mithras Liturgy*

The dynamic of the gods is psychic energy. This is our immortality, the link through which man feels inextinguishably one with the continuity of all life . . . The psychic life-force, the libido, symbolizes itself in the sun. [2]

—C.G. Jung

The sun in the landscape

The *sunthemata* of the Sun form a recurrent theme in *Liber Novus*, from specific solar symbols and landscapes to figures who embody the radiant life-force of what medieval astrological texts referred to as the 'Great Light'. Jung's understanding of the solar realm grew from his early definition of the Sun as a libido-symbol to an interpretation of the symbol of the noetic Sun as equivalent to the Self, the centre of the individual psyche and the orchestrator of the individuation process. Late antique perceptions of the physical Sun as the material expression of a transcendent divinity were incorporated into Jung's psychological understanding of this most important of astrological symbols. He drew ideas from Neoplatonists, Gnostics, Hermeticists, and the *Mithras Liturgy*, as well as from nineteenth-century anthropologists and historians of myth; and Mead's interpretations of the older texts, focusing more on the interior spiritual life than on a pantheon of objective celestial divinities, helped Jung to build up his psychological model of a numinous centre of the personality. Jung insisted that solar power, or libido, tends to be perceived in the human imagination in the form of a solar hero, who seeks immortality through a 'treasure hard to attain'. This conviction is evident from his earliest descriptions of solar 'astro-mythology'. Richard Noll has argued that Jung was attempting to found a 'solar cult'.[3] But it is apparent from Jung's own statements that his apparent Sun-worshipping proclivities were always symbolic rather than literal, and focused on the idea of individuation as a psychological process reflecting a meaningful pattern of individual development.

Over time, once he began to explore the symbolism of alchemy more deeply, Jung gradually began to reject the idea that the Sun, in itself, was the most important of all astrological factors:

> You know, the Sun is just one of the planets in ancient astrology, as it is in alchemy. It is in a position that is certainly prominent but not dominant. There is the Sun and the Moon and the host of planets – and it is precisely in alchemy that the Sun is not the main point. In fact, the *coniunctio soli et lunae* is the main point. And, what is more, Mercury is more important. Or, in certain older forms of alchemy, it is Saturn.[4]

But in Jung's early studies, the Sun dominated the stage. Because of his involvement with astrology and his receptivity to the solar emphasis accorded by Alan Leo, there is an obvious relationship between Neoplatonic and Mithraic ideas about the 'central spiritual Sun' and Jung's perception of the meaning of the Sun in the horoscope. Moreover, he was born under the Sun-ruled zodiacal sign of Leo, and he seems to have been convinced of the relevance of Leonine *sumbola* to the core of his own nature. It is therefore not surprising that themes reflecting the astrology and mythology of the Sun form the backbone of *Liber Novus*.

Jung's initial meeting with the old prophet Elijah in Book One of *Liber Novus* happens on 'a dazzling bright day', and introduces the symbolism of the Sun through the landscape in which the encounter occurs. This conjoining of a Saturnian *senex* figure with a solar landscape occurs later in *Liber Novus* with the Anchorite Ammonius, but it is in the encounter with Elijah that the significant juxtaposition first appears. Jung and the prophet climb to the top of a high mountain, with 'a wonderful flood of sunlight all around'. On the peak is a circular embankment made of huge blocks of stone. Elijah, standing on a 'mighty boulder' at the centre of the structure, explains to Jung:

> This is the temple of the sun. This place is a vessel, that collects the light of the sun.[5]

The resemblance of this landscape image to ancient centres of solar worship such as Delphi and Stonehenge is striking; the circular nature of Elijah's 'temple of the sun' is echoed by these two great archaeological sites as well as by numerous other shrines to the Sun-god,[6] and mirrors the Sun's apparent circular movement through the heavens during the course of the day and its apparent circular passage through the zodiac (the ecliptic) in the course of the year. The form of the temple also echoes Jung's reference to Plotinus' description of the soul's natural circular movement 'around something interior, around a centre', which Jung identified with the Self.[7] Equally relevant, Elijah's 'temple of the sun' portrays in three-dimensional form the ancient glyph for the Sun, which since Byzantine times has been represented in horoscopes by a point at the centre of a circle, and which appears on coins from Delphi dated from the fifth century BCE.[8] Alan Leo described this solar glyph in terms that clearly resonated with Jung's own understanding:

> As a factor in astrological symbology, the circle is taken to represent Spirit in general, abstract and unindividualised . . . When a point is placed in the centre of the circle, something is coming into existence out of the depths of the incomprehensible No-thing; Light is beginning to shine forth out of the darkness . . . This stands for God manifest . . . Although omnipresent, His life and power are more especially manifested through the Sun, which great luminary this symbol represents astrologically.[9]

Although Elijah himself is not a solar figure, he reveals solar secrets to Jung and, in the course of Jung's meeting with the old prophet's daughter Salome, Jung is transformed into the Leontocephalus, the lion-headed god of the Mithraic mysteries.[10] Later in Book One, not long after the encounter with Elijah, Jung meets a Tramp, and once again the Sun is an important factor in the landscape setting: 'A gray evening sky covers the sun'. The Tramp is 'poor and dirtily clothed' and possesses only a single eye, the other one having been gouged out in a fight.[11] During the course of Jung's interchange with the Tramp, the life-giving Sun is concealed; moonlight floods the room in the inn to which Jung has brought him, and the Tramp dies coughing with blood flowing from his mouth. The Tramp is without Sun, and thus without meaning or a sense of connection with the Self. In the first layer of *Liber Novus*, Jung recorded the stark details of his vision:

> He [the Tramp] worked, lazed about, laughed, drank, ate, slept, gave his eye . . . he lived the human myth after a fashion . . . And then – then he miserably died – like everyone else.[12]

In the reworking of this episode, Jung inserted a passage that reflected his growing comprehension of the importance of a sense of individual significance and destiny in order to rise above the 'endlessness of being'. The absence of the Sun in the landscape has assumed a more explicit symbolic significance.

> Your heights are your own mountain, which belongs to you and you alone. There you are individual and live your very own life . . . you do not live the common life, which is always continuing and never-ending, the life of history

> and the inalienable and ever-present burdens and products of the human race. There you live the endlessness of being, but not the becoming.[13]

Jung's use of landscape to highlight the symbolic significance of the Sun continues more overtly in his dialogue with Ammonius the Anchorite, whom he meets directly after his experience with the Tramp. Before he encounters Ammonius, Jung describes his own longing for the Sun, for 'light dry air', and for the psychic transition 'from being to becoming': the only remedy for meaninglessness and the pathos of the inevitability of death.[14] Ptolemy's description of the potency of the astrological Sun reflects Aristotle's elemental categories: the Sun's power is found in heat and dryness.

> The active power of the sun's essential nature is found to be heating and to a certain degree, drying. This is made more easily perceptible in the case of the sun than any other heavenly body by its size and by the obviousness of its seasonal changes, for the closer it approaches to the zenith the more it affects us in this way.[15]

It is in an extreme solar landscape, filled with 'hot red rocks', that Jung meets the Anchorite, who takes his daily walks at dawn and at sunset. Ammonius is a deeply introverted Saturnian figure who dwells in a solar world:[16]

> The life of the solitary would be cold were it not for the immense sun, which makes the air and rocks glow. The sun and its eternal splendor replace for the solitary his own life warmth. His heart longs for the sun. He wanders to the lands of the sun . . . In the desert the solitary is relieved of care and therefore turns his whole life to the sprouting garden of his soul, which can flourish only under a hot sun.[17]

It is directly after his first confrontation with Ammonius that Jung has a dream of Helios rising in the eastern sky, driving his chariot drawn by four white horses with golden wings. Jung then offers an invocation – the first of many in *Liber Novus* – to this solar divinity who is also the individual Self:

> Give us your light, you are flame-curled, entwined, crucified and revived; give us your light, your light![18]

The giant Izdubar

The first figure in *Liber Novus* to whom Jung dedicated a full-page painting is the giant Izdubar, whom he meets in Book Two (see Plate 2). Although the giant has both astrological and mythic connotations, Izdubar is also a profoundly personal figure in the parade of inner images in *Liber Novus*. The Sun and solar mythology provided the backbone of Jung's understanding of both deity and the psychological idea of the Self, but his dialogues with Izdubar also dramatise with great clarity the severe internal conflict between rational science and intuitive vision – the 'Spirit of This Time' and the 'Spirit of the Depths' – that helped to precipitate Jung's psychological collapse. The encounter with Izdubar, which extends for many pages and encompasses some of the most beautiful and dramatic images in *Liber Novus* as well as some of the most overtly magical incantations, describes what Jung seems to have experienced as an irreconcilable antipathy between his imaginative and rational faculties, and the apparently mutually exclusive world-views these faculties reflected. Jung's conflict was intensely felt and experienced, somatically as well as psychologically. Although the tension might be viewed solely within the context of his upbringing and the culture in which he lived and worked, this conflict is as alive today on a collective level as it was in the early decades of the twentieth century, and accounts in large part for why Jung's commitment to astrology has been ignored in so many analytic training programmes and biographies of his life and work. Jung's dialogues with Izdubar reveal with great poignancy a drastic and painful dilemma within a man who was both a visionary communing with imaginal realms, and an empiric thinker determined to be accepted within the scientific community of his time and the social and religious structures of the late nineteenth-century Swiss-German milieu in which he was raised.

The name 'Izdubar' is based on the published mistranslation in 1872 of the cuneiform ideograph for Gilgamesh,[19] as the decipherment of cuneiform texts was still in its infancy at that time.[20] By 1906 the mistake had been recognised in scholarly literature,[21] and Jung, who was well aware of this, used the corrected form when describing the ancient Babylonian hero in *Wandlungen* in 1912.[22] But he chose the older, apparently 'wrong' name for his own imaginal figure, painted in 1915. Sonu Shamdasani suggests that Jung's use of the earlier form 'was a way of indicating that his figure, while related to the Babylonian epic, was a free elaboration'.[23] Jung's giant Izdubar exhibits many of the attributes of the Babylonian hero as presented in the *Epic of Gilgamesh*, particularly Gilgamesh's persistent quest for immortality.[24] Gilgamesh, according to Jung, is a 'sun-hero',[25] as is Izdubar. The giant bears bull's horns on his head, and Jung refers to him as 'Izdubar, the mighty, the bull-man'.[26] Gilgamesh, in turn, is described in Tablet I of the *Epic* as 'a savage wild bull in Uruk-the-Sheepfold . . . lording it like a wild bull'.[27] In the *Epic*, Gilgamesh slaughters the Bull of Heaven, sent against him by his mortal enemy, the goddess Ishtar; in *Liber Novus*, Izdubar carries a 'sparkling double axe in his hand, like those used to strike bulls'.[28]

Shamdasani has pointed out that Jung's painting of Izdubar resembles Roscher's drawing of the Babylonian hero (whom Roscher called Izdubar-Nimrod) in the *Ausfürliches Lexikon*.[29] Roscher's illustration, based on an Assyrian relief from the palace of King Sargon II at Khorsabad, presents the hero carrying a serpent in his right hand, associated by the Babylonians with their

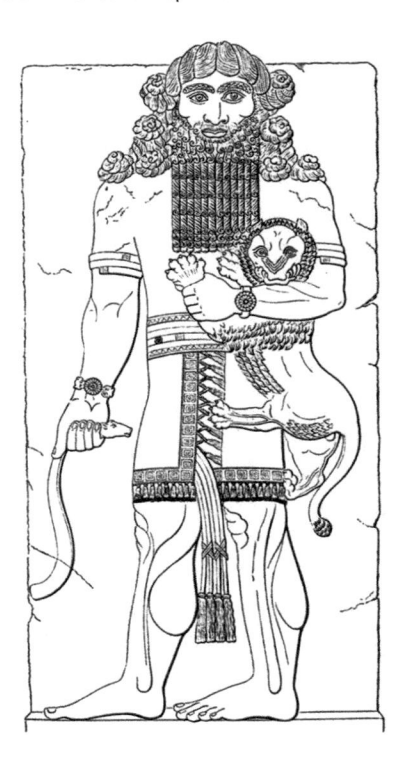

FIGURE 2.1 Left, Roscher's drawing of Izdubar-Gilgamesh. Right, an eighth-century BCE Assyrian version of Gilgamesh.[30]

constellation of the Serpent, sacred to the Lord of the Underworld.[31] In his left hand, Gilgamesh holds a benign-looking small lion, which the Babylonians associated with the zodiacal constellation they called 'The Great Lion'.[32] The serpent and the lion appear together nine centuries later as a *unio oppositorum* in the iconography of the Mithraic lion-headed god Aion, in the initiation ritual described in Apuleius' *Metamorphoses* (which Jung frequently cited),[33] and in Jung's vision of his own symbolic crucifixion in *Liber Novus*.[34] In the *Epic of Gilgamesh*, the Babylonian hero pursues the secret of immortality in Dilmun, a land blessed by the gods; this secret appears in the form of a flower from the plant of eternal youth, which Gilgamesh manages to eventually discover and claw from the sea-bed after many dangerous adventures. Like Izdubar, Gilgamesh craves the light of the Sun:

> Now let my eyes look on the sun so I am sated with light.
> The darkness is hidden, how much light is there?
> When may a dead man see the rays of the sun?[35]

Also like Jung's giant, Gilgamesh is advised – in the case of the Babylonian hero, by the Sun-god himself – to abandon his quest and accept his mortality:

> O Gilgamesh, where are you wandering?
> You cannot find the life that you seek.[36]

Gilgamesh and Izdubar share a craving for solar immortality. Roscher, describing Gilgamesh (who was still called Izdubar at the time the *Detailed Lexicon* was written), noted: 'As a God, Izdubar [Gilgamesh] is associated with the Sun-God'.[37] But there are critical differences between the Babylonian hero and Jung's giant. Whereas the source of eternal life for Gilgamesh is the flower of immortality hidden beneath the sea, for Izdubar it is the Sun itself, setting in the West. And while Gilgamesh is ultimately thwarted in his quest by the goddess Inanna, Izdubar, in *Liber Novus*, is initially thwarted by Jung's 'I', but eventually achieves apotheosis through a rebirth which Jung portrayed in a series of extraordinary paintings.[38] Izdubar seeks the Western land 'where the Sun goes to be reborn'. But Jung's 'I', still serving the scientific 'Spirit of This Time' despite his earlier transformative encounters with The Red One, Elijah, Salome, and the Anchorite, scoffs at the giant, reminding him that as a mortal he can never reach the Sun – which is, after all, merely a star circling in empty space, orbited by the Earth and the other planets. According to this overbearingly rational, scientific Jung, there is no 'Western land'.[39]

The idea that immortality can be found in the West, where the Sun vanishes at dusk, is ubiquitous in myth.[40] The 'Western land' which Izdubar seeks is the place 'where the sun and the maternal sea are united in an eternally rejuvenating embrace'.[41] Jung's description of the setting Sun in *Psychology of the Unconscious* is as poetic as it is psychological:

> Just as the sun, guided by its own internal laws, ascends from morn till noon, and passing beyond the noon descends toward evening, leaving behind its splendor, and then sinks completely into the all-enveloping night, thus, too, does mankind follow his course according to immutable laws, and also sinks, after his course is completed, into night, in order to rise again in the morning to a new cycle in his children.[42]

In Jung's birth horoscope, the Sun is placed in its own zodiacal sign of Leo and is located precisely at the Western horizon, as Jung was born at the exact moment of sunset. Since he understood astrological symbolism as the imaginal portrayal of the qualities of time, this natal horoscopic placement would have been of immense symbolic significance to him as a myth of his own personal journey, since the Sun, according to Alan Leo's descriptions, is the 'vessel' for the divine spark in a particular lifetime and reflects, through its position by zodiacal sign and relationship to the four cardinal points, the inner spiritual qualities and destiny of the individual. The giant Izdubar, seeking immortality through the setting Sun, is cast in the mould of archetypal solar heroes such as Gilgamesh; but he is also the questing solar spirit of Jung himself, portrayed earlier in his encounter with Elijah and the 'temple of the sun'. That Jung was familiar with the traditional astrological relationship between the Sun and the sign of Leo is stated explicitly in *Psychology of the Unconscious*. Here he noted that Leo is 'the Zodiacal sign of the sun's greatest heat',[43] and described the destructive as well as beneficial attributes of this ambivalent solar symbol:

> The zodiacal representation of the August heat is the herd-devouring lion whom the Jewish hero Samson killed in order to free the parched earth from this plague.[44]

Jung's fascination with solar mythology at the time he envisioned Izdubar, and his understanding of the mythic Sun as a symbol of the life-force or libido, are clearly demonstrated in *Psychology of the Unconscious*. But the physical Sun and the noetic Sun were not identical in late antique religious philosophy, nor were they for Jung. The planets, in Jung's view, are not a plurality of independent powers, but are also 'libido-symbols' and 'representations of the sun'.[45] This echoes the Neoplatonic view of the physical Sun as the great chorus-master of the heavens, orchestrating the motions of the planets, while the noetic Sun orchestrates the realm of the planetary daimons on the level of the soul. This perception is also described in Mead's discussion of the *Chaldean Oracles*, which, along with the *Mithras Liturgy*, Jung was reading at the time:[46]

> Proclus, however, tells us that the real Sun, as distinguished from the visible disk, was trans-mundane or super-cosmic . . . it belonged to the Light-world proper, the monadic cosmos, and poured forth thence its 'fountains of Light' . . . The Sun's 'wholeness' . . . was to be sought on the trans-mundane plane; 'for there', he [Proclus] says, 'is the "*Solar Cosmos*" and the "*Whole Light*"', as the Oracles of the Chaldaeans say, and I believe'.[47]

Eliding this idea with the solar divinity of the *Mithras Liturgy*, Jung observed: 'Mithra seems to be the divine spirit, while Helios is the material god . . . the visible lieutenant of the divinity'.[48] It was this view that Alan Leo applied to the Sun in the horoscope when he declared that it 'symbolises cosmic life or consciousness' and 'stands beyond and above the form side of manifestation'.[49] Moreover, according to Leo, over many incarnations the solar influence becomes stronger and stronger as the individual becomes more 'self-consciously individualised':

> The Sun's positions, aspects, and influence will now dominate his horoscope and he will no longer be classed as an ordinary man, but as a progressive individual.[50]

In 1911, Jung had written to Freud that the signs of the zodiac were images of the cycle of the libido. Now the entire solar system began to appear to Jung as an extension of the central light and potency of the 'libido-symbol' of the Sun; the zodiac is, after all, an imaginal portrayal of the ecliptic, the apparent path of the Sun around the earth, and the planets travelling through the twelve zodiacal signs can only express their meanings through this solar circle as 'representations of the sun'. Jung seems to have combined older Neoplatonic perceptions of the noetic spiritual Sun with Alan Leo's understanding of the astrological Sun as a symbol of what he called the 'Individuality' – the 'divine spark' within the individual – an idea which, via Blavatsky, was itself based on Neoplatonic conceptions. Izdubar is an archetypal solar hero reflecting the 'immutable laws' of the human journey from birth to death to rebirth. But he is also entirely specific to Jung's own natal horoscope, and reveals in imaginal form Jung's understanding of what it might mean to be an individual born with the Sun in Leo setting in the West.

Izdubar's *sunthemata*

In his painting of Izdubar, Jung reproduced one of the most important features of his birth horoscope. A more careful inspection of the image of the giant reveals a multitude of golden-winged salamanders surrounding the figure of Izdubar; two

FIGURE 2.2   Glyphs for the zodiacal sign of Leo. From left to right: glyph from a horoscope dated 28 October 497 CE, during the reign of the emperor Diocletian; hand-drawn glyph by Alan Leo; hand-drawn glyph by Jung; glyph generated by the Time Cycles Research Io astrological computer programme in 2013.[52]

FIGURE 2.3   Izdubar with Leo glyphs highlighted in black. The style of the glyph resembles most closely the one drawn by Alan Leo.

of these winged, four-legged, striped creatures crown Izdubar's horns and create a kind of headpiece. Together, they form repeating images of the astrological glyph for Leo, the continuity of which is reflected in horoscopes from the sixth century to the present day.[51]

As Jung had been studying astrology intensively for at least four years before he produced his painting of Izdubar, it is unlikely that this repeated appearance of a specific astrological symbol is accidental. Jung had, after all, ample opportunity to draw as well as study the glyph of Leo. This zodiacal sign is described by astrological authors from Vettius Valens onward as belonging to the fiery trigon. The salamander, according to Paracelsus, is one of the chief symbols of the element of fire; it is an 'elemental', the animating spirit or daimon of the element.[53] Later alchemists distinguished between this natural elemental spirit and a more interior spiritual potency related to transformation and immortality, in much the same way that the physical Sun for the Neoplatonists was a symbol of, but not identical with, the noetic Sun of the divine realm. The 'Salamander of the Philosophers', according to the seventeenth-century alchemist Michael Maier, is not the ordinary 'creeping worm' of nature, nor even a 'natural' elemental spirit such as Paracelsus described, but is 'born in Fire' and 'rejoyces in Fire'. The salamander portrayed in the engraving accompanying Maier's text is clearly meant to represent this spiritual, celestial salamander: it bears stars along its spine.

Although Maier's 'Salamander of the Philosophers', unlike Jung's, has no wings, the image of the winged dragon was often used synonymously in alchemical texts as a fiery symbol of the spiritual unity of life hidden in the *prima materia* or primal substance.[55] These dragons have webbed wings like those Jung painted on Izdubar's salamanders. For Maier, the salamander-dragon was an emblem of the secret spiritual heart of matter and of the human being, identical with the alchemical gold or Philosophers' Stone: 'As the Salamander lives in fire, so also the Stone'.[56]

In *Liber Novus*, following his final encounter with Ammonius and The Red One, Jung wrote about the chameleon, whose Greek name – ΧΑΜΑΙΛΕΩΝ – means 'crawling lion', and which Jung described as 'a crawling shimmering lizard, but precisely not a lion, whose nature is related to the sun'. The salamander-like chameleon, for Jung, symbolises the solar spirit trapped in the cycle of repeated incarnations:

> After all the rebirths you still remain the lion crawling on the earth . . . I recognized the chameleon and no longer want to crawl on the earth and change colors and be reborn; instead I want to exist from my own force, like the sun which gives light and does not suck light.[57]

Jung identifies himself with the chameleon, declaring that he recalls his 'solar nature' and 'would like to rush to my rising'. He hurries toward the East to experience this rising and encounters the giant Izdubar hurrying the other way, heading toward the West to pursue his immortality. The striped salamanders in the painting are also chameleons which, like Izdubar, are solar spirits trapped in mortal life.

EMBLEMA **XXIX.** *De fecretis Naturæ.*
Ut Salamandra vivit igne fic lapis:

EPIGRAMMA **XXIX.**

D*Egit in ardenti Salamandra potentiori igne,*
Nec Vulcane tuas æstimat illa minas:
Sic quoque non flammarum incendia fæva recufat,
Qui fuit affiduo natus in igne Lapis.
Illa rigens æstus extinguit, liberáque exit,
At calet hic, fimilis quem calor inde juvat.

Q 3   I

FIGURE 2.4   Michael Maier's 'Salamander of the Philosophers'[54]

These creatures, shaped in the form of the astrological glyph for Leo, suggest that Izdubar is a fiery elemental spirit, a *daimon* who embodies in mythic form what Jung seems to have understood as the core of this Sun–ruled zodiacal sign: the intuitive knowledge of, and yearning for, a direct experience of celestial immortality. Alan Leo declared that the zodiacal sign of Leo, from an esoteric point of view, represents 'the perfected man, the Christ, the Buddha, realising himself as the son of the Cosmic Self'.[58] The individual born under the sign of Leo might thus, in Alan Leo's view, be driven by a greater need than others to experience – or, as Plato might have understood it, to recollect – the 'One Life which permeates all things' as the central theme of the life-journey. Jung rephrased this idea in a psychological context:

> The sun is adapted as is nothing else to represent the visible God of this world . . . Our source of energy and life is the Sun. Thus our life substance, as an energic process, is entirely Sun.[59]

During the time Jung worked on *Liber Novus*, he seems to have relied more on myth than on alchemy for his understanding of dragons, serpents, salamanders, crocodiles, and other related symbols. But the creatures in the painting – whose stripes, like those in Jung's images of the Orphic god Phanes later in *Liber Novus*, suggest a conjoining of opposites[60] – also imply that, like the *prima materia* in the alchemical *opus*, the giant must be subjected to a transformation before his divine solar essence can be revealed. The crocodiles on Izdubar's left and right in the lower part of the painting continue this theme. Jung described the crocodile as an archetypal 'mother-image', which may also appear as 'other salamander-like, saurian creatures';[61] but the crocodile may equally signify the solar divine child, if the image is derived from 'earlier, non-Christian levels'.[62] Izdubar, whose prototype originates in Babylon, is certainly 'earlier' and 'non-Christian'. Jung also pointed out that a number of Egyptian deities bearing various animal guises were associated with the Sun-god Ra:

> Even the water-god Sobk, who appeared as a crocodile, was identified with Ra.[63]

The divine spark

Alan Leo called the Sun the 'positive and primal fount of all existence'.[64]

> There is but one life, and that is the life of the Logos . . . The planetary spirits and the planetary bodies have their own specialised forms of this ONE life, and humanity in its turn holds this life in a separate form while moving in the great whole . . . Potentially we are all sons of God, sparks from the great flame.[65]

The Sun is also mirrored in Christlike qualities:

> The Sun . . . is the body of God, the Logos of this solar system, through which He gives His Love, Light and Life . . . The Sun, giving life, light and heat to the world, stands in each nativity as the symbol of vitality and activity, mind and intellect, love and feeling.[66]

The relationship between the Sun, love, and the 'inner Christ' appealed to Jung's unorthodox but nevertheless firm allegiance to Christ as a symbol of the Self.[67] In 1943, Jung noted that 'this light of the Sun becomes the light of John's logos, which shines out in the darkness and undoubtedly means spiritual illumination . . . It is the light of the *gnosis theou*'.[68] The idea of the human spirit as a 'spark from the great flame' is expressed in a number of Gnostic texts, and it appears in Book One of *Liber Novus* when the voice of the Spirit of the Depths calls upon the ambiguous god of the new Aion, who is 'hateful-beautiful', 'evil-good', 'laughable-serious', 'sick-healthy', 'inhuman-human', and 'ungodly-godly':

> You new spark of an eternal fire, into which night were you born? . . .
> The constellation of your birth is an ill and changing star.[69]

The phrase appears again when Jung adjures the Serpent: 'Oh holy spirit, grant me a spark of your eternal light!'[70] And finally, Philemon, in 'Scrutinies' (Book Three of *Liber Novus*) announces to Jung: 'I myself am of the eternal fire of light'.[71]

The original text of 'Scrutinies' was written and privately published in 1916 as *Septem sermones ad mortuos*, and was presented as a pseudepigraphic treatise purportedly written by the second-century Gnostic teacher Basilides. Revised in 1917 and retitled 'Scrutinies', the teacher is Jung's own personal daimon, Philemon, who is himself 'of the eternal fire of light'. The perception of the Sun as the 'eternal light', and of both humans and gods as 'sparks' of that divine fire, directly link these references to Jung's declaration:

> Just as the greening earth and every living body needs the sun, so we as spirits need your light and your warmth. A sunless spirit becomes the parasite of the body. But the God feeds the spirit.[72]

Jung calls the newly reborn Izdubar 'the sun, the eternal light'.[73]

The human soul as a 'spark' of the eternal solar light dominates a number of Kabbalistic texts of the late sixteenth century,[74] which were published in a Latin translation by Christian Knorr von Rosenroth at the end of the seventeenth century in a work called *Kabbala denudata*.[75] Jung was familiar with this work and frequently cited it in later volumes of the *Collected Works*.[76] In Sermon VII of *Septem sermones*, Jung referred to a 'solitary star':

> In immeasurable distance there glimmers a solitary star on the highest point of heaven . . . This star is man's God and goal. It is his guiding divinity; in it man finds repose. To it goes the long journey of the soul after death; in it shine all things which otherwise might keep man from the greater world with the brilliance of a great light. To this One, man ought to pray . . . Such a prayer builds a bridge over death.[77]

In Sermon II, the identity of this 'solitary star' is stated explicitly: it is the Sun-god Helios.[78] Jung's references to the divine spark within the individual – a microcosm of the 'central spiritual Sun' – suggest that, as a psychological paradigm, it contributed significantly to his idea of individuation. Alan Leo understood the astrological Sun as 'the vehicle through which the Solar Logos is manifesting',[79] and all the other astrological significators in a birth chart ultimately owe their development and teleology to the Sun as the focus of the natal horoscope. The idea that the Sun infuses meaning into the rest of the planets appears regularly in Neoplatonic and Hermetic literature; the theurgy of Iamblichus and Proclus, as well as that of the *Mithras Liturgy*, was solar-focused.[80] The Hermetic treatise known as *The Definitions of Asclepius unto King*

Ammon, which appears in translation in Mead's *Thrice-Greatest Hermes*, describes the central role of the Sun as the charioteer of the 'cosmic team' of planetary *daimones*:

> He [the Sun] safely drives the cosmic team, and holds them in unto Himself lest they should run away in dire disorder . . . And under Him is ranged the choir of daimons . . . they are the ministers of each one of the Stars . . . The soul's rational part is set above the lordship of the daimons – designed to be receptacle of God. Who then doth have a Ray shining upon him through the Sun within his rational part . . . on them the daimons do not act; for no one of the daimons or of Gods has any power against one Ray of God.[81]

Consciousness of solar light, according to this treatise, frees the soul from planetary *Heimarmene*. Jung, embedding this idea in a psychological framework, seems to have elided the Hermetic concept with Leo's astrological perspective, and understood the Sun in the horoscope as the vehicle through which the entire horoscope, as the vessel for the Self, expresses itself in an individual life. It is this theme that underpins the transformation of Izdubar, from a wounded mortal seeker to an immortal solar divinity.

The transformation of Izdubar

Solar myths, as Jung understood them, are archetypal and universal. But from his astrological perspective, they are reflected in the individual in unique ways according to where the astrological Sun was placed at the moment of birth, because this moment encapsulates the qualities of the Sun's expression in its specific relationship to other planets and zodiacal signs. This relationship of macrocosm to microcosm – the great contained in the small – was fully articulated in Jung's cosmological diagram, the *Systema Munditotius*, discussed more fully below in Chapter 7. The idea, with its accompanying underpinning of *sumpatheia*, can be found in Neoplatonic, Hermetic, and Gnostic cosmologies, as well as in the literature of alchemy and the Kabbalah in the medieval period. It is also the dominant theme in Alan Leo's astrological approach. His various comments about the Sun in the horoscope describe a transpersonal core or 'Individuality' which represents, not the personal daimon or 'Master of the House', but the essential nature of the incarnated individual who is called upon by the daimon to fulfil a particular destiny.

Alan Leo had a great deal to say about the Sun as a dynamic process. In his view, one is not born with the Sun fully shining; it requires effort, consciousness, and suffering to facilitate its meaningful expression in life. According to Leo, the unconscious or 'unevolved' individual expresses the Sun instinctually. Its power first pours through Mars as 'blind forces' that must eventually be transmuted.[82] This mirrors Jung's idea that Mars is the 'principle of individuation': it is the instinctual, unconscious form of the nascent Sun. When Jung first encounters Izdubar, the giant is a raw instinctual force, 'elementally powerful' but afflicted with 'blindness and unknowingness'. He is 'a primordial grown child that required human Logos'.[83] Jung lames and nearly destroys him with the 'poison of science',[84] but compassion and an increasing realisation of Izdubar's true nature demand that the giant be saved and healed:

> Divinity and humanity should remain preserved, if man should remain before his God, and the God remain before man. The high–blazing flame is the middle way, whose luminous course runs between the human and the divine.[85]

Both The Red One and Ammonius, respectively Martial and Saturnine figures, are seen running away just before the giant's transformation, as though solar revelation has now superseded and absorbed all other planetary processes. Jung's experiences with Izdubar emphasise the importance and necessity that he attributed to the giant's apotheosis, which he seems to have understood as the only way to heal the intolerable rift in his own nature: the 'high–blazing flame' of the Sun is the 'middle way' that can connect human and divine, allowing both science and intuitive vision to cohabit in a world where each is valued because both are expressions of the central Self. The conflict between the truth of science and the truth of the imagination forms the dominant motif of Jung's dialogues with the giant. Jung's 'I' eventually acknowledges to Izdubar that the 'wisdom of the astrologers . . . is that which comes to you from inner things'.[86]

When Jung and the giant arrive at the tiny secluded house where the healing can occur, Jung enables Izdubar to shrink, and the giant becomes encapsulated within an egg. He emerges transformed into the Sun itself (see Plate 3). Jung facilitates the giant's apotheosis through a series of ritual 'incantations' which any practitioner of ceremonial magic, from antiquity to the present, would immediately recognise as a rite of adjuration.[87] Before the incantations begin, Jung declares:

> Do not speak and do not show the God, but sit in a solitary place and sing
>   incantations in the ancient manner:
> Set the egg before you, the God in his beginning.
> And behold it,
> And incubate it with the magical warmth of your gaze.[88]

The rite is successful: 'Christmas has come'.[89] Astonished at the results, Jung declares in amazement: 'Oh Izdubar! Divine one! How wonderful! You are healed!' The giant replies: 'Healed? Was I ever sick? Who speaks of sickness? I was sun, completely sun. I am the sun'.[90]

The mythic motif of the solar god emerging from the cosmic egg is found in both the Orphic and Mithraic cosmologies in which Jung was immersed at the time.[91] Phanes, the Orphic primal deity, rose from an egg filled with fire; Mithras likewise burst from an egg, surrounded, like Phanes, by the circle of the zodiac.[92] Izdubar's transformation, in terms of Jung's understanding of astrology, seems to reflect the idea that the microcosmic Sun in the natal horoscope − in Jung's case, the Sun in Leo, setting in the West − reflects the individual 'God-image': a symbol of the Self that reveals its meaning as 'the greatest value' over time, and exhibits different faces according to changes in individual consciousness. Izdubar's nature is fiery and visionary, and does not accord with the rational 'poison' of Jung's intellect. A complex process must occur through which the giant's essence can be recognised, valued and, eventually, acknowledged as an image of the divine:

> The renewed God signifies a renewed attitude, that is, a renewed possibility for intensive life, a recovery of life, because psychologically God always denotes the greatest value, thus the greatest sum of the libido, the greatest intensity of life the optimum of psychological life's activity.[93]

Jung's discovery that Izdubar is not only 'real', but also a vessel for the universal life-force, suggests that he perceived the astrological Sun in much the same way Alan Leo did: as the individual embodiment of the 'divine spark' that constitutes the transpersonal centre of the personality. Awareness of this spark, according to both Jung and Leo, is not automatic, and it can be suppressed or remain unconscious through too much rationality and identification with the world-view of the 'spirit of this time', which has the power to destroy even the immortal gods. For Jung, this spirit was the 'poison' of what is currently referred to as 'scientism': the belief that science alone can provide truths about the nature of reality.[94]

Jung seems to have understood the impact of the Hermetic solar 'Ray of God', described by Mead as shining on the 'rational part' of the human soul, as the conscious ego's direct experience of the Self.[95] If such an experience can be achieved, it could, in Jung's view, facilitate a transformation of the personality, and release the individual from much of the suffering of *Heimarmene*: the compulsions of the unconscious libido. The astrological symbol for this process, for Jung, lies in the Sun in the natal horoscope. The 'maximal consciousness' that such an experience brings, however brief, is akin to the experience of temporary 'divinisation' described in the *Mithras Liturgy*, in which the soul of the initiate briefly experiences union with Helios-Mithras.[96] Although the ecstatic moment passes, the individual is permanently changed by the experience. Mead compared the Hermetic idea of the Sun with the Orphic Phanes, whose primal egg symbolises 'the two hemispheres above and below'.[97] Izdubar's apotheosis as a solar divinity, ritually invoked out of the cosmic egg, links him firmly with the Orphic primal divinity, who appears later in *Liber Novus* as 'he who brings the Sun': the god-image of the new astrological Aion. Izdubar is also absorbed into another figure, the *coniunctio oppositorum* of Saturn and the Sun whom Jung called Philemon, and who, in a vision Jung experienced in 1917, informed him: 'My name was Izdubar'.[98]

Notes

1 G.R.S. Mead (trans.), *A Mithraic Ritual*, VIII:1–2–XI:1, in G.R.S. Mead, *Echoes from the Gnosis*, Vol. VI (London: Theosophical Publishing Society, 1907), pp. 221–22.
2 Jung, CW5, ¶¶296–7.
3 See Richard Noll, *The Jung Cult* (Princeton, NJ: Princeton University Press, 1994).
4 Jung, *The Solar Myths and Opicinus de Canistris*, pp. 78–79.
5 Jung, *Liber Novus*, p. 251.
6 For architectural circularity associated with the solar deity in ancient cultures, see Brian Hobley, *The Circle of God* (Oxford: Archaeopress, 2015); Fritz Graf, *Apollo* (London:

Routledge, 2009). For Stonehenge as a 'solar temple', see John D. North, *Stonehenge* (New York: Simon and Schuster, 1996), pp. 221–27 and 393–408.

7 Jung, CW9ii, ¶342, citing Plotinus, Ennead VI, in Stephen Mackenna (trans.), Plotinus: *The Enneads*, 6 volumes (London: Medici Society, 1917–30).

8 See Otto Neugebauer and H.B. van Hoesen, *Greek Horoscopes* (Philadelphia, PA: American Philosophical Society, 1987), p. 163. For the coins, see *British Museum Catalogue of Greek Coins, Central Greece* (1963), Plate 14, nos. 4, 24, and 33.

9 Alan Leo, *Esoteric Astrology* (London: Modern Astrology Office, 1910), p. 2.

10 For more on Elijah, see Chapter 4. For more on Salome, see Chapter 3. For the Leontocephalus, see Greene, *Jung's Studies in Astrology*, chapter 6.

11 Jung, *Liber Novus*, p. 265.

12 Jung, *Liber Novus*, p. 266.

13 Jung, *Liber Novus*, p. 266. The distinction between the two 'layers' in this passage was given by Sonu Shamdasani in a personal communication.

14 Jung, *Liber Novus*, p. 267.

15 Ptolemy, *Tetrabiblos,* I.4. See Jung, CW8, ¶869; Jung, CW9ii, ¶¶128, 149; Jung, CW14, ¶576.

16 For more on the Saturnine qualities of Ammonius, see Chapter 4.

17 Jung, *Liber Novus*, p. 269.

18 Jung, *Liber Novus*, p. 270.

19 See George Smith, 'The Chaldean Account of the Deluge', *Transactions of the Society of Biblical Archaeology* 1–2 (1872), pp. 213–34. The error was later perpetuated in Leonidas le Cenci Hamilton's translation of the epic, *Ishtar and Izdubar* (London: W.H. Allen, 1884), and in Alfred Jeremias, *Izdubar-nimrod* (Leipzig: B.G. Teubner, 1891). The discovery of a lexicographic tablet by T.G. Pinches in 1890 eventually allowed the literal translation of the ideograph – *iz* (or *gish*), *du*, and *bar* – to be rendered phonetically as 'Gilgamesh'. See Morris Jastrow, *The Religion of Babylonia and Assyria* (Boston, MA: Athenaeum Press, 1898), p. 468.

20 For recent works on the history of the decipherment of cuneiform, see C.B.F. Walker, *Cuneiform* (Berkeley: University of California Press, 1987); Karen Radnor and Eleanor Robson (eds.), *The Oxford Handbook of Cuneiform Culture* (Oxford: Oxford University Press, 2011).

21 See Peter Jensen, *Das Gilgamesh-Epos in der Weltliteratur* (Strasbourg: Karl Trübner, 1906), p. 2.

22 See, for example, Jung, *Psychology of the Unconscious*, p. 106, n. 1.

23 Shamdasani, *C. G. Jung: A Biography in Books*, p. 93.

24 For *The Epic of Gilgamesh,* see Andrew R. George (ed. and trans.), *The Babylonian Gilgamesh Epic*, 2 volumes (Oxford: Oxford University Press, 2003).

25 Jung, *Psychology of the Unconscious*, p. 106, n. 1.

26 Jung, *Liber Novus*, p. 278.

27 George (trans.), *The Babylonian Gilgamesh Epic,* 64 and 81, p. 543.

28 Jung, *Liber Novus*, p. 278.

29 Shamdasani, *C. G. Jung: A Biography in Books*, p. 92.

30 Roscher, *Ausfürliches Lexikon*, Vol. 2, p. 776; bas-relief of Gilgamesh, eighth century BCE, Musée du Louvre, photo by Urban.

31 See Gavin White, *Babylonian Star-Lore* (London: Solaria, 2008), pp. 81–82 and 183–85.

32 See White, *Babylonian Star-Lore*, p. 140; Richard Hinckley Allen, *Star Names* (New York: Dover, 1963 [1899]), pp. 252–63; David H. Kelley and Eugene F. Milone, *Exploring Ancient Skies* (New York: Springer, 2011), pp. 479–81.

33 See Jung, *Liber Novus*, p. 252, n. 211. The passage in Apuleius is marked by a line in the margin in Jung's German translation of the work.

34 Jung, *Liber Novus*, p. 252.

35 George (trans.), *The Babylonian Gilgamesh Epic*, I:13–15, Vol. 1, p. 277.

36 George (trans.), *The Babylonian Gilgamesh Epic*, I:7–8, Vol. 1, p. 277.

37 Roscher, *Ausfürliches Lexikon*, Vol. 2, p. 774, cited by Shamdasani in *Liber Novus*, p. 284, n. 136.

38 Jung, *Liber Novus*, pp. 59–64.

39 Jung, *Liber Novus*, 278.

40 See Jung, CW5, ¶357; Jung, CW5, ¶364 and n. 67.

41 Jung, CW5, ¶364.

42 Jung, *Psychology of the Unconscious*, p. 106. The revised version is found in Jung, CW5, ¶251.

43 Jung, *Psychology of the Unconscious*, p. 559, n. 50.

44 Jung, *Psychology of the Unconscious*, p. 70.

45 Jung, *Psychology of the Unconscious*, p. 501, n. 27.

46 See Jung, *Psychology of the Unconscious*, p. 503, n. 45; p. 504, n. 60. Jung noted (*Psychology of the Unconscious*, p. 225) that, according to the 'Chaldean view', the planetary gods are grouped in triads. This doctrine is explicitly stated in the *Chaldean Oracles*, where the fiery 'Supreme Being' emanates a primary trinity of power, intellect, and will. For this primary triad, see Hans Lewy, *Chaldaean Oracles and Theurgy: Mysticism, Magic, and Platonism in the Later Roman Empire* (Paris: Institut d'Études Augustiniennes, 2011 [1956]), pp. 76–83.

47 G.R.S. Mead, *Chaldean Oracles* (London: Theosophical Publishing Society, 1908), p. 333.

48 Jung, *Psychology of the Unconscious*, pp. 501–502, n. 21.

49 Leo, *Esoteric Astrology*, p. 23.

50 Leo, *Esoteric Astrology*, pp. 146–7.

51 For a similar portrayal of the serpentine symbols as well as the crocodiles, see the frontispiece in Wolfgang Schultz, *Dokumente der Gnosis* (Jena: E. Diederichs, 1910), a work which Jung probably acquired not long after its publication. For the comparison, see Lance Owens' Foreword in Alfred Ribi, *The Search for Roots: C. G. Jung and the Tradition of Gnosis* (Los Angeles, CA: Gnosis Archive Books, 2013), p. 19. However, Schultz' serpents do not form the astrological glyph for Leo, and they are not salamanders, as they do not have legs.

52 Late fifth-century glyph: Neugebauer and van Hoesen, *Greek Horoscopes*, p. 156. Alan Leo's glyph: Leo, *The Key to Your Own Nativity*, p. xiv. Jung's glyph: horoscope drawn by Jung, reproduced in Greene, *Jung's Studies in Astrology*, chapter 2. The computer font is Io Wizardry from Time Cycles Research.

53 Theophrastus von Hohenheim (Paracelsus), *Sämtliche Werke*, 1:14.7, ed. Karl Sudhoff and Wilhelm Matthiessen (Munich: Oldenbourg, 1933).

54 Michael Maier, *Atalanta fugiens* (Frankfurt, 1617), Emblem 29; Private Collection/ Bridgeman Images.

55 See the various images reproduced in Jung, CW12 and Jung, CW13.

56 Maier, *Atalanta fugiens*, caption for Emblem XXIX.

57 Jung, Liber Novus, p. 277.

58 Leo, *Esoteric Astrology*, p. 90.

59 Jung, *Psychology of the Unconscious*, 70–71.

60 See the striped garments of the Orphic god Phanes in Jung, *Liber Novus*, pp. 113, 123, and 125.

61 Jung, CW9i, ¶310.

62 Jung, CW9i, ¶270.

63 Jung, CW5, ¶147, n. 35.

64 Alan Leo, *Astrology for All* (London: Modern Astrology, 1910), p. 10.

65 Leo, *Astrology for All*, pp. 10–11.

66 Alan Leo, *How to Judge a Nativity, Part One* (London: Modern Astrology, 1908).

67 For Jung's equation of solar symbolism with Christ and with the Self, see Jung, CW9ii, ¶¶68–126; Jung, CW5, ¶¶158–9, 638; Jung, CW12, ¶¶112, 314, 497; Jung, CW9i, ¶¶106, 661; Jung, CW13, ¶296.

68 Jung, *The Solar Myths and Opicinus de Canistris*, p. 86.

69 Jung, *Liber Novus*, p. 243.

70 Jung, *Liber Novus*, p. 329.

71 Jung, *Liber Novus*, p. 354.

72 Jung, *Liber Novus*, p. 286.

73 Jung, *Liber Novus*, p. 286.

74 For these texts, known as 'Lurianic' after the influential Kabbalist Isaac Luria (1534–1572), see Lawrence Fine, *Physician of the Soul, Healer of the Cosmos* (Stanford, CA: Stanford University Press, 2003); Louis Jacobs, 'Uplifting the Sparks in Later Jewish Mysticism', in Arthur Green (ed.), *Jewish Spirituality, Vol. 2* (New York: Crossroad, 1987), pp. 99–126;

Gershom Scholem, *Kabbalah* (New York: Keter Publishing House, 1974), pp. 128–44, 420–28, 443–48; Moshe Idel, *Hasidism* (Albany: SUNY Press, 1995), pp. 33–43.

75 Christian Knorr von Rosenroth, *Kabbala denudata*, 3 volumes (Sulzbach/Frankfurt: Abraham Lichtenthal, 1677–1684).

76 For Jung's many citations of the *Kabbala denudata*, see, for example, Jung, CW12, ¶313; Jung, CW13, ¶411; Jung, CW14, ¶¶592–93; Jung, CW9i, ¶¶557n, 576n, 596n. See also Jung's Kabbalistic vision, described in *MDR*, p. 325, and based on a text by the sixteenth-century Kabbalist Moshe Cordovero, which is included in a Latin translation in the *Kabbala denudata*. Jung directly associated his vision with Cordovero's text.

77 Jung, *Septem sermones*, in Hoeller, *The Gnostic Jung*, p. 58.

78 Jung, *Septem sermones*, in Hoeller, *The Gnostic Jung*, p. 50.

79 Leo, *How to Judge a Nativity*, p. 29.

80 See Gregory Shaw, *Theurgy and the Soul: The Neoplatonism of Iamblichus* (University Park: Penn State University Press, 1995).

81 G.R.S. Mead (ed. and trans.), *Thrice-Greatest Hermes: Studies in Hellenistic Theosophy and Gnosis*, 3 volumes (London: Theosophical Publishing Society, 1906), Vol. 2, pp. 266–84 (*CH* XVI, 'The Definitions of Asclepius unto King Ammon', Text R, 348–54, 7–16).

82 Alan Leo, *The Art of Synthesis* (London: Modern Astrology Office, 1912), p. 32.

83 Jung, *Liber Novus*, pp. 280–81.

84 For the 'poisoning' of Izdubar, see Jung, *Liber Novus*, pp. 278–79.

85 Jung, *Liber Novus*, p. 281.

86 Jung, *Liber Novus*, p. 278.

87 For late antique adjuration rituals and their characteristic phrasing, see Michael D. Swartz, *Scholastic Magic* (Princeton, NJ: Princeton University Press, 1996); Rebecca Macy Lesses, *Ritual Practices to Gain Power* (Harrisburg, PA: Trinity Press, 1998); Betz, *The Greek Magical Papyri*; Peter Schäfer, *The Hidden and Manifest God*, trans. Aubrey Pomerance (Albany: SUNY Press, 1992). These ancient rituals of adjuration were taken up in later grimoires such as *Abramelin* and the *Sixth and Seventh Books of Moses*; see Owen Davies, *Grimoires* (Oxford: Oxford University Press, 2009). See also the magical invocation of the 'boundless Light' in Mead (trans.), *Pistis Sophia*, 142:375.

88 The incantations appear in Jung, *Liber Novus*, pp. 49–61. For the translation, see pp. 284–85.

89 Jung, *Liber Novus*, p. 284.

90 Jung, *Liber Novus*, p. 286.

91 For the elision of Phanes and Mithras through the motif of the egg, see David Ulansey, *The Origins of the Mithraic Mysteries: Cosmology and Salvation in the Ancient World* (Oxford: Oxford University Press, 1991), pp. 120–21; Franz Cumont, 'Mithra et l'Orphisme', *Revue de l'histoire des religions* 109 (1934), pp. 64–72. In *Psychology of the Unconscious*, p. 289, Jung cited Leo Frobenius, *Das Zeitalter des Sonnengottes* (1904), in which various myths of the Sun-god incubating in an egg are given. For further references to the cosmic egg, see Jung, *Psychology of the Unconscious*, pp. 388, 394, 415, 468, 540 n. 36, 547 n. 55.

92 See, for example, the relief from the Roman Mithraeum at Housesteads Roman fort (Vercovium/Borcovecium) on Hadrian's Wall (CIMRM 860), from the third century CE, now at the Museum of Antiquities, University of Newcastle upon Tyne. Mithras is shown emerging from the cosmic egg, holding a dagger and a torch and surrounded by the circle of the zodiac.

93 Jung, CW6, ¶301.

94 For 'scientism', see Gregory R. Peterson, 'Demarcation and the Scientist Fallacy', *Zygon* 38:4 (2003), pp. 751–61; Olav Hammer, *Claiming Knowledge: Strategies of Epistemology from Theosophy to the New Age* (Leiden: Brill, 2004), pp. 205–208.

95 Mead, *Thrice-Greatest Hermes*, 2:282–83.

96 For a similar experience, see also *Corpus Hermeticum* X, described in Fowden, Garth, *The Egyptian Hermes: A Historical Approach to the Late Pagan Mind* (Princeton, NJ: Princeton University Press, 1993), p. 83, n. 38.

97 Mead, *Thrice-Greatest Hermes*, 2:282.

98 See Shamdasani's comments in Jung, *Liber Novus*, p. 305, n. 232.

3

THE ANIMA, THE MOON, AND THE SERPENT

The common view that man is a composite creature is correct, but it is not correct that he is composed of two parts only . . . Now the union of soul with body makes up the emotional part, the further union [of soul] with mind produces reason . . . When these three principles have been compacted, the earth contributes body to the birth of man, the moon soul, the sun reason, just as he contributes light to the moon.[1]

—Plutarch

But humankind is masculine and feminine, not just man or woman. You can hardly say of your soul what sex it is. But if you pay close attention, you will see that the most masculine man has a feminine soul, and the most feminine woman has a masculine soul. The more manly you are, the more remote from you is what woman really is, since the feminine in yourself is alien and contemptuous.[2]

—C.G. Jung

The anima as fate

A great deal has been written about Jung's concept of the anima: the feminine 'soul' in men that serves as a mediator between the archetypal realm of the collective unconscious and the daylight realm of the conscious ego.[3] Jung devoted a number of essays to this theme, as well as discussing it more briefly in various passages throughout the *Collected Works*.[4] For Jung, the anima was not a mere intellectual construct, as he pointed out in the preface to a work titled *Anima as Fate*, written by one of his students:

> Whenever psychological concepts are introduced, such as Anima, we must not see this as a theoretical presupposition, since Anima, in this case, is meant

to be, not an abstract idea, but an empirical concept or name designating an array of observable and typical events.[5]

This 'array of observable and typical events' provides the emotional substratum for the entire narrative of *Liber Novus*. Like the idea of the Sun as the symbol of a transpersonal centre or 'spark', the idea of the Moon as a symbol of the soul occurs repeatedly, in images of female figures and in descriptions of the Moon in the heavens, whose 'clear and cold' gaze 'remains luminous and embraces the entire horror and the earth's round'.[6]

Since the 1970s, Jung's ideas about the anima have been viewed by some as seriously limited by the cultural values of his time. Switzerland was, after all, the last European country to offer women the vote, only conceding defeat in 1971, and in the early decades of the twentieth century, the social suppression and undervaluing of many of the qualities that Jung understood as 'feminine' – feeling, imagination, receptivity to the invisible world – contributed to his formulation of a sharp psychological dichotomy between the sexes that might be deemed increasingly inappropriate for twenty-first-century Western society with its blurring of traditional gender roles.[7] Whether the psychological dichotomy that Jung described is an innate reflection of human biology, a social construct, or a mixture of the two, comprises a discussion beyond the scope of this book to explore. But whatever the political and social implications such ideas might carry today, when Jung began working on *Liber Novus* the stereotypical assumptions against which the feminist movement of the late twentieth century fought so vigorously were still firmly in place in German-speaking Protestant Switzerland.

As a denizen of that world, Jung was acutely aware of the imprisonment of his imaginal faculties by the scientific and social constrictions of his time, as well as by his own temperament with its emphasis on rational thought. Moreover, many of the older astrological texts to which Jung had access supported the dichotomy by assigning the Sun to men and the Moon to women. Ptolemy, for example, suggested that the Moon signifies the wife in a man's horoscope, rather than an expression of his own inner nature, while the Sun signifies the husband in a woman's.[8] Jung, in his astrological 'experiment' on synchronicity, examined the statistical evidence for Ptolemy's recommendations for harmony in marriage, beginning with the relationship between the Sun in a woman's chart (representing 'the husband') and the Moon in a man's chart (representing 'the wife').[9] But although Jung assigned the Sun to the masculine principle and the Moon to the feminine, and insisted on a sharp psychological distinction between the sexes, he was more concerned with understanding these symbols as inner factors rather than as 'husband' and 'wife':

> We know that the moon is a favourite symbol for certain aspects of the unconscious – though only, of course, in a man. In a woman the moon corresponds to consciousness and the sun to the unconscious. This is due to the contrasexual archetype in the unconscious: anima in a man, animus in a woman.[10]

Jung's interiorisation of the male and female attributes of the Sun and Moon found support in Alan Leo's approach. Leo, well in advance of his time – perhaps in part because Blavatsky provided him with such an unconventional model of feminine psychology – did not follow the traditional dichotomy in his interpretation of the Moon, and did not describe it as 'the wife' in a man's horoscope. He viewed the natal placement of the Moon as relevant to every individual's experience of the mother,[11] but understood Sun and Moon to reflect aspects of the inner life of both sexes: the solar 'individual self' or spiritual core, and the lunar 'personal self', expressed through feelings, instincts, and physical interaction with everyday mundane life.[12]

There are several feminine characters in *Liber Novus*, and they are connected by symbols that Jung specifically mentioned elsewhere in his writings as aspects of lunar mythology. Although Jung's Soul is the first personal figure with whom he engages at the beginning of *Liber Novus*,[13] this inner voice, which initially has no face, is later revealed as that of the Serpent, who, toward the end of the book, also appears as a bird.[14] The Serpent, in turn, is closely related to the figure of Salome, whom Jung acknowledges as his Soul.[15] These three figures – Soul, Salome, and the Serpent – form a lunar triad that portrays the multiple meanings Jung attributed to the Moon in his published work.[16] Salome's name is connected, not only to the bloodthirsty daughter of Herodias in the biblical story of John the Baptist, but also to the companion, disciple, and midwife of Jesus who is described in a number of Gnostic texts.[17] Another female figure in *Liber Novus*, the Cook, does not initially seem to be related to the ambiguously erotic and sometimes sinister figure of Salome; but the Cook too is an image of the astrological Moon through her role as a provider of food.[18] As a heavenly body, the Moon itself is the subject of a number of discourses in *Liber Novus* and, like the Sun, contributes a particular significance to the 'composition of place' in which Jung engages in his dialogues with various characters.

The question might be asked whether the Moon and its female representatives in *Liber Novus* are specifically astrological, or whether the significance of this lunar symbolism lies in the wider range of mythic associations with which Jung was so familiar, and which he understood as unconscious portrayals of psychological dynamics. But it is impossible to separate the mythic from the astrological in ancient lunar lore, since cosmology and astrology were so intimately interrelated; ancient lunar goddesses were invariably connected with both the cycles of the Moon in the heavens and with earthly cycles such as vegetation, female menstruation, and human birth and death.[19] Nor is it possible to separate cosmological and astrological domains in the imagery of alchemy, as Jung himself noted; the metal silver, the Moon in the heavens, and the cycles of nature were one and the same. Jung seemed to view the two modes of perception, mythic and astrological, as inextricably entwined; both are symbolic representations of the archetypal dominants of the collective unconscious. As Jung wrote to Freud in 1911, astrology provided him with the key to myth, since the earliest mythic narratives were woven around the observation and interpretation of the heavenly bodies; and myth likewise appears to have provided him with the key to astrology, as demonstrated in his analysis of the horoscope of Miss X.[20] Astrology and myth are frequently paired in Jung's published descriptions of the Moon, as in the following passage from *Mysterium Coniunctionis*:

> In ancient tradition Luna is the giver of moisture and ruler of the water-sign Cancer . . . The relation of the moon to the soul, much stressed in antiquity, also occurs in alchemy.[21]

Just as solar myth cannot be separated from the astrological Sun in Jung's heroic giant Izdubar, lunar myth cannot be separated from the astrological Moon in the figure of Salome. She is not only an image of the archetypal Moon; she is also a particular dimension of the Moon in Jung's own horoscope.

Salome

After Jung's Soul, who initially has no image or description, Salome is the first female figure to appear in *Liber Novus*. Jung painted her in Book One, in the section titled 'Mysterium' (see Plate 4).[22] Salome is the daughter of Elijah, the wise old prophet who presides over the 'temple of the sun'.[23] In the painting, accompanied by Elijah, the black serpent, and Jung's 'I', she has long black hair and wears a blood-red robe. In the darkened heavens a 'blood Moon' is visible, as it purportedly was at the time of Jesus' crucifixion.[24] When they are introduced, Jung immediately associates Salome's name with 'the daughter of Herod, the bloodthirsty woman', and recoils from her in horror; but Elijah sternly informs him, 'My wisdom and my daughter are one'.[25] Jung's Salome, unlike the daughter of Herodias, is blind,[26] a motif which Jung associated with inner vision:

> What is described here as an outward event [blindness] is really a symbol for the inward turning towards the centre . . . towards the archetype of man, towards the self . . . It is an act of realization on a higher level, establishing a connection between the consciousness of the individual and the supraordinate symbol of totality.[27]

Symbols of a specifically lunar nature appear throughout the encounter. When he first meets Elijah, Jung is lying 'in a dark depth'.[28] 'Darkness reigns' inside the old prophet's house, in which Jung perceives glittering walls and discovers 'a bright stone the color of water' in which he sees a vision of 'the mother of God with the child' and 'a many-armed bloody Goddess' – the Hindu dark mother-goddess Kali, whose festivals occur at the new Moon – who is also Salome.[29] The stone is a scrying crystal suggestive of aquamarine, a type of beryl that, according to Pliny, is 'the pure green of the sea'.[30] Aquamarine was sacred to the Moon, and was believed to protect those who travelled by sea.[31] At one point Jung experiences 'wild music, a tambourine, a sultry moonlit night';[32] then he is plunged into the dark of the Moon, 'pitch black all around me'. He has 'fallen into the source of chaos, into the primordial beginning'.[33] He is led into a cave where he hears 'the rippling of a spring'.[34] Night, darkness, water, and the phases of the Moon repeatedly provide the 'composition of place' that reveals the nature of this deeply ambivalent female planetary daimon Jung experienced directly in imaginal form.

Salome and her father Elijah are invariably accompanied by a black serpent. Not surprisingly, Jung had a good deal to say about the serpent, one of the most ancient, sacred, and ubiquitous of symbols, as both an archetypal image and in terms of its specific role as the companion and double of Salome. Discussing his vision of Salome at a seminar given in 1925, Jung equated the serpent with the anima:

> Inasmuch as the serpent leads into the shadows, it has the function of the anima; it leads you into the depths, it connects the above and the below . . . The serpent is the personification of the tendency to go into the depths and to deliver oneself over to the alluring world of shadows.[35]

The serpent is also closely associated with an ancient deity who encapsulates the entire spectrum of lunar myth: Triple-Bodied Hecate, discussed in greater detail below, whom Jung described as 'a real spectral goddess of night and phantoms . . . guardian of the door of Hades'.[36] Hecate, whose tripartite nature reflects Jung's understanding of the threefold nature of the soul, was linked with the underworld goddess Persephone in early Greek myth, and was seen as the patroness of drugs and poisons.[37] Hecate was also a birth-goddess and a goddess of marriage who, in the Orphic cosmogonies, 'occupies the centre of the world as Aphrodite and Gaia, if not as the world soul itself'.[38] She thus incorporates all the dimensions of lunar myth, symbolised by the phases of the Moon: the dark of the Moon with its witches and sorceries and triune goddesses of fate; the crescent Moon as the virginal, unworldly or otherworldly Kore-Persephone; and the full Moon as the fecund Demeter-Aphrodite. The astrological Venus, it seems, was viewed by Jung, as well as by the alchemists, as only one dimension of this all-encompassing archetype of the Moon.

The invisible planet

In *Liber Novus*, Jung's perception of the domain of the feminine is heavily weighted on the side of the underworld. This is not a conventional reading of the astrological Moon. Salome, as an anima-figure, is always accompanied by her magical black serpent, and there are numerous references in *Liber Novus* relating the Moon to the gateway to Hades, the 'realm of the Mothers', and the dark chaos of the collective unconscious. Although Salome exhibits an erotic dimension that fascinates Jung, she remains primarily a lunar rather than a Venusian figure, and is more aligned with Hecate's world of ghosts, spells, incantations, and blood-sacrifices than with the 'nourishing good Mother' usually described in astrological texts. When the 'good Mother' does appear in the form of the Cook, she turns out to be the guardian of a kitchen that is a passageway into the underworld.

Modern astrologers interpreting Jung's natal horoscope in the twenty-first century have noted the close alignment of Jung's Moon with the trans-Neptunian celestial body known as Pluto, and this conjunction is interpreted as an indicator, not only of Jung's 'uncanny' mother, but also of his lifelong preoccupation with the depths of the psyche.[39] But Pluto was only discovered in 1930, after Jung had completed most of his work on *Liber Novus*.[40] Later, when he became aware of this newcomer to the planetary pantheon, he still referred in published works only to the mythic deity, and not to the astrological symbolism of the planet.[41] However, Pluto was mentioned in the interpretation of Jung's horoscope offered by his daughter Gret Baumann-Jung at the Psychological Club of Zürich in 1974.[42] In her paper, Baumann-Jung referred to her father's Moon-Pluto conjunction as a symbol of the ways in which Jung had perceived his mother. He wrote in his autobiography that he had once dreamed of her as 'a guardian of departed spirits',[43] but in waking life her real nature 'remained hidden beneath the semblance of a kindly, fat old woman':

> She held all the conventional opinions a person was obliged to have, but then her unconscious personality would suddenly put in an appearance. That personality was unexpectedly powerful: a sombre, imposing figure possessed of unassailable authority . . . I was sure that she consisted of two personalities, one innocuous and human, the other uncanny.[44]

An interesting conundrum arises from the apparent presence of the 'invisible' Pluto in *Liber Novus*. From the astrologer's perspective, it might be argued that Jung intuitively expressed the qualities and attributes of his Moon-Pluto configuration in the visions of Salome and the Cook, even though he did not know he had a Moon-Pluto conjunction. In Jung's own words, the planets 'are the gods, symbols of the powers of the unconscious';[45] and Plutonian 'power' would have manifested in his life even if Jung was unaware of its planetary symbol. It might equally be argued that lunar myths, with which Jung was thoroughly familiar when he invoked, painted, and wrote about Salome, encompass the underworld domain and do not need the addition of a newly discovered heavenly body, or a belief in the veracity of astrology, to explain Jung's focus on the depths. Moreover, his ongoing interest in the psychology of mediumship and trance phenomena accorded with particular trends in the psychiatric milieu of his time, which was prepared to explore and experiment with occult literature and practices as well as the methods of medical science.

In the *Jahreshoroskop* or solar return chart that Liliane Frey prepared for Jung in 1939,[46] Pluto appears as an important significator, as it was moving into the early part of the zodiacal sign of Leo on Jung's birthday in 1939, and during the course of the subsequent year entered into an exact alignment with his natal Sun. Frey did not offer a written interpretation of this configuration, although she and Jung no doubt discussed it. But it is possible that Jung requested the *Jahreshoroskop* from Frey because he was aware of the dramatic nature of the upcoming configurations in 1939 – the year of the outbreak of the Second World War – and was concerned about its possible meanings. By that time, Pluto was not invisible any more.

The High Priestess

Elaborating on the exquisitely detailed image in *Liber Novus* of an unnamed female figure that he later referred to as 'the anima' (see Plate 5),[47] Jung, in an essay written nearly forty years later, displayed the Mercurial spirit which has so often annoyed his critics,[48] and attributed the image to the dream of a patient rather than admitting that it was his own.

> Then she [the anima] appears in a church, taking the place of the altar, still over-life-size but with veiled face.[49]

An inscription in Latin is written along the border of the painting:

> The wisdom of God is a mystery, even the hidden wisdom, which God ordained before the world unto our glory . . . For the Spirit searcheth all things, yea, the deep things of God.[50]

Along the right side of the image, Jung wrote: 'The Spirit and the Bride say, Come'. This quote from Revelation 22:17 may be related to Jung's understanding of the Kabbalistic *Shekhinah* as the Bride or feminine face of the godhead and the manifestation of God's glory in the world, symbolised by the Moon.[51] The *Shekhinah* is Nature herself, through which God's immanence may be perceived and directly experienced. The woman in Jung's painting is unnamed, and her white robe and veil do not correspond to Salome's red robe, although her hair, just visible, is black like Salome's. She may be an amalgam of all the female figures in *Liber Novus*, or a vision of the *Mater coelestis* described later in 'Scrutinies'; but whoever she is, she clearly belongs to the realm of the Moon, as indicated by the lunar crescent to the right of her head. Jung was familiar with at least some of the major themes of the Kabbalah and, although he did not refer to this Jewish esoteric lore in his early publications, it is evident, from the knowledge he exhibited in private seminars given in English in Zürich between 1928 and 1930,[52] that he had encountered the Kabbalah no later than the mid-1920s and probably much earlier, while he was still working on *Liber Novus*.[53] He had also acquired both the original publication (1912) and the later, revised edition (1929) of A.E. Waite's lengthy work on the Kabbalah, which specifically describes the *Shekhinah* as the Bride of God.[54]

Jung's painting, according to his own interpretation, 'restores the anima to the Christian church, not as an icon but as the altar itself'.[55] The altar, as Jung pointed out, may be understood as the 'place of sacrifice' and the 'receptacle for consecrated relics'.[56] It is the liminal zone of transformation, the *mundus imaginalis* where the ineffable becomes visible, and human and divine meet and recognise each other through the mediation of symbols. It is on the altar that the wine is transformed into blood, the wafer into flesh, and the smoke of the burnt offering into food for the gods. The altar, like the anima, is an intermediary; it is the imagination or organ of *phantasia* as Iamblichus understood it.

There is an interesting family resemblance between Jung's image, with her association with 'hidden wisdom' and the 'deep things of God', and the image of The High Priestess in Waite's Tarot deck, published in 1910.[57] Both figures are personifications of secret wisdom and are shown with lunar crescents; both appear beneath an arch supported by two columns. Waite's portrayal of The High Priestess differs from Jung's painting in a number of visual details. The High Priestess is alone and unveiled, while Jung's anima-figure, her face veiled, is surrounded by a crowd of worshippers; the crescent Moon is beneath the feet of The High Priestess, while it shines to the right of the head of Jung's figure. But the similarities in the interpretations made by the two men are striking. According to Waite,

> She [The High Priestess] is the spiritual Bride and Mother, the daughter of the stars and the Higher Garden of Eden. She is the moon nourished by the milk of the Supernal Mother.[59]

FIGURE 3.1   A.E. Waite's Tarot card of The High Priestess[58]

Waite also related The High Priestess directly to the Kabbalistic *Shekhinah*, and hinted at her role as an inner spiritual mediator:

> Her truest and highest name in symbolism is *Shekinah* – the co-habiting glory. According to Kabalism, there is a *Shekinah* both above and below . . . Mystically speaking, the *Shekinah* is the Spiritual Bride of the just man, and when he reads the Law she gives the Divine meaning.[60]

Originally a member of the Hermetic Order of the Golden Dawn, Waite was a prolific author whose scholarly books and articles on esoteric traditions such as alchemy, magic, Tarot, Kabbalah, and Grail lore are referenced in a number of Jung's *Collected Works*.[61] Through Waite's books, as well as a late nineteenth-century work on the Tarot by the French occultist Papus,[62] Jung became familiar with, and respectful of, the imagery of the Tarot, which he referred to as 'descended from the archetypes of transformation'.[63]

> They [the Tarot cards] are psychological images, symbols with which one plays . . . For example, the symbol of the sun, or the symbol of the man hung up by the feet, or the tower struck by lightning, or the wheel of fortune, and so on. Those are sort of archetypal ideas, of a differentiated nature, which mingle with the ordinary constituents of the flow of the unconscious, and therefore it is applicable for an intuitive method that has the purpose of understanding the flow of life.[64]

In a private conversation recorded by Hanni Binder, Jung even offered 'keyword' interpretations of the twenty-two cards of the Major Arcana.[65] He gave the following interpretation for The High Priestess:

> Sitting Priestess. She wears a veil. On her knees is a book. This book is open. She stands in connection with the moon. Occult wisdom. Passive, eternal woman.

Jung's High Priestess, unlike Waite's, 'wears a veil', as does the figure in his painting. Whether Jung intended to depict Salome or a more universal lunar potency in his painting, his image seems to have a strong connection with the Tarot card of The High Priestess. Both figures are guardians of secret mysteries and stand at the gateway to the underworld; and both are personifications of the Moon.

The Scholar's Daughter

The meeting of Jung's 'I' with Salome and Elijah, to which he gave the title 'Mysterium', concludes the first part of *Liber Novus*. The next female figure Jung encounters is the pale and ghostly Scholar's Daughter, whom Jung discovers in a small castle surrounded by 'quiet, dark swamp water' in a dark forest.[66] Even without the later lunar references in the text, Jung's painting of the castle portrays a landscape dominated by the crescent Moon, just as his painting of Salome is dominated by the 'blood Moon' of a lunar eclipse (see Plate 6).

When he first enters the castle, Jung's 'I' believes the Scholar lives alone. But as he turns and tosses in an attempt to sleep, a 'slim girl, pale as death', appears in the doorway of his chamber. She gives no name, but tells Jung that she is the old man's daughter, and that the Scholar 'holds me here in unbearable captivity' because she is his only child and the image of her mother, who died young. Jung immediately falls in love with her:

> She is beautiful. A deep purity rests in her look. She has a beautiful and unworldly soul, one that wants to come into the life of reality . . . Oh this beauty of the soul![67]

But she is not as unworldly as Jung assumes; her understanding of the value of ordinary life is greater than his own. Their ensuing brief conversation focuses on the importance of the incarnate versus the purely abstract and philosophical. The girl informs Jung: 'Only what is human and what you call banal and hackneyed contains the wisdom that you seek'.[68] As she leaves him, she tells him that she brings greetings from Salome. Her form then dissolves into the darkness:

> Dim moonlight penetrates the room. Where she stood something shadowy lies – it is a profusion of red roses.[69]

Jung's description of the girl, slim and pale like the young crescent Moon with which the virginal Persephone was associated in Greek myth, belongs to the lunar realm; so does the 'composition of place'. The 'quiet, dark swamp water' surrounding the castle is reminiscent of Waite's Tarot image of The Moon, with its pale light shining on an 'abyss of water'.[70] Jung, discussing the meaning of this Tarot card with Hanni Binder, informed her: 'A crayfish comes out of the water. It is night. The door to the unconscious is open'.[71]

But the red roses hint at another, specifically erotic planetary association with the Scholar's Daughter: Aphrodite, known to the Romans as Venus, whose flower, according to poets from the first-century BCE Greek lyric poet Bion to Shakespeare and Spencer, is the red rose.[72] The Scholar's Daughter appears to contain the attributes of Venus in nascent form, without overtly displaying them as does Salome in her red robe, whom Jung described as 'the erotic element'.[73] Jung's exegesis on masculinity and femininity following his encounter with the Scholar's Daughter makes clear that she, as well as Salome, is an image of the soul. He concludes:

> As a man you have no soul, since it is in the woman; as a woman you have no soul, since it is in the man. But if you become a human being, then your soul comes to you.[74]

FIGURE 3.2 Waite's Tarot card of The Moon

Jung later pointed out the archetypal nature of the mythic pairing of an old man and a young woman, which occurs in *Liber Novus* in the relationship between Salome and Elijah, and between the Scholar and his daughter:

> In such dream wanderings one frequently encounters an old man who is accompanied by a young girl, and examples of such couples are to be found in many mythic tales. Thus, according to Gnostic tradition, Simon Magus went about with a young girl whom he had picked up in a brothel.[75]

According to Jung, this 'young girl', called Helen or Selene (an epithet for the Moon), is

> *ennoia* [consciousness or thought], *sapientia* [wisdom], and *epinoia* [design or purpose].[76]

An earthly version of the Gnostic celestial potency Sophia, who is both a divinity and a harlot, Simon Magus' Helen, like Jung's Salome, embodies the wisdom of the unconscious. Later, when Jung's deeper understanding of alchemy had provided him with a greatly enlarged symbolic vocabulary for the process of individuation, he reiterated the pairing of the *senex* and the anima in astrological/alchemical language:

> The moon also has a relation to Saturn, the astrological maleficus. In the 'Dicta Belini' Saturn is, as it were, the 'father-mother' of the moon:'I am the light of all things that are mine and I cause the moon to appear openly from within my father Saturn'.[77]

The idea of Saturn 'fathering' the Moon is not mentioned in astrological texts, although the two heavenly bodies are said to rule opposite signs (Capricorn and Cancer respectively) and therefore symbolise two sides of a single formative principle, reflected in the fluid maternal matrix of water and the structured formality of earth, which 'moves by slow steps'.[78] Jung described this polarity by remarking:'The old prophet expresses persistence, but the young maiden denotes movement'.[79] Alan Leo described a more complex relationship between the Moon and Saturn that focused on the need for the lunar 'personality' to be aligned with the solar goal of 'individuality' through the mediation of Saturn:

> So is the Moon, the representative of the personality, centred in Saturn, the planet controlling the path of discipleship or freedom from irresponsibility.[80]

From this perspective, Salome on her own would remain no more than the bloodthirsty daughter of Herodias – the sinister eclipsed Moon, unconscious and compulsive – but under the governance of her father Elijah, she can fulfil her role as the principle of Eros. Jung, however, commenting later on his vision, expressed dissatisfaction with the psychological imbalance reflected in Salome's 'inferior' position, and suggested that, as long as she remained subordinate and blind, she was 'an incorrect allegory for Eros', reflecting that aspect of Jung's own nature in which 'Logos undoubtedly has the upper hand'.[81] Salome's healing, as well as his own, thus becomes an urgent necessity, but it can only occur through a great sacrifice: his own crucifixion and resurrection. At the end of Jung's torment, Salome cries, 'I see light!', and Elijah announces to Jung: 'Your work is fulfilled here'.[82]

The Cook

Jung's 'I' encounters the Cook in Book Two of *Liber Novus*, at the same time that he meets her master, the Librarian, another Saturnine figure. After leaving the Librarian's sanctuary, Jung enters a vast kitchen with an immense chimney over the stove. Unlike the ethereal Scholar's daughter, the Cook is large and fat – a full rather than a crescent Moon – and wears a chequered apron.[83] Immediately solicitous, she invites Jung to take a seat, and wipes the table in front of him. They have a conversation about Thomas à Kempis' *Imitation of Christ*,[84] a book that the Cook's mother has bequeathed to her and which Jung also happens to be reading at the time; he values it because 'it is written from the soul'. The Cook, despite her homely, rather stereotypical appearance, is a woman who aligns herself with an interior approach to the spirit, albeit a doctrinally conventional one. This is not because of any great intellectual insight, but because this was the view held by her mother and her grandmother: an instinctual, inherited sense of feeling-based rightness rather than an individual conviction arrived at through philosophy or science. But their dialogue is interrupted, and Jung loses the Cook in the midst of a chaotic crowd.

She reappears a few pages later, when Jung awakens from a kind of sleep or trance-state and finds himself in 'blind darkness' with a 'gray worm of twilight' crawling along a great wall.[85] He has once again entered a dark lunar landscape. He has a vague impression of a round face emerging from this 'worm of twilight', and hears convulsive laughter. He opens his eyes and 'the fat cook is standing before me'. It seems that Jung has fallen asleep in the kitchen.

> Have I slept? I must have dreamed, what a dreadful play! Did I fall asleep in this kitchen? Is this really the realm of mothers?[86]

The 'realm of mothers' refers to the first act in Part Two of Goethe's *Faust*, in which Faust must descend into the underworld realm of 'the Mothers'. In Scene Five of this act, Mephistopheles informs Faust:

> Unwilling, I reveal a loftier mystery. –
> In solitude are throned the Goddesses,
> No Space around them, Place and Time still less.
> Only to speak of them embarrasses . . .
> Delve in the deepest depths must thou, to reach them . . .
> Descend, then! I could also say: Ascend!
> 'Twere all the same.[87]

Jung later interpreted Goethe's 'realm of the Mothers' as the collective unconscious, below as well as above, which can 'irrupt violently into consciousness' and confront the individual with 'strange and seemingly incomprehensible contents'. The 'realm of the Mothers' is also the anima, who 'personifies the collective unconscious'.[88] The Cook initially appears as a caricature of the round, kindly, nurturing and nourishing Good Mother: the full Moon as the symbol of 'fecundation' and 'sustenance'.[89] But the Cook also presides over the gateway to the underworld, revealing herself as close kin to those wilder, bloodier dimensions of the sinister dark of the Moon described in Jung's first encounter with Salome.[90] Jung compares the Cook to Kundry, the female protagonist in Wagner's last opera, *Parsifal*: a highly ambivalent figure who serves both the black magician Klingsor and the spiritual community of the Knights of the Holy Grail. Like Salome, Kundry displays both a dark eroticism and a compassionate spirituality. After Jung's awakening in the kitchen, he and the Cook part ways, and she makes no further appearances in *Liber Novus*.

Triple-bodied Hecate

The resemblance between the Cook and Jung's autobiographical description of his mother needs no elaboration. But the Cook, although their encounter is brief, is also an important figure in terms of Jung's understanding of astrology, because she reveals his capacity to view any symbol, including astrological ones, as an encapsulation of apparently antithetical expressions connected through a single thread of meaning.

> An archetypal content expresses itself, first and foremost, in metaphors. If such a content should speak of the sun and identify with it the lion, the king, the hoard of gold guarded by the dragon, or the power that makes for the life and health of man, it is neither the one thing nor the other, but the unknown third thing that finds more or less adequate expression in all these similes, yet – to the perpetual vexation of the intellect – remains unknown and not to be fitted into a formula.[91]

For Jung, the realm of the astrological Moon encompasses at the same time Salome, the Scholar's Daughter, and the Cook, because all three figures emerge from the same archetypal core, which the Greeks personified as Triple-bodied Hecate. The entire spectrum of lunar myth, from the darkest and most chthonic to the lightest and most noetic, appears in these imaginal women. There is no suggestion of neatly divided 'malefic' and 'benefic' planets in *Liber Novus*; each astrological symbol can appear through a number of characters, all of them ambivalent. Although Jung does not mention the ancient lunar goddess Hecate by name in *Liber Novus*, he wrote about her extensively elsewhere, particularly in *Psychology of the Unconscious*, and it seems that her portrayals in antiquity – not least that presented in the *Chaldean Oracles*, in which she personifies the World Soul[92] – inspired much of the symbolic material Jung incorporated in the three female figures in *Liber Novus*.

According to Carl Kerényi, Jung's collaborator in *Essays on a Science of Mythology*, Triple-bodied Hecate is 'often held to be the representative of the moon'. She encompasses the attributes of both Demeter the Great Mother (who resembles the Cook) and her daughter Persephone or Kore (who resembles the Scholar's Daughter). Hecate is 'Mistress of Spirits' and presides over the world of ghosts and witchcraft; but she also possesses 'a sort of motherliness'. She is both nurse and nourisher, and at the centre of her sphere of influence 'there stands the moon'.[93] Jung affirmed these associations in his own essay on Kore (the Maiden), which follows Kerényi's in their collaborative work. Both the Maiden and the Mother can be represented as serpents (as are Salome and Jung's Soul), and they are often 'adorned with a sickle moon' (as are the anima-figure and the Old Scholar's castle in Jung's paintings).[94] Moreover, the 'fruitful good Mother', whom 'naive man' perceived as related to the Moon,[95] may equally preside over 'drinkings of blood and bathings in blood',[96] as the biblical Salome did at the death of John the Baptist. In *Psychology of the Unconscious*, Jung pointed out that Triple-bodied Hecate is 'related to the moon (waxing, full, and waning moon)';[97] moreover, she has 'snake-like feet'.[98] Jung then cited Plotinus' equation of the Moon with the World Soul, and suggested that this equation continued into early Christianity:

> Certain early Christian sectarians attributed a maternal significance to the Holy Ghost (world-soul, moon).[99]

Alan Leo's astrological interpretation of the Moon is entirely in accord with Jung's, and it is likely that Leo's work contributed significantly to the lunar figures in *Liber Novus* as well as to Jung's understanding of the lunar anima as an intermediary between the collective unconscious and consciousness. In most of his books, Leo was fairly conventional in his descriptions of the Moon, referring to its traditional relationship with family, parents, and nourishment.[100] But in *Esoteric Astrology*, Leo spread his Theosophical wings, and declared:

> It [the Moon] signifies therefore, a state of duality, a mean between two extremes . . . and in this way it is employed as the symbol of the Soul, regarded as intermediate between Spirit above and Body below . . . It [the semi-circle or crescent] signifies the Moon in its dual phases of light and dark, waxing and waning; the representative of the personal soul with its varying moods, which can rise up to and become one with the spiritual consciousness above, or can descend and be bound to body below.[101]

According to Leo, the Moon, because it 'signifies all things intermediate', also plays an important part in mediumship as 'the missing link between the living and the dead'.[102] For Jung, in turn, the Moon is 'the gathering place of departed souls, the guardian of seeds'.[103] After the death of the Tramp, whom Jung meets directly after his encounter with the Scholar's Daughter,[104] Jung refers to the Moon as the abode of dead souls:

> Your soul went to the moon, to the preserver of souls. Thus the soul moved toward death.[105]

It is precisely this role of mediator between the daylight world and the 'realm of the Mothers' – between the living and the dead, the domain of consciousness and the domain of the unconscious – that the various lunar figures play in *Liber*

Novus, and that Jung assigned to the anima as the archetype of the feminine soul in men.

Toward the end of *Liber Novus*, after Jung's transformative meeting with the magician Philemon, Salome, once again accompanied by Elijah, reappears. She is offered to Jung by her father, but Jung points out that, although he loves her, he is already married. Desperate to be with him, she promises to serve him, sing and dance for him, and 'pick roses for you each day',[106] but he continues to refuse her. Jung has now 'stolen' the Serpent, which he has recognised as his own Soul, and for a time he believes he has appropriated all the magical power once held by Elijah and his daughter.[107] Like Izdubar, Salome herself has undergone transformation through Jung's encounter with her, just as she has transformed him: after Jung has accepted his sacrifice at her hands and experiences a form of crucifixion, she is no longer blind.[108] He, in turn, has been able to access his own depths and the intuitive powers of the unconscious:

> As I became aware of the freedom in my thought world, Salome embraced me and I thus became a prophet, since I had found pleasure in the primordial beginning, in the forest, and in the wild animals.[109]

The reference to the forest and the 'wild animals' hints at yet another aspect of lunar myth: the goddess Artemis, protector of beasts, whom Jung described as 'the wild nocturnal huntress', and who bears 'a close relation' with Hecate as a goddess of the Moon.[110]

In *Liber Novus*, Jung eventually realises that 'Salome is where I am', and that 'Salome is my soul'.[111] He achieves this gradual integration through another experience of suffering: he now hangs suspended from the summit of the 'tree of life', a form of self-sacrifice 'less noble' than crucifixion 'but no less agonizing'.[112] Jung has become the Hanged Man of the Tarot, about which Waite commented with his usual sybilline ambiguity:

> It expresses the relation, in one of its aspects, between the Divine and the Universe. He who can understand that the story of his higher nature is imbedded in this symbolism will receive intimations concerning a great awakening that is possible, and will know that after the sacred Mystery of Death there is a glorious Mystery of Resurrection.[113]

The sacrifice reflected in the imagery of this card seems to be related to the patient waiting required after a willing relinquishment of the conscious will; the figure hangs with his head at the bottom, his feet at the top, and his hands free to achieve release if he so wishes. Waite offered only an oblique reference to mystical rebirth, but more recent Tarot commentators have emphasised the 'voluntary' nature of the sacrifice, the 'serene and composed' expression on the figure's face, and the meaning of the card as the exchange of 'the mundane for the spiritual' through

FIGURE 3.3 Waite's Tarot card of The Hanged Man

trusting to an unknown transpersonal power over which one has no conscious control.[114] Jung's own brief interpretation was that the card signified 'powerlessness, sacrifice, test, proof'.[115] On the mythic motif of hanging, he had considerably more to say:

> The whole series of hanged gods teaches us that the hanging of Christ on the cross is not a unique occurrence in religious mythology . . . The cross

of Christ is the tree of life, and equally the wood of death . . . *As one striving backwards toward the mother, he* [the hero] *must die hanging or suspended on the mother tree.*[116]

Through 'hanging on the tree of life', Jung further noted, the Teutonic god Wotan obtained 'the inspiring, intoxicating drink which invested him with immortality'.[117] The goal of this voluntary sacrifice of conscious control, like the theurgic ritual of the *Mithras Liturgy*, is the transformation resulting from willing receptivity to a direct experience of the Self. In *Liber Novus*, Jung declares his reason for undergoing such a painful process when he declares to Salome: 'I am hanging for your sake and for mine'.[118]

From the perspective of Jung's understanding of astrology, the various conversations, events, emotional upheavals, and dark visions accompanying his encounters with the representatives of the Moon, that most ambivalent of astrological symbols, ultimately resulted in the recognition and at least partial integration of an archetypal principle that had previously been entirely projected onto women and suppressed by the intellectual bias and social conventions dominating his personal and professional life. Jung never claimed that his visions, experienced through active imagination and processed through the lens of a variety of symbolic systems, resulted in a perfectly whole and miraculously healed personality. But it seems that his understanding of the astrological Moon, initially through reading and intellectual analysis and eventually through a direct encounter with powerful living images that he may have deliberately invoked, shaped his understanding of male psychology and of that archetypal principle which he called the anima, and which he experienced as his soul.

Notes

1 Plutarch, *The Face Which Appears on the Orb of the Moon*, trans. A.O. Prickard (London: Simpkin & Co., 1911), XXVII:943, pp. 44–45. Jung's library contained all of Plutarch's works in German: Plutarch, *Lebensbeschreibungen*, trans. Hanns Floerke, 6 volumes (Munich: Georg Müller, 1913).
2 Jung, *Liber Novus*, p. 263.
3 For works on various aspects of the anima, see, among others, Esther Harding, *The Way of All Women* (London: Longmans, Green, 1933); Marie-Louise von Franz, *The Feminine in Fairy Tales* (Putnam, CT: Spring, 1972); Cornelia Brunner, *Anima as Fate,* trans. Julius Heuscher and Scott May (Dallas, TX: Spring, 1986)
4 For Jung's essays on the anima, see Jung, CW7, ¶¶296–340; Jung, CW13, ¶¶57–63; Jung, CW9i, ¶¶111–47; Jung, CW9ii, ¶¶20–42. See also the lengthy discussion of the 'lunar' psychology of women in CW14, ¶¶214–33.
5 Jung, 'Preface', in Brunner, *Anima as Fate*, p. xiii. This work was originally published in German as *Die Anima als Schicksalsproblem des Mannes* (Zürich: Rascher Verlag, 1963); Jung's preface was first written in German in 1959.
6 Jung, *Liber Novus*, p. 267.
7 For discussions of Jung's concept of the anima from a feminist perspective, see, among others, Susan Rowland, *Jung* (Cambridge: Polity Press, 2002); Demaris S. Wehr, *Jung and*

Feminism (Boston, MA: Beacon Press, 1989); Naomi R. Goldenberg, 'A Feminist Critique of Jung', *Signs* 2:2 (1976), pp. 443–49.

8 Ptolemy, *Tetrabiblos* IV.5.

9 Jung, CW8, ¶869 and n. 65, citing Ptolemy's *Tetrabiblos* and Jerome Cardanus' *Commentarium in Ptolemaeum de astrorum iudiciis*.

10 Jung, CW14, ¶159.

11 See, for example, Leo, *Astrology for All*, p. 64, where the Moon in Aries indicates that 'the mother will play a prominent part in the life in some way, often not a sympathetic or fortunate one'.

12 See, for example, Leo, *Esoteric Astrology*, p. 5.

13 Jung initially has dialogues with the Spirit of the Depths and the Spirit of This Time, which might be viewed as collective rather than personal.

14 Jung, *Liber Novus*, p. 358.

15 See Jung, *Liber Novus*, pp. 327, 357, and p. 251, n. 196.

16 For Jung's understanding of the soul as 'tripartite', see Shamdasani, 'Introduction', in Jung, *Liber Novus*, p. 207.

17 Salome appears regularly in the Apocrypha as the disciple of Jesus; see, for example, the *Gospel of Thomas*, the *Secret Gospel of Mark*, the *Greek Gospel of the Egyptians*, and the *Protovangelium of James*, XIV, in which she plays the role of a midwife at Jesus' birth. In the canonical gospels, in Mark 6:3 she is Jesus' sister, and in Matthew 27:56 she is the sister of Mary, Jesus' mother. See Richard Bauckham, 'Salome the Sister of Jesus, Salome the Disciple of Jesus, and the Secret Gospel of Mark', *Novum Testamentum* 33:3 (1991), pp. 245–75.

18 For more on the Cook, see below.

19 For a discussion of lunar symbolism in a range of contexts, see Jules Cashford, *The Moon: Myth and Image* (London: Cassell, 2003).

20 See Greene, *Jung's Studies in Astrology*, chapter 1.

21 Jung, CW14, ¶155.

22 A female figure who is presumably also Salome (she has the same long black hair and wears the same red robe) appears later in a mandala in *Liber Novus*, p. 105. She is polarised with a woman in a blue robe and a white head-covering who represents the spiritual face of the anima.

23 Jung, *Liber Novus*, p. 245.

24 A 'blood Moon' or lunar eclipse in April, 33 CE purportedly coincided with the crucifixion of Jesus; see Acts 2:14–21. For more on 'blood Moons' and the death of Jesus, see B.E. Schaeffer, 'Lunar Visibility and the Crucifixion', *Quarterly Journal of the Royal Astronomical Society* 31:1 (1990), pp. 52–67.

25 Jung, *Liber Novus*, p. 246.

26 See Jung, *Liber Novus*, p. 245: 'A beautiful maiden steps out of the door. She walks uncertainly and I see that she is blind'.

27 Jung, CW11, ¶425.

28 Jung, *Liber Novus*, p. 245.

29 Jung, *Liber Novus*, p. 248. For Kali and her festivals, see Rachel Fell McDemott and Jeffrey John Kripal (eds.), *Encountering Kali* (Berkeley: University of California Press, 2003).

30 Pliny the Elder, *The Natural History*, trans. Henry T. Riley (London: H.G. Bohn, 1855), 37:20.

31 For aquamarine's lunar associations, see Agrippa, *De occulta philosophia*, I.24–27.

32 Jung, *Liber Novus*, p. 246.

33 Jung, *Liber Novus*, p. 247.

34 Jung, *Liber Novus*, p. 251.

35 Jung, *Analytical Psychology*, pp. 94–95.

36 Jung, *Psychology of the Unconscious*, p. 404.

37 See Timothy Gantz, *Early Greek Myth: A Guide to Literary and Artistic Sources* (Baltimore, MD: Johns Hopkins University Press, 1993), pp. 26–27.

38 Jung, CW5, ¶577. Accompanying this lengthy paragraph is a drawing of a 'Gnostic' gem portraying Hecate in her triple-headed form (Fig. 34).

39 See, for example, Dane Rudhyar, 'Carl Jung's Birthchart', at <www.mindfire.ca/Astrology%20and%20The%20Modern%20Psyche/Chapter%20Six%20-%20Carl%20Jung's%20Birthchart.htm>; Elizabeth Spring, 'Obama's Astrological Chart; Jung's Astrological Chart', at <http://northnodeastrology.blogspot.co.uk/2008/11/obamas-astrological-chart-jungs.html>.

40 Although the search for Pluto began in 1906, its existence was not confirmed until 1930. It was originally classified as the ninth planet from the Sun. In 2006 it was demoted by the International Astronomical Union to the new category of 'dwarf planet', as it is only one-sixth of the mass of the Moon. Contemporary astrologers have not been impressed by Pluto's demotion, nor have some astronomers; see, for example, Adam Gorwyn and Alan Stern, 'A Chihuahua is still a dog, and Pluto is still a planet', *EarthSky*, 18 February 2010. For more on Pluto's discovery, see Ken Croswell, *Planet Quest: The Epic Discovery of Alien Solar Systems* (New York: Free Press, 1997); Allen Stern and Jaqueline Mitton, *Pluto and Charon* (New York: John Wiley and Sons, 1998).

41 Jung, CW5, ¶572; Jung, CW9i, ¶169; Jung, CW10, ¶394; Jung, CW12, ¶209, n. 83, 505; Jung, CW14, ¶144, n. 157. None of these references implies an astrological connection.

42 Gret Baumann-Jung, 'Some Reflections on the Horoscope of C.G. Jung', *Quadrant* (Spring 1975), pp. 35–55. See especially pp. 46–48.

43 Jung, *MDR*, p. 241.

44 Jung, *MDR*, pp. 65–66.

45 Jung, Letter to André Barbault, 26 May 1954, in Jung, *C. G. Jung Letters*, Vol. 2, pp. 175–77.

46 See Greene, *Jung's Studies in Astrology*, chapter 2.

47 The painting appears in Jung, *Liber Novus*, p. 155.

48 See Wouter J. Hanegraaff, *New Age Religion and Western Culture: Esotericism in the Mirror of Secular Thought* (Leiden: Brill, 1996), p. 507 and n. 429; Richard Noll, *The Jung Cult* (Princeton, NJ: Princeton University Press, 1994), pp. 181–84.

49 C.G. Jung, 'The Psychological Aspects of the Kore', in Jung and Kerényi, *Essays on a Science of Mythology*, pp. 175–76, repr. in Jung, CW9i, ¶¶306–83.

50 The quote is from 1 Corinthians 2:7–10. See Shamdasani's comments in Jung, *Liber Novus*, p. 317, n. 283.

51 For Jung's references to the *Shekhinah*, see Jung, CW9i, ¶576; Jung, CW9ii, ¶425; Jung, CW11, ¶727; Jung, CW14, ¶¶18, 652. For the *Shekhinah* as the Bride, the manifestation of God's glory in the world, the personification of God's wisdom, and the Moon, see Gershom Scholem, 'The Feminine Element in Divinity', in Gershom Scholem, *On the Mystical Shape of the Godhead*, trans. Joachim Neugroschel (New York: Schocken Books, 1991), pp. 140–96; Arthur Green, 'Shekhinah, the Virgin Mary, and the Song of Songs', *AJS Review*, 26:1 (2002), pp. 1–52. For lunar associations, see also Wolfson, *Through a Speculum*, pp. 267n, 359; Moshe Idel, *Kabbalah and Eros* (New Haven, CT: Yale University Press, 2005), pp. 69, 91, 261n; Gershom Scholem, *On the Kabbalah and Its Symbolism*, trans. Ralph Mannheim (New York: Schocken Books, 1965), pp. 107–8, 151–53.

52 Jung, *Dream Analysis*, pp. 504–6.

53 For Jung's probable early acquaintance with the Kabbalah, see Sanford L. Drob, 'Towards a Kabbalistic Psychology', *Journal of Jungian Theory and Practice* 5:2 (2003), 77–100. For Freud's absorption of Kabbalistic concepts into his psychoanalytic theories, see David Bakan, *Sigmund Freud and the Jewish Mystical Tradition* (Princeton, NJ: Van Nostrand, 1958; repr. Boston: Beacon Press, 1975).

54 A.E. Waite, *The Secret Doctrine of Israel: A Study of the Zohar and Its Connections* (London: William Rider & Son, 1912); A.E. Waite, *The Holy Kabbalah: A Study of the Secret*

Tradition in Israel (London: Williams & Norgate, 1929). For Waite's discussion of the *Shekhinah*, see Waite, *The Holy Kabbalah*, pp. 377–405.

55 See Jung, *Liber Novus*, p. 317, n. 283.

56 Jung, CW9i, ¶380.

57 A.E. Waite, *The Pictorial Key to the Tarot* (London: William Rider & Son, 1910). For a detailed history of this Tarot deck, see K. Frank Jensen, *The Story of the Waite-Smith Tarot* (Melbourne: Association of Tarot Studies, 2006).

58 Waite, *Pictorial Key*, p. 77.

59 Waite, *Pictorial Key*, pp. 76–79. At one point in *Liber Novus* (p. 249), Salome claims to be the daughter of Mary, the *Mater Coelestis* or 'heavenly mother' (for this latter reference see *Liber Novus*, p. 352, n. 113).

60 Waite, *Pictorial Key*, p. 79.

61 See, for example, Jung's citing of various of Waite's works in Jung, CW12, ¶490; Jung, CW14, ¶¶18, 27, 312; Jung, CW16, ¶¶417, 500.

62 Papus [Gérard Encausse], *Le Tarot des Bohémiens* (Paris: Flammarion, 1889). Papus' interpretations are based on links between the Tarot and the Kabbalah, and Jung had the German translation of a work by Papus titled *Die Kabbala*, published in 1910; this suggests an even earlier introduction to the Kabbalah than the seminars Jung gave in the 1920s.

63 Jung, CW9i, ¶81.

64 C.G. Jung, *Visions*, ed. Claire Douglas, Vol. 2 (Princeton, NJ: Princeton University Press, 1997), 923.

65 <http://marygreer.wordpress.com/2008/04/18/carl-jung-on-the-major-arcana/>. Mary Greer states that the definitions of the cards consist of brief notes Hanni Binder took of Jung's descriptions in German when he spoke to her about the Tarot cards. According to Greer, the deck Jung used was 'based on the Grimaud Tarot de Marseilles, which he felt most closely contained properties he recognized from his reading of alchemical texts'.

66 Jung, *Liber Novus*, p. 261. Jung described this vision in 'Psychological Aspects of the Kore', p. 174, attributing it, like the painting of Salome, to a patient.

67 Jung, *Liber Novus*, p. 262.

68 Jung, *Liber Novus*, p. 262.

69 Jung, *Liber Novus*, p. 263. Jung discussed this encounter in his essay, 'On the Psychological Aspects of the Kore Figure', in Jung, CW9i, §361.

70 Waite, *Pictorial Key to the Tarot*, p. 143.

71 See <http://marygreer.wordpress.com/2008/03/31/carl-jung-and-tarot/>. The crayfish was the conventional way of portraying the crab associated with the zodiacal sign of Cancer during the medieval period. An actual crab is rarely seen in astrological iconography until the modern era, although it appears on amulets from the Greco-Roman world.

72 Bion of Smyrna, *Lament of Adonis*, cited in Marie Louise von Glinski, *Simile and Identity in Ovid's Metamorphosis* (Cambridge: Cambridge University Press, 2012), p. 42. For further connections between the rose and Aphrodite, see *Pausanias' Guide to Ancient Greece*, trans. Christian Habicht (Berkeley: University of California Press, 1998), 6:24.6–7; David Kinsley, *The Goddesses' Mirror* (Albany: SUNY Press, 1989), p. 189; H. David Brumble, *Classical Myths and Legends in the Middle Ages and Renaissance* (London: Routledge, 2013), p. 344.

73 Jung, *MDR*, p. 207.

74 Jung, *Liber Novus*, p. 264.

75 Jung, *MDR*, p. 206.

76 Jung, CW14, ¶160.

77 Jung, CW14, ¶226, n. 359. The 'Dicta Belini' is a treatise purportedly authored by Apollonius of Tyana (c. 15–100 CE), a Greek Neopythagorean philosopher reputed to be a

magician and often associated with Hermes Trismegistus in medieval Arabic alchemical writings. Jung found the text in the alchemical collection known as *Theatrum chemicum*, V, p. 97. For Apollonius, see Maria Dzielska, *Apollonius of Tyana in Legend and History* (Rome: L'Erma, 1986); Philostratus, *Apollonius of Tyana*, trans. Christopher P. Jones (Cambridge, MA: Loeb Classical Library, 2006). In the Arabic text of the *Turba Philosophorum*, another alchemical work which Jung cited frequently, the 'water of the moon and of Saturn' are identical; see Jung, CW14, ¶493. See also Nathan Schwartz-Salant, *The Mystery of Human Relationship* (London: Routledge, 2003), pp. 132–33.

78 Jung, CW14, ¶2. The Moon governs the watery sign of Cancer, while Saturn governs the earthy sign of Capricorn. For Jung's reference to these rulerships, see Jung, CW14, ¶6.

79 Jung, *Liber Novus*, p. 365.

80 Leo, *Esoteric Astrology*, p. 27.

81 Jung, *Liber Novus*, p. 366.

82 Jung's symbolic crucifixion occurs in *Liber Novus*, p. 252.

83 Jung, *Liber Novus*, p. 294.

84 Thomas à Kempis, *The Imitation of Christ*, trans. B. Knott (London: Fount, 1996). Jung had a German translation of the work: *Das Buchlein von der Nachfolge Christi* (Leipzig: Karl Tauchnitz, 1832).

85 Jung, *Liber Novus*, p. 302.

86 Jung, *Liber Novus*, p. 302.

87 Johann Wolfgang von Goethe, *Faust: A Tragedy,* trans. Bayard Taylor (New York: Modern Library, 1950 [1870]), pp. 53–54. See Shamdasani's n. 217 on p. 302 of *Liber Novus*.

88 Jung, CW10, ¶714.

89 Max Heindel, *Message of the Stars*, pp. 6 and 32.

90 For Jung's observations on the sinister, dangerous nature of the new Moon, see Jung, CW14, ¶¶21–30.

91 Jung, CW9i, ¶267.

92 For Hecate as the World Soul in the *Chaldean Oracles*, see Sarah Iles Johnston, *Hekate Soteira* (Oxford: Oxford University Press, 2000); Lewy, *Chaldean Oracles*, pp. 83–98.

93 Carl Kerényi, 'Kore', in C.G. Jung and Carl Kerényi, *Essays on a Science of Mythology* (Princeton, NJ: Princeton University Press, 1969), pp. 101–155, on pp. 110–13.

94 C.G. Jung, 'The Psychological Aspects of the Kore', in Jung and Kerényi, *Essays*, pp. 156–77, on pp. 158–59.

95 Jung, *Psychology of the Unconscious*, p. 25.

96 Jung, 'Psychological Aspects of the Kore', p. 158.

97 Jung, *Psychology of the Unconscious*, p. 549, n. 50.

98 Jung, *Psychology of the Unconscious*, p. 404.

99 Jung, *Psychology of the Unconscious*, pp. 147–48.

100 See, for example, Leo, *The Key to Your Own Nativity*, p. 10.

101 Leo, *Esoteric Astrology*, pp. 2–3.

102 Alan Leo, *How to Judge a Nativity* (London: Modern Astrology, 1908), pp. 69–70.

103 Jung, *Psychology of the Unconscious*, p. 352, referring to a passage in Firmicus Maternus, *Mathesis*, I.5.9.

104 For the narrative of the Tramp, see Jung, *Liber Novus*, pp. 265–66.

105 Jung, *Liber Novus*, p. 267.

106 Jung, *Liber Novus*, p. 323.

107 Jung, *Liber Novus*, pp. 317 and 324.

108 Jung, *Liber Novus*, p. 252.

109 Jung, *Liber Novus*, p. 251.

110 Jung, *Psychology of the Unconscious*, p. 405 and p. 530, n. 53.

111 Jung, *Liber Novus*, pp. 327, 357, and p. 251, n. 196.

112 Jung, *Liber Novus*, p. 325.

113 Waite, *Pictorial Key*, pp. 118–19.

114 See, among others, Juliet Sharman-Burke, *Understanding the Tarot* (London: Eddison/ Sadd, 1998), p. 43; John D. Blakeley, *The Mystical Tower of the Tarot* (London: Watkins, 1974), p. 55.

115 <http://marygreer.wordpress.com/2008/04/18/carl-jung-on-the-major-arcana/>.

116 Jung, *Psychology of the Unconscious*, pp. 264 and 402. Italics original. For the revised version, see Jung, CW5, ¶¶349, 398–99, 594, 659.

117 Jung, *Psychology of the Unconscious*, p. 559, n. 54.

118 Jung, *Liber Novus*, p. 325.

4

SATURN IN THE HERMITAGE, PART ONE

The solitaries

By withdrawal from earthly things, by leisure, solitude, constancy, esoteric theology and philosophy, by superstition, magic, agriculture, and grief, we come under the influence of Saturn.[1]

—Marsilio Ficino

O exalted lord whose name is great and who stands above the heavens of every other planet, whom God made subtle and exalted! You are the lord Saturn, who is cold and dry . . . whose knowledge reaches far and deep, truthful in your words and promises, single in your operations, solitary, remote from others, near to suffering and sorrow, far from joy and celebration; you are old, ancient, wise . . . You are the author of good and evil.[2]

—*Picatrix*

Grey and black correspond to Saturn and the evil world; they symbolize the beginning in darkness, in the melancholy, fear, wickedness, and wretchedness of ordinary human life . . . The darkness and blackness can be interpreted psychologically as man's confusion and lostness.[3]

—C.G. Jung

Prophecy and magic: Elijah

Several male figures make their appearance on Jung's journey in the first part of *Liber Novus*. All are old, and all exhibit a specific form of wisdom or scholarly learning. These figures seem to portray different aspects of the image of the *senex* or 'Old Man', whom Jung equated directly with Saturn, 'the coldest, heaviest, and most distant of the planets'.[4] The three characters eventually achieve their full potential in the more nuanced and complex figure called Philemon, discussed in the next chapter. But these early versions of the *senex* are nevertheless important aspects of what Jung came to understand as his personal daimon, astrologically defined as Saturn, the ruler of his horoscope.

The first of the *senex* figures, Elijah, bears the name of the biblical prophet who defended the worship of the Hebrew god Yahweh against the Canaanite god Baal, and was taken up to heaven in a whirlwind in a chariot drawn by horses of fire.[5] According to Jung, the figure of Elijah was the chief trigger for his realisation that the images of *Liber Novus* 'had a psychological reality in their own right, and were not merely subjective fragments'.[6] As Elijah himself testily informs Jung in *Liber Novus*: 'We are real and not symbols'.[7] When Elijah makes his first appearance, Jung describes him as looking 'like one of the old prophets'. Elijah's house is built at the foot of a sheer wall of rock, and contains a scrying-stone of the kind in which John Dee, in the sixteenth century, saw visions of the forms of angels.[8]

Along with the watery, lunar references discussed in the previous chapter in relation to Salome, stones and mountains appear repeatedly in the setting that Elijah inhabits. Gemstones form the walls of his house,[9] and huge stone blocks were used to build the 'temple of the sun' at the top of a mountain. Stones and foundations, in both a literal and a metaphorical sense, likewise figure in the mythology and iconography of Saturn, known to the Greeks as Kronos, from Hesiod and the Orphics through the alchemy of the early modern period. Kronos, according to Hesiod's *Theogony*, was given a stone to swallow by his sister-wife Rhea as a substitute for the baby Zeus when the old Titan attempted to devour his children to preserve his own power; Rhea then hewed a sickle out of stone for Zeus to overthrow and castrate his father.[10] In Orphic doctrines, Kronos was perceived as the architect of the solid material world.[11] The first-century CE Roman astrologer Marcus Manilius stated that Saturn 'ruled the foundations of the universe', while Vettius Valens, in the second century, declared that the planet 'rules lead, wood, and stone'.[12] The alchemist Heinrich Khunrath, whom Jung believed to have foreseen the Aquarian Aion, referred to the planet as 'an old man on a mountain' who resides in 'Saturn's mountain cave'.[13] And Alan Leo, in modern times, continued these associations by declaring that Saturn governs the mineral world.[14] Jung, who was familiar with all these sources, did not overlook this consistent historical chain of Saturnian correspondences, and remarked that the Sabaeans, an ancient people from the first millennium BCE who lived in what is now Yemen, worshipped an image of Saturn 'made of lead or black stone'.[15]

Stones were profoundly important to Jung, from his childhood to the end of his life. In his autobiography, he discussed in detail both his early experiences of 'my stone' in the garden of his childhood home, and the stone he carved at Bollingen, which he also called 'my stone'. On this latter object, decorated on one side with astrological symbols, Jung inscribed a Latin paraphrase from various alchemical texts, intended to represent the voice of the stone itself as the *lapis philosophorum*, the central symbol of alchemy:[16]

> I am an orphan, alone; nevertheless I am found everywhere. I am one, but opposed to myself. I am youth and old man at one and the same time. I have known neither father nor mother, because I have had to be fetched out of the

deep like a fish, or fell like a white stone from heaven. In woods and mountains I roam, but I am hidden in the innermost soul of man. I am mortal for everyone, yet I am not touched by the cycle of aeons.[17]

The underground setting of Elijah's house is itself Saturnian, since this divinity, as Jung pointed out, was, like Pluto, a god of the underworld who 'rules over the dead';[18] his earthy, rocklike, Titanic nature belongs to the realm of dark caves, black fires, and underground vaults full of treasure.[19] Elijah's age, wisdom, and gift of prophecy – an attribute long associated with the melancholic frenzy of Saturn's 'black bile' – all point directly to that planetary god who figured so powerfully in alchemy as the 'Old King', the primal form of the alchemical gold.[20]

Jung referred to Elijah as a symbol of 'the factor of intelligence and knowledge'.[21] Saturn's power, in Jung's view, was chiefly experienced through the faculty of mind, an attribute described by Firmicus Maternus, who declared that Saturn was the patron of deep thinkers.[22] Alan Leo concurred:

> Saturn inclines toward the scientific attitude, giving an intense desire to find out the true state of things . . . Gifted with a mind that is watchful and wary, his chief delight will consist in study and research, or in any work requiring a studious, contemplative, and reflective attitude of mind.[23]

According to Leo, if Saturn is placed in the zodiacal sign of Aquarius, as it was at the time of Jung's birth,

> Saturn is here the bridge between the will of the Higher Self and the Lower. To the awakened it gives the ability to judge character, to fix the attention, and to meditate on subjective or abstract thoughts.[24]

Leo, through his reliance on Blavatsky's writings, drew on ancient antecedents for this perception of Saturn as a planet of the 'higher mind'. It was largely through the Neoplatonists that the planet came to be associated with the highest intellectual faculties, rather than being interpreted solely as a 'malefic' influence; and a number of the sources Jung regularly consulted at the time he wrote about Elijah expressed this view. Plotinus understood Saturn as a symbol of the higher intellect (νους),[25] and Firmicus Maternus credited Saturn with the power to produce 'famous magicians and philosophers, as well as excellent soothsayers and *mathematici* [astrologers] who always prophesy correctly, and whose words possess, as it were, divine authority'.[26]

Frances Yates has noted that, during the Renaissance revival of Neoplatonic doctrines in the late fifteenth and early sixteenth centuries, all celestial influences were viewed as ultimately 'good', and it was up to the individual to make a good rather than a bad use of the horoscope. There were no intrinsically 'bad' or 'malefic' planets, and Saturn was perceived as the planet of great thinkers and prophets:

> Saturn, unfortunate and bad in normal astrological theory, is placed highest in the list. Being the outermost or highest planet in the cosmic order, he is nearest

to the divine source of being and therefore associated with the loftiest con-templations. 'Saturnians' are not those poor and unfortunate characters of tra-ditional astrology but inspired students and contemplators of highest truths.[27]

It was this Neoplatonic understanding of Saturn that coloured the planet's cen-tral, albeit ambiguous, role in alchemical literature, as well as influencing Alan Leo and Jung himself. Given these associations, it is not surprising that Jung referred to Elijah as a figure representing 'predetermination' or 'forethinking'. This quality, according to Jung, is associated with the mythic figure of Prometheus, an earthy Titan like Kronos-Saturn, whose name in Greek means 'foresight', and who 'brings the chaotic to form and definition'.[28] Elijah inhabits and embodies a recognisably Saturnian universe: stones, scrying, prophecy, and the bringing of form to chaos all traditionally belong to this planetary god.[29]

On the third night of Jung's meeting with Elijah, he finds himself standing 'before a steep ridge in a wasteland'. Elijah, like the mountain goat that symbolises Saturn's 'night' sign, Capricorn,[30] leads Jung on a climb to the very high summit on which Jung finds the circular 'temple of the sun', built of gigantic stones. The old prophet then transforms into a dwarf: a figure whom Jung associated with the mythic Greek dwarf-gods known as the Kabeiroi, as well as with the Nibelungen or dwarf-smiths of Teutonic myth. Jung also related the image of the dwarf to the Anthroparion or 'leaden homunculus' of alchemy, which he defined as none other than 'the leaden spirit or planetary demon Saturn'.[31] Elijah promises to show Jung 'the wellsprings', leading him into the utter solitude of a dark cave. Here Jung expe-riences visions in Elijah's crystal. The old prophet then vanishes from the narrative for a long time (Jung states that it was two years).[32] But he reappears toward the end of *Liber Novus*, offering his daughter to Jung as a gift. Like so many of Jung's *dramatis personae*, he has transformed in the interim, apparently for the worse: he has 'lost the power of his wisdom', and is now weak and poor. He tells Jung: 'An excess of my power has gone to you'.[33] He has evidently been at least partly integrated into consciousness; but the root of his power as the archetypal 'Wise Old Man' is now vested in his later incarnation, the magician Philemon.

Solitude and grief: the Old Scholar

Elijah possesses the power to reincarnate in new forms and reveal many levels and dimensions, as the archetypal planetary symbols in Jung's astrological world are wont to do. The old prophet appears next in the more personal guise of the Old Scholar, whose castle, built of stone, is secreted in the middle of a dark forest. Like the 'composition of place' surrounding Elijah and Salome, the landscape of the Old Scholar's castle is a combination of stone, the Saturnian substance, and water, the lunar substance. Jung noted the parallel between Elijah and the Scholar:

> In the adventure I experienced what I had witnessed in the Mysterium. What I saw there as Salome and Elijah became in life the old scholar and his pale, locked-up daughter.[34]

Like Elijah, the Scholar lives in isolation with his daughter, far from the world with its extraverted, banal life. Unlike Elijah, he is neither a prophet nor a magus; he is a grief-stricken recluse, echoing Ficino's association of Saturn with grief as well as solitude. In the 'small, old castle', the hall is lined with 'black chests and wardrobes' – a colour Jung associated directly with Saturn – while the Old Scholar's study reveals 'bookshelves on all four walls and a large writing desk, at which an old man sits wearing a long black robe'.[35] The sheets in the tiny chamber in which Jung is offered a bed are 'uncommonly rough', and the pillow is hard. Associations of the colour black with Saturn abound in antiquity as well as throughout the medieval and early modern periods, and today the association still lingers in the present-day attribution of black gemstones such as jet, obsidian, and black onyx to this planetary god.[36]

The air in the room is heavy, and the Old Scholar seems 'careworn'. He has given himself tirelessly 'to the material of science and research, anxiously and equably appraising, as if he personally had to represent the working out of scientific truth'. In this description Jung seems to be recreating the portrayal of Saturn given by a long list of astrological authors over many centuries, but in an extreme and highly personalised form. Jung at first believes the Old Scholar leads 'an ideal though solitary existence'. Although no image of him appears in *Liber Novus* – only his stone castle – his description mirrors Waite's image of The Hermit in the Major Arcana of the Tarot, standing alone in a barren, mountainous landscape with a lantern and a staff.

But the Scholar, although he belongs to the same chain of *senex* images as Elijah, is a sad and self-destructive figure. His personality is lopsided, and he seems to personify what Jung experienced as his own rigidity of intellect – the same rigidity that 'poisoned' the giant Izdubar. The Scholar is 'petrified in his books, protecting a costly treasure and enviously hiding it from all the world'.[38] The old man keeps his daughter imprisoned, fearful of allowing her to confront the dangers of worldly life. At this point in the narrative, Jung has evidently begun to realise that the intellect, driven by scholarly ambition and unsupported by any emotional engagement of the soul with life, results in a dry and barren existence:

> Perhaps you think that a man who consecrates his life to research leads a spiritual life and that his soul lives in larger measure than anyone else's. But such a life is also external, just as external as the life of a man who lives for outer things . . . Go to the meetings of scholars and you will see them, these lamentable old men with their great merits and their starved souls famished for recognition and their thirst which can never be slaked.[39]

The relationship between the 'Wise Old Man' and his daughter – or, in Jung's astrological understanding, between Saturn and the Moon – is fluid and fruitful in the case of Elijah and Salome, but constricting and damaging in the case of the Old Scholar and his Daughter. Interestingly, in the horoscope prepared for Jung by Max Heindel's Rosicrucian Fellowship during the 1920s, Saturn and the Moon are

FIGURE 4.1 Waite's Tarot card of The Hermit[37]

presented as forming a difficult angle to each other,[40] which Heindel interpreted rather gloomily in *Message of the Stars*:

> Saturn square or opposition to the Moon is one of the signatures of sorrow in life, for it makes the mind melancholy and full of worries so that the person is constantly carrying an atmosphere of gloom with him . . . These aspects make the mind bitter and selfish . . . In the man's horoscope they either deny marriage or indicate the death of the marriage partner.[41]

Jung was not known as a gloomy or bitter person, and he did not lose his wife until his eighty-first year. But the Old Scholar has lost his own wife while still young. It seems that Jung's portrayal of the relationship between the Scholar and his Daughter reflects his understanding of a particular psychological conflict in his own horoscope, which is presented in a more creative manner in the figures of Elijah and Salome – although he later noted the 'inferiority' of Salome's subordinate position.

Alan Leo was as negative as Heindel about this planetary conflict between Saturn and the Moon, although he offered the possibility of constructive effort to mitigate its worst effects:

> Being the aspect of fate, as a rule it brings misfortune and sorrow into the life. You will do well to exterminate all the selfishness from your nature, avoiding discontent, as this aspect limits and binds those who come under its influence.[42]

The Old Scholar appears to embody not only Jung's experience of his own melancholy, loneliness, and intellectual isolation at the time, but also the astrological descriptions of Leo and Heindel, which present the qualities of this unhappy figure with great precision. After Jung's meeting with him, the Old Scholar makes no further appearance in *Liber Novus*. But the Saturnine *senex* resurrects himself once again, this time in the stern religiosity of Ammonius the Anchorite.

Theology and philosophy: the Anchorite

Jung begins the section of *Liber Novus* titled 'The Anchorite' with an entirely different 'composition of place'.

> I found myself on new paths; hot dry air flowed around me, and I saw the desert, yellow sand all around, heaped up in waves, a terrible irascible sun, a sky as blue as tarnished steel.[43]

Without the cold, moist lunar presence, the heat and dryness of the Sun beat down on this landscape with intolerable ferocity. But the barren rocks and stones once again evoke Saturn's world. Jung finds a small hut made of reeds and mud bricks, where 'a haggard man covered in a white linen mantle' sits on a mat with his back leaning against the wall. He appears to be reading a Greek gospel, and Jung realises that he is 'with an anchorite of the Libyan desert'. According to Herodotus, whose *Histories* Jung cited many times in the *Collected Works*, white linen was worn by the ancient Egyptian priests.[44] One of the figures in Zosimos' Hermetic-alchemical visions, which Jung translated and eventually published, is Ion, the 'priest of the inner sanctuaries', who is clothed 'in a white robe reaching to his feet'.[45] Jung's Anchorite is called Ammonius, a name he based on an actual individual from late antiquity; in a letter written in 1913, Jung noted that Ammonius lived in the third century CE.[46] There is, in fact, a choice of four late antique historical figures of that name who might have provided the prototype for the Anchorite.[47] Given Jung's inclination to link images and symbols through a common theme or meaning, it is possible that his Ammonius is a distillation of aspects of all four historical figures, each of whom reflected, in one way or another, a religious syncretism and confusion similar to that which beset Jung himself at the time of his imaginal encounter.

In a letter to Pastor Tanner, written in 1959, Jung discussed the phenomenon of the anchorite in the context of religious experience and the language in which it is communicated.

> The solitude of religious experience can be, and will be, an unavoidable and necessary transitional phase for everyone who seeks the essential experience, that is to say the *primordial* religious experience . . . But once he has attained this certitude, he will in the normal course of things be unable to remain alone with it . . . But what language shall he choose? . . . For practical reasons he will not invent a new idiom . . . but will be bound to make use of the immemorial myth, in this case the Christian myth.[48]

It seems that this is the case with Jung's Anchorite, who used to be a pagan but has converted to the Christian faith. Ammonius talks to Jung's 'I' about the multiple meanings that can be derived each time one reads a holy text:

> Men strive to assign only a single meaning to the sequence of words . . . On the higher levels of insight into divine thoughts you recognize that the sequence of words has more than one valid meaning. Only to the all-knowing is it given to know all the meanings of the sequence of words.[49]

Initially this approach seems highly promising to Jung, who speaks glowingly of the Anchorite's solitary life:

> He looks at the whole and at inner meaning . . . No cloudiness of the sky, no haze or mist is allowed to be around him, otherwise he cannot look at the distant manifold in the whole. Consequently the solitary loves the desert above all, where everything nearby is simple and nothing turbid or blurred lies between him and the far-away.[50]

Jung's 'I' learns a great deal from Ammonius, particularly about the subtleties of language:

> A succession of words does not have only one meaning. But men strive to assign only a single meaning to the sequence of words, in order to have an unambiguous language. This striving is worldly and constricted . . . On the higher levels of insight into divine thoughts, you recognize that the sequence of words has more than one valid meaning. Only to the all-knowing is it given to know all the meanings of the sequence of words.[51]

But Jung ultimately rejects the idea of life as a solitary, which, he declares, 'would be cold were it not for the immense sun . . . *His heart longs for the sun*'. This longing for the Sun is, as Jung explained it in *Psychology of the Unconscious*, 'astral-mythological, or, to express it better, of astrological character': the Sun is the 'only rational representation of God', and is the only way to resolve the discord 'into which the soul of man has fallen'.[52] Ammonius, a Saturnine solitary seeking intellectual truths in the meanings he discovers hidden in holy texts, proves unable to interiorise true solar light. He worships a 'God of words'. Jung's 'I' expresses his eventual disappointment with the path of the solitary by describing its ultimate disconnection from the fullness of life:

> The solitary fled the world; he closed his eyes, plugged his ears and buried himself in a cave within himself, but it was no use. The desert sucked him dry, the stones spoke his thoughts, the cave echoed his feelings, and so he himself became desert, stone, and cave. And it was all emptiness and desert, and helplessness and barrenness, since he did not shine and remained a son of the earth who sucked a book dry and was sucked empty by the desert.[53]

Too much Saturn without any inner Sun evidently results in 'emptiness and desert'. Jung's 'I' concludes that a different kind of solitude is required of him, in which the sensual, Venusian dimension of life – implied by the reference to the perfume of roses – replaces the aridity of the desert:

> And you yourself want to be that solitary who strolls with the sun in his garden, his gaze resting on pendant flowers and his hand brushing a hundred-fold of grain and his breath drinking the perfume from a thousand roses.[54]

After his encounter with the Anchorite, Jung comes across another Saturnian figure in the desert:

> Someone is standing there, on the last dune. He is wearing a black wrinkled coat; he stands motionless and looks into the distance . . . He is gaunt and with a deeply serious look in his eyes.[55]

Jung calls him 'dark one'. The man tells him, 'I am cold and my heart has never beaten'. Jung replies: 'You are ice and the end; you are the cold silence of the stones; and you are the highest snow on the mountains and the most extreme frost of outer space'. Although the identity of this figure is unclear, he resembles an Ammonius with his inner world revealed, wearing black rather than white, and revealing the absolute coldness of the void in a man whose heart has never been awakened.

The final appearance of Ammonius in *Liber Novus* is rather ignominious. Jung meets two figures whom at first he does not recognise: an old monk and a tall gangly man with a childish gait and discoloured red clothes.[56] The gangly man is The Red One, who has radically changed: he has grown old, his red hair has become grey, and his fiery red clothes are shabby and worn out. The other man has a paunch, and turns out to be Ammonius. In a bizarre reversal of roles, both of them accuse Jung of paganism, and Ammonius insists that his downfall is due to Jung's persistent curiosity, which has undermined the anchorite's hard-won Christian faith. The Red One likewise blames Jung for his own deterioration, declaring that, after his encounter with Jung, he became too serious and joined a monastery. Although The Red One then quietly reveals that he is in disguise, the disguise is not altogether attractive, as it involves constant dissimulation. Ammonius wears no disguise; his Saturnine nature has crystallised, and his thinking has become rigid in its orthodoxy. After this brief meeting, Jung leaves them behind for good.

The Librarian and the Professor

Jung's association of the negative face of the Saturnine *senex* with 'scholarly ambitions', 'scholarly conceit', and 'wounded scholarly vanity' reappears in the Librarian, 'a small thin man of pale complexion' whom Jung discovers sitting in the reading room of a large library.[57] When asked what he wants, Jung replies that he would like to have a copy of Thomas à Kempis' *Imitation of Christ*. This surprises the Librarian, a 'modern' thinker who dismisses Christianity as 'just a religion'. The Librarian is evidently Saturn dressed in the garb of the sceptical, scientistic 'Spirit of This Time'. Jung's ensuing discussion with him is, inevitably, about theological issues. The Librarian believes that people 'can no longer get involved in Christian dogmatics these days', and insists that Nietzsche, as an alternative to more conventional religious approaches, 'interiorizes man exceptionally well', and 'confers a precious feeling of superiority' upon those who need more freedom in life. Jung finds himself adopting a more traditional stance, insisting:

> There seem to be all sorts of things in Christianity that maybe one would do well to keep. Nietzsche is too oppositional. Like everything healthy and long-lasting, truth unfortunately adheres more to the middle way, which we unjustly abhor.[58]

Jung then leaves the library with the copy of Thomas à Kempis in his hand, and enters the large kitchen in which he encounters the Cook.

The Librarian and his Cook echo the Saturn-Moon pairing of Elijah and Salome, and the Old Scholar and his Daughter. But this pairing is different because the Cook is not the Librarian's daughter, nor is she his wife; nor, it seems, does he have any comprehension of the mysterious depths over which she secretly presides. The Cook informs Jung that the Librarian is a gourmet who 'loves good cooking', and that she has been with him 'for many years'.[59] Upon leaving the Cook and contemplating the strange underworld journey that he experienced falling asleep in her kitchen, Jung declares:

> So that was the librarian's cook. Does he really know what food is prepared inside? He has certainly never gone in there for a temple sleep.[60]

Deciding to return his copy of Thomas à Kempis to the library, Jung once again meets the Librarian, and informs him that he fell asleep in the kitchen. The

Librarian suggests that prayer books such as that of Thomas à Kempis 'are terribly boring'. In response to Jung's question of whether the Librarian has ever experienced an 'incubation sleep' in his kitchen, he replies that he has never entertained 'such a strange idea'. The Librarian's utter disconnection from the real identity of his Cook, and from any glimmering of an inner spiritual spark, suggests a shallow, rigidly intellectual, emotionally arid figure entirely dissociated from, and contemptuous toward, the hidden lunar depths that provide him with his nourishment.

Between his two encounters with the Librarian, Jung meets yet another form of Saturnine rigidity in the figure of the Professor. The Professor, like the Librarian, is an ironic personification of Saturn as a facet of the 'Spirit of This Time', as well as a mocking parody of the spirit of the conventional psychiatry of Jung's professional milieu. This 'small, fat man', like the Librarian, is deeply sceptical about religion, declaring: 'The imitation of Christ leads to the madhouse'. He suggests that Jung might be suffering from an illness because he hears voices that follow him, to which Jung replies with insouciance: 'Oh no, Heaven forbid, I summoned them'.[61] Although Jung protests that he is 'not at all sick', he is nevertheless temporarily incarcerated in a psychiatric ward. He expresses a deep concern about the nature of madness in general and his own madness in particular, which he perceives as a 'higher form' of the solar life-force, akin to Plato's divinely inspired *mania*:[62]

> The problem of madness is profound. Divine madness – a higher form of the irrationality of the life streaming through us – at any rate a madness that cannot be integrated into present-day society – but how?[63]

When Jung eventually returns to the curtained anteroom where he first found the entrance to the library, he pushes the curtains aside and discovers he is in a theatre. The Librarian and his Cook are 'part of the play'; it is the only time in the narrative when these two figures appear together. The Librarian is 'ailing and pale' and has a 'bad stomach', while the Cook is 'disappointed and furious'.[64] It seems that the Cook has, deliberately or not, poisoned the Librarian; the rich and complex food she provides has made him ill. As the play proceeds, it transforms into Wagner's final opera, *Parsifal*, and Jung, who finds himself playing more than one part, eventually takes off 'my armor layered with history and my chimerical decoration', and puts on a white penitent's shirt. In the long monologue following this sequence, Jung reveals the profound repercussions of his meetings with the Librarian, the Professor, and the Cook. The Saturnian boundaries have been breached, the gateway to the unconscious has opened, and he has become a prophet.

> Unrest has moved in, a quiet underground earthquake, a distant great roaring. Ways have been opened to the primordial and to the future. Miracles and terrible mysteries are close at hand. I feel the things that were and that will be. Behind the ordinary the eternal abyss yawns. The earth gives me back what it hid.[65]

The paintings: (1) the mandala

Three full-page paintings follow Jung's realisation that the doors to the underworld have opened, although the paintings do not seem to be related in any obvious way to the specific part of the text in which they are embedded.[66] The first painting, dated November 1919, is what Jung referred to as a 'mandala', with a faceted gemstone at its centre.[67] The mandala is divided into sixteen segments, with the horizontal and vertical axes demarcated by serpentine lines representing rivers.

The image legend for the mandala makes clear its astrological–alchemical content. It refers to the central gemstone as the Philosophers' Stone, and equates the four rivers with the 'four streams' of Aquarius, whose ruler is Saturn:

> This stone, set so beautifully, is certainly the Lapis Philosophorum. It is harder than diamond. But it expands into space through four distinct qualities, namely breadth, height, depth, and time. It is hence invisible and you can pass through it without noticing it. The four streams of Aquarius flow from the stone.[68]

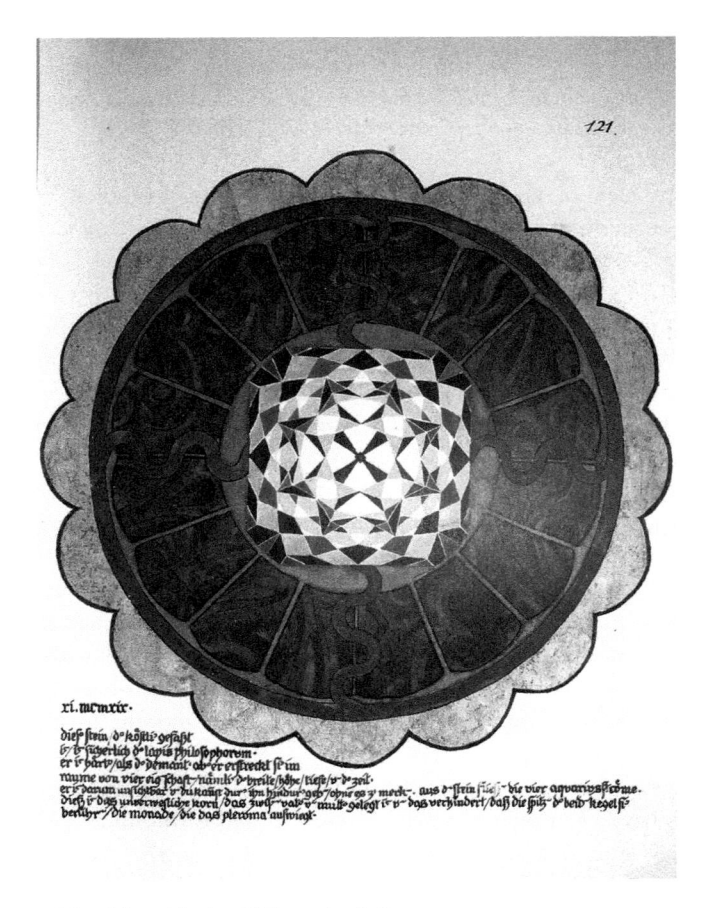

FIGURE 4.2 Mandala with the Philosopher's Stone

The four rivers, which reflect a biblical reference to the rivers of the Garden of Eden in Genesis 2:10–14, have been given an astrological connotation in *Liber Novus*. The astrological reference seems to hint at Jung's understanding of the possibilities for humanity inherent in the new Aquarian Aion: integration of the individual personality with the Self, for which he came to view the *lapis philosophorum* of alchemy as a primary symbol.[69] The quaternity of rivers may also relate to Jung's perception of the potentials offered by the more personal mythology and psychology of the zodiacal sign that was rising at the time of his birth. While Jung had one eye firmly focused on the understanding and resolution of his own internal conflicts, the other eye was fixed on the collective and the 'Way of What Is to Come'.

The paintings: (2) Atmavictu

The second painting is unlike any other image Jung created for *Liber Novus* (see Plate 7). It portrays a quasi-human, quasi-animal face, bearded and long-nosed, and apparently constructed of mottled rocks and stones. Small budding horns spring from the head. The pupils of the eyes are horizontal, a feature limited to only a few mammals – the mongoose, the hippopotamus, the sheep, and the goat[70] – and, of these, the combination of long black beard and stubby horns suggests that the goat is the creature that Jung had in mind. This face, staring out at the viewer, floats bodiless against a backdrop of greyish stones, and is surrounded by ancient flint or obsidian knives and the fossils of ammonites and other prehistoric creatures. The colours are those of the earth: grey, rusty brown, ochre, and black. Both the image legend and the goatlike features suggest specific symbolic references to Saturn.

> This is the back side of the gem.[71] He who is in the stone has this shadow. This is Atmavictu, the old one, after he has withdrawn from the creation. He has returned to endless history, where he took his beginning. Once more he became stony residue, having completed his creation.[72]

Sonu Shamdasani notes that Atmavictu first appeared to Jung as a vision in 1917, although the painting was not completed until December 1919. In the *Black Book* dated for 1917, Jung wrote:

> The serpent says that Atmavictu was her companion for thousands of years. He was first an old man, and then he died and became a bear. Then he died and became an otter. Then he died and became a newt. Then he died again and came into the serpent. The serpent is Atmavictu. . . . The serpent says that she is the kernel of the self. From the serpent, Atmavictu transformed into Philemon.[73]

A year after he produced this painting, Jung created a sculpture of Atmavictu, whose name, he noted, came to him while he worked on the stone:

> Only while I was doing this work did the unconscious supply me with a name. It called the figure Atmavictu – the 'breath of life' . . . the creative impulse.[74]

There appears to be a deliberate link between the Saturnian nature of the stone figure of Atmavictu and the solar reference of the 'creative impulse'; this relationship between Saturn and the Sun appears first in Elijah, whose stony landscape culminates in a circular temple to the Sun, and in the cold, dry Anchorite, who inhabits a hot, dry solar landscape and longs for the light of the Sun. Jung's carving of Atmavictu, which he placed in his garden in Küsnacht, presents a bearded old man with a thin, elongated form like that of an ancient Greek herm, with arms extending into a serpent-like coil around his body. He echoes the figure of the Mithraic god Aion-Kronos as well as the figures of Elijah – invariably accompanied by the black serpent – and Philemon, whose image in *Liber Novus* portrays the

FIGURE 4.3   The sculpture of Atmavictu in Jung's garden[75]

serpent to the left of the old magician's feet. Jung's assertion that both Atmavictu and Elijah transform into Philemon, and that all three are embodiments of the serpent, suggests a single archetypal core revealing itself in various images, all pointing to a Saturnian core.

The chain of associations Jung portrayed and described in relation to the painting of Atmavictu – old man, serpent, shadow, stone, demiurge, goat, *prima materia* – are, without exception, symbols that he viewed as Saturnian *sunthemata*. Even the animals representing Atmavictu's various incarnations, according to Jung, are Saturnian. He associated the bear with 'the *nigredo* of the *prima materia*', identical with Saturn;[76] the serpent, who appears in *Liber Novus* as Jung's soul, is also, like Saturn, the 'kernel of the self'; and the newt, like the toad and the dragon, is akin to the salamander, an image of the Saturnian *prima materia* that must be purified in the fire to produce the alchemical gold.[77] In this careful gathering of a network of correspondences, closely mirroring the planetary 'chains' described by Iamblichus and Proclus, Jung displayed a unique understanding of astrological symbols, their relationship to mythic narratives and images, and their capacity to reveal unsuspected connections with other planetary archetypes to form specific relationship dynamics, such as Saturn-Moon and Saturn-Sun.

Although Jung might not have understood the full psychological significance of alchemy when he worked on his painting of Atmavictu, he was familiar with Greco-Egyptian alchemical texts and their astrological correspondences. Jung was also well acquainted with the ancient Greek goat-god Pan, with the god's accompanying train of wild satyrs and his significance as a libido-symbol.[78] Pan reflects an 'absolute connection with nature',[79] and the satyr, according to Jung, 'is an allusion to the goat God, or the goat man; he is emblematic, almost divine'.[80] Pan, in Gnostic texts, was also the 'utterance of god' and the 'shepherd of white stars', which Jung understood as synonyms for the Self, the matrix and organizing principle of consciousness.[81] Citing a passage from Nietzsche, Jung also revealed one of the possible inspirations for the image legend accompanying the painting of Atmavictu, who has 'returned to endless history':

> The moment of eternity is the noonday hour, sacred to Pan: 'Hath time flown away? Do I not fall? Have I not fallen – hark! – into the well of eternity?'[82]

Jung also noted that the goat is the astrological symbol for Capricorn, Saturn's 'night' domicile:

> The symbol for that portion of the zodiac in which the sun re-enters the yearly cycle at the time of the winter solstice is Capricorn, originally known as the "Goat-Fish" (αιγοχερως, 'goat-horned'): the sun mounts like a goat to the tops of the highest mountains, and then plunges into the depths of the sea like a fish.[83]

Jung's many associations for the symbol of the goat point to a now familiar archetypal potency. According to Jung, the goat is, like Saturn, associated with the devil and the dark side, since 'the unruly and lascivious nature of goats makes them an image of evil'.[84] In alchemy, however, the blood of the goat is 'a synonym for the divine water',[85] reflecting the profound paradox inherent in this symbol; the he-goat, like Atmavictu, is a symbol of the 'creative mana', the 'power of healing and fertility'.[86] Although Jung made no direct allusion between Pan and Saturn, the Saturnian goat is clearly related to the Great God Pan, who was, according to Aeschylus, the son of Kronos-Saturn.[87] In *Liber Novus*, Jung linked the goat to the scapegoat in Leviticus:

> We are still seeking the goat that should bear our sin. Everything that becomes too old becomes evil, the same is true of your highest ... One can also betray and crucify a God, namely the God of the old year. If a God ceases being the way of life, he must fall secretly.[88]

The 'God of the old year', as Jung indicated, dies at the winter solstice, at the moment when the Sun enters the zodiacal sign of Saturn-ruled Capricorn and the God of the new year is born.

The face of Atmavictu seems to be Jung's portrayal of the Titanic face of Saturn-Kronos, surrounded by his *sunthemata*. The original vision may not have contained all these *sunthemata*, but by the time he completed the painting, Jung had evidently made sufficient associations between his vision and the various symbols belonging to Saturn to justify their inclusion as a means of deepening his understanding of the vision, as well as of his own planetary ruler. Even the fossils in the background, according to one of the earliest Greek lapidaries, are associated with Saturn, particularly the petrified shells of sea-creatures such as oysters.[89] This Saturnian daimon is Jung's ruling planet, the 'Master of the House'. He is not the exclusively malefic Saturn of traditional astrological texts, but seems to represent to Jung a dynamic principle capable of expressing itself through numerous forms and symbols, and whose paradoxical nature, as the undifferentiated unconscious and the scapegoat for the human projection of darkness and evil, demands its own transformation and the release of its divine essence. The 'old one', in myth, is both the demiurge who creates manifest reality (like the Gnostic planetary archon Ialdabaoth, equivalent to Saturn) and the dark or shadowy matrix, the 'saturnine *prima materia*' which is the 'kernel of the self'.[90] Jung apparently understood Saturn as his personal daimon, and his early encounters with the various old men in *Liber Novus* may constitute a direct experience of something within him that he later identified as the most problematic and fateful, yet ultimately most fruitful, dimension of his own horoscope.

The paintings: (3) the water-bearer

The third painting in the series portrays a youthful figure dressed in black, green, and white stripes, with the red disc of the Sun behind him and another disc, made up of seven concentric bands of colour, beneath his feet (see Plate 8).[91] He is pouring water from a jug, and the water is painted in a zig-zag pattern identical to the astrological glyph of Aquarius (♒). This Aquarian stream of water nourishes seven plants that grow from the green body of a serpent-dragon rooted in the earth below.

The similarity of this figure to traditional representations of the Aquarian water-bearer, portrayed in virtually every medieval manuscript concerned with astrology, relates the painting directly to the 'four streams of Aquarius' that flow from the stone in the Mandala painting. The figure in striped garb is apparently the alchemical stone, the Self, in anthropormophised form. The image legend for the painting states:

> This is the caster of holy water. The Cabiri grow out of the flowers which spring from the body of the dragon. Above is the temple.[92]

This enigmatic pronouncement does not clarify the identity of the figure, other than that he casts 'holy water'. But he is clearly a representation of the spirit of Aquarius. The numerology of the painting – seven plants, seven concentric circles – hints at the figure of a noetic cosmocrator who nourishes the seven planetary spheres and their earthly counterparts. The *sunthemata* are once again Saturnian. Aquarius is Saturn-ruled; the Cabiri (Kabeiroi) emerging from the flowers are the dwarf smith-gods of Greek myth, whom Jung associated with Saturn; and the green dragon, ubiquitous in alchemical texts, is the Saturnian *prima materia* out of which they grow and flower, nourished by both water and the light of the Sun. The figure's harlequin garb, apparently signifying a *coniunctio oppositorum* of darkness and light combined with the green of the earth, appears later in *Liber Novus* in the figure of Phanes, discussed below in Chapter 6, whom Jung understood as the god of the new Aquarian Aion. Phanes thus appears to be a reborn and transformed Saturn as ruler of Aquarius and, in the context of Jung's idiosyncratic but deeply rooted Christian beliefs, he is also a new and more complete form of Christ, as suggested in John 4:14:

> But whosoever drinketh of the water that I shall give him shall never thirst; but the water that I shall give him shall be in him a well of water springing up into everlasting life.[93]

All three of the paintings seem to involve Jung's perception of the incoming Aquarian Aion, as well as the nature of Saturn as ruler of this constellation. Jung's predilection for linking diverse symbolic motifs that point to a shared meaning might be daunting to more literally minded astrologers as well as more literally minded psychologists. Nevertheless, this predilection reflects Jung's particular approach to astrology, which formed an essential aspect of his psychological understanding. The paintings also suggest a relationship with what is described in *Liber Novus* as Jung's newly awakened gift of prophecy, which emerges after his journey into the 'realm of the Mothers'. The 'Caster of Holy Water' is a kind of personification of the new Aion, 'The Way of What Is to Come': the title of the first section of *Liber Novus*, in which the very first painting that Jung included in the work portrays the Sun at its equinoctial point, represented as a star, moving from the constellation of Pisces to that of Aquarius.[94]

The Saturnian Librarian and his lunar Cook might seem insignificant figures in *Liber Novus*, as Jung's meetings with them are brief. But the insights that Jung describes immediately following his encounters with them involve a lengthy dialogue with his Soul, a complete reorientation of his understanding of the nature of God, and his realisation of the necessity, despite the unique nature of his gifts, to 'be content and cultivate your garden with modesty'.[95] The paintings, although their insertion in this particular section of the text may appear to be arbitrary, nevertheless convey Jung's increasing understanding of the new Aquarian Aion, the ambiguous qualities of its planetary lord, and the role in which he believed himself to be cast through his painful and isolating insights into the human depths.

Notes

1 Marsilio Ficino, *De vita triplici* III.2, in Marsilio Ficino, *Opera omnia* (Basel: Heinrich Petri, 1576), p. 534. The translation cited above is from Raymond Klibansky, Erwin Panofsky, and Fritz Saxl, *Saturn and Melancholy* (New York: Basic Books, 1964), p. 261. For an alternative translation, see Marsilio Ficino, *The Book of Life*, trans. Charles Boer (Irving, TX: Spring, 1980), p. 93. For Jung's reference to this specific work by Ficino, see CW13, ¶170, n. 4. Jung cited Ficino's *Opera omnia* regularly throughout the *Collected Works*, especially CW12, 13, and 14.

2 Invocation to the planetary god Saturn in *The Picatrix*, trans. John Michael Greer and Christopher Warnock (Iowa City, IA: Renaissance Astrology/Adocentyn Press, 2010), pp. 159–60. Jung did not cite *Picatrix* in the *Collected Works*, nor does the work appear in his library catalogue, but it was frequently quoted by Agrippa, one of Jung's important sources on astrology, alchemy, and magic. For another translation of the invocation to Saturn, see Seznec, *The Survival of the Pagan Gods*, p. 53.

3 Jung, CW14, ¶306.

4 Jung, CW14, ¶298.

5 For the biblical personage of Elijah, see 1 Kings 17. The name Elijah means 'My God is Yahweh'.

6 See Shamdasani's introduction to the translation in Jung, *Liber Novus*, p. 210, and Jung, *Analytical Psychology*, p. 95.

7 Jung, *Liber Novus*, p. 246.

8 For the watery colour of this stone, see Chapter 3. For an account of scrying contemporary with the writing of *Liber Novus*, see Theodore Besterman, *Crystal-Gazing* (London: Rider, 1924). For John Dee's experiments with scrying, see Deborah E. Harkness, *John Dee's Conversations with Angels* (Cambridge: Cambridge University Press, 1999); Deborah E. Harkness, 'Shows in the Showstone', *Renaissance Quarterly* 49 (1996), pp. 707–37. For scrying as an ancient and widespread method of divination, see Sarah Iles Johnston, 'Introduction: Divining Divination', in Sarah Iles Johnston and Peter T. Struck (eds.), *Mantikê* (Leiden: Brill, 2005), pp. 1–28; Georg Luck, *Arcana Mundi* (Baltimore, MD: Johns Hopkins University Press, 1985), p. 254.

9 Jung, *Liber Novus*, p. 246.

10 Hesiod, *Theogony* 453–91. Jung was familiar with the *Theogony* and cited it in CW5, ¶¶198 and 577, and CW12, ¶456.

11 See Klibansky, Saxl, and Panofsky, *Saturn and Melancholy*, p. 154.

12 Manilius, *Astronomica*, II.929; Vettius Valens, *Anthologium*, I.1.

13 Jung, CW13, ¶¶274–75. For Jung's reference to Khunrath's purported prediction, see Greene, *Jung's Studies in Astrology*, chapter 6.

14 Alan Leo, *Saturn: The Reaper* (London: Modern Astrology Office, 1916), p. 20.

15 Jung, CW9ii, ¶128.

16 For more on the stone at Bollingen, see Chapter 5.

17 Jung, *MDR*, pp. 253–55. For Jung's childhood stone, see *MDR*, pp. 35–36.

18 Jung, CW10, ¶394.

19 See, for example, Lucan I.652, in R.J. Getty, 'The Astrology of P. Nigidius Figulus (Lucan I, 649–65)', *Classical Quarterly* 45:1–2 (1941), p. 17. For Saturn as an underworld deity, see Peter Kingsley, *Ancient Philosophy, Mystery, and Magic* (Oxford: Clarendon Press, 1995), p. 71, n. 1 and p. 355.

20 For Saturn's association with 'black bile' and prophecy, see the various references in Klibansky, Saxl, and Panofsky, *Saturn and Melancholy*, pp. 10–49. The connection between melancholy and prophetic frenzy first appears in Plato, *Timaeus* 71a. For Saturn as old and wise and the patron of deep thinkers, see Firmicus Maternus, *Matheseos* 3:2; Ptolemy, *Tetrabiblos* 3. For Saturn as the nascent philosophers' stone, see the various references in Jung, CW12, 13, and 14.

21 See Jung, *Liber Novus*, p. 245 n. 157, and Jung, CW18, ¶¶1518–31.

22 Firmicus Maternus, *Matheseos* 3:2.

23 Leo, *The Art of Synthesis*, p. 89.

24 Leo, *Saturn*, p. 65.

25 Plotinus, Ennead V.1:4.

26 Firmicus Maternus, *Matheseos* 3:2.

27 Frances A. Yates, *The Occult Philosophy in the Elizabethan Age* (London: Routledge & Kegan Paul, 1979), p. 33.

28 Jung, *Liber Novus*, p. 247.

29 See, for example, Leo, *Saturn*, p. viii: 'The planetary sphere of Saturn is largely concerned with the crystallisations of the Mineral Kingdom . . . Saturn governs the bony structure in man and his concrete or scientific mind'. For Saturn as the bringer of form and structure to chaos in an individual sense, see Leo, *Saturn*, p. 12: 'Saturn represents the scaffolding around the real self while the edifice of the individuality is in the process of building'.

30 For Saturn's dual rulership of Aquarius and Capricorn, see Leo, *Saturn*, pp. 41–42.

31 Jung, CW11, ¶350. The dwarf into whom Elijah transforms is Mime, the wily mastercraftsman of Wagner's operatic cycle, *Der Ring des Nibelungen*. Wagner derived his character from the Icelandic Mimir, known in the thirteenth-century Icelandic *Prose Edda* as 'the wise one', guardian of the Well of Wisdom. See Padraic Colum, *The Children of Odin* (New York: Palgrave Macmillan, 1920), pp. 74–76. For Jung's fascination with the symbolism of the dwarf, see, for example, Jung, CW9i, ¶¶406–7; CW12, ¶¶203 and 302; CW13, ¶392. For Jung, the dwarf is the guardian of the threshold of the unconscious, a role also occupied by Saturn in occult literature as the 'Dweller on the Threshold'; see, for example, Dion Fortune, *The Mystical Qabalah* (London: Ernest Benn, 1976), p. 218. Max Heindel described Saturn as 'the door to Chaos' (Heindel, *Message of the Stars*, p. 6).

32 Jung, *MDR*, pp. 338–39.

33 Jung, *Liber Novus*, p. 324.

34 Jung, Liber Novus, p. 263.

35 Jung, *Liber Novus*, p. 261.

36 For Jung's references to Saturn as a 'black star' or 'black sun' in alchemy, see, among others, Jung, CW9ii, ¶307; Jung, CW12, ¶140; Jung, CW13, ¶337; Jung, CW14, ¶¶113, 117, 229–30, 330–32. For ancient associations of Saturn with the colour black, see Firmicus Maternus, *Mathesis*, II:1. Proclus, *The Six Books of Proclus*, trans. Thomas Taylor (London: A.J. Valpy, 1816), X:1.5, p. 333; Ptolemy, *Tetrabiblos*, III:11. See also Samuel L. Macey, *Patriarchs of Time* (Athens: University of Georgia Press, 2010), pp. 23–36. For modern associations of Saturn with jet, obsidian, and black onyx, see William Thomas Pavitt and Kate Pavitt, *The Book of Talismans, Amulets and Zodiacal Gems* (1914), p. 245; Diane Stein, *The Women's Book of Healing* (New York: Random House, 2011), p. 176; Raven Kaldera, *Pagan Astrology* (Rochester, VT: Inner Traditions/Destiny Books, 2009), p. 143. For websites with these gemstone associations, see, among

many others, <http://gemstonemeanings.us/black-onyx-meaning/>; <www.jewelinfo4u.com/Black_Onyx.aspx#sthash.LfzMTVsO.dpbs; <www.jewelrynotes.com/heres-what-you-should-know-about-onyx/>.

37 Waite, *The Pictorial Key to the Tarot*, p. 105.

38 Jung, *Liber Novus*, p. 262.

39 Jung, *Liber Novus*, p. 264.

40 The horoscope indicates Saturn and the Moon in a quadrate or square (90°) aspect. This planetary aspect is also indicated in the horoscope prepared for Jung by W.C. Bond. It is not mentioned in van Ophuijsen's chart for Jung, probably because the 'orb' or allowable margin for two planets in an inexact aspect is debated among astrologers. Thorburn does not mention the aspect. For these horoscopes, see Greene, *Jung's Astrological Studies*, Chapter 2.

41 Heindel, *Message of the Stars*, p. 236.

42 Leo, *The Key to Your Own Nativity*, p. 95.

43 Jung, *Liber Novus*, p. 267.

44 Herodotus, *Herodotus, Book II*, ed. Alan B. Lloyd (Leiden: Brill, 1976), II:81–82, and the editor's commentary on this passage on p. 343. See also Ian S. Moyer, *Egypt and the Limits of Hellenism* (Cambridge: Cambridge University Press, 2011), p. 208.

45 Jung, CW13, 'The Visions of Zosimos', III.v, p. 63.

46 See Jung, *Liber Novus*, p. 267, n. 45, where the possible historical figures on which Ammonius was based are discussed.

47 For the various historical possibilities for Ammonius, see Shamdasani in Jung, *Liber Novus*, p. 267, n. 45.

48 C.G. Jung, Letter to Pastor Tanner, 12 February 1959, in *Jung Letters*, Vol. 2, pp. 482–88.

49 Jung, *Liber Novus*, p. 268.

50 Jung, *Liber Novus*, p. 269.

51 Jung, *Liber Novus*, p. 268.

52 Jung, *Psychology of the Unconscious*, p. 70.

53 Jung, *Liber Novus*, p. 273.

54 Jung, *Liber Novus*, p. 269.

55 Jung, *Liber Novus*, p. 273.

56 Jung, *Liber Novus*, p. 275.

57 Jung, *Liber Novus*, p. 292.

58 Jung, *Liber Novus*, p. 293.

59 Jung, *Liber Novus*, p. 302.

60 Jung, *Liber Novus*, p. 302.

61 Jung, *Liber Novus*, p. 295.

62 Plato, *Phaedrus*, 244a; *Ion*, 534b-3.

63 Jung, *Liber Novus*, p. 295.

64 Jung, *Liber Novus*, p. 302.

65 Jung, *Liber Novus*, p. 305.

66 Jung, *Liber Novus*, pp. 121–23.

67 For Jung's discussions on the nature of the mandala as a symbol of the Self, see Jung, CW9i, ¶¶627–718; Jung, CW12, ¶¶122–331.

68 Jung, *Liber Novus*, p. 305, n. 229.

69 For Jung's equation of the *lapis philosophorum* with the Self, see, among many references, Jung, CW12, ¶¶447–515; Jung, CW9ii, ¶¶194, 257, 264, 387, 426; Jung, CW14, ¶¶364, 524, 649, 716, 776.

70 See M.F. Land, 'Visual Optics: The Shapes of Pupils' *Current Biology*, 16:5 (2006), pp. 167–68.

71 'The gem' is the gemstone portrayed in the previous painting.

72 Jung, *Liber Novus*, p. 305, n. 231.

73 Jung, *Liber Novus*, p. 303, n. 222.

74 Jung, *MDR*, pp. 38–39.

75 Photograph by Steven Herrmann, used with his kind permission.

76 Jung, CW12, ¶726; Jung, CW14, ¶172.

77 Jung, CW12, ¶404, n. 8; Jung, CW13, ¶177; Jung, CW14, ¶172, n. 264.

78 For Pan as a libido-symbol, see Jung, CW5, ¶298.

79 Jung, *The Visions Seminars*, Vol. 1, p. 62.

80 Jung, *The Visions Seminars*, Vol. 1, p. 68.

81 Jung, CW9ii, ¶310.

82 Jung, CW9i, ¶210.

83 Jung, CW5, ¶290.

84 Jung, CW6, ¶389; Jung, CW9i, ¶¶413 and 597.

85 Jung, CW14, ¶77, n. 211.

86 Jung, CW16, ¶340.

87 Aeschylos, Fr. 25b R, cited in Gantz, *Early Greek Myth*, p. 110. The Roman god Faunus, who was identified with the Greek Pan, was the son of Saturn. Pan, according to *Homeric Hymn* 19, was the son of Hermes. He is a creature of the mountains in the *Hymn*, and is referred to as a daimon. See Gantz, *Early Greek Myth*, p. 110.

88 Jung, *Liber Novus*, p. 241. The ritual of the scapegoat is given in Leviticus 16:7–10.

89 For *ostrachitis* as the stone of Saturn, see Damigeron, *De Virtutibus Lapidum*, trans. Patricia Tahil, ed. Joel Radcliffe (Seattle, WA: Ars Obscura, 1989), p. 4.

90 For Jung's equation of Saturn with the planetary archon and demiurge Ialdabaoth, see Jung, CW9ii, ¶128.

91 Jung, *Liber Novus*, p. 122.

92 Jung, *Liber Novus*, p. 306, n. 233.

93 John 4:14, *King James Bible*.

94 See Greene, *Jung's Studies in Astrology*, chapter 6.

95 Jung, *Liber Novus*, p. 306.

5

SATURN IN THE HERMITAGE, PART TWO

ΦΙΛΗΜΩΝ and the 'personal daimon'

> All is concealed in Saturn . . . The Stone called the Philosopher's Stone, comes out of Saturn.[1]
>
> —Johann Isaac Hollandus

> As God [contains] all the treasure of his godhead . . . hidden himself as in an archetype . . . in like manner Saturn carries the similitudes of metallic bodies hidden in himself.[2]
>
> —*Tractatus aureus*

> He can find Mercurius only through the rite of the ascent and descent, the 'circular distillation', beginning with the black lead, with the darkness, coldness, and malignity of the malefic Saturn; then ascending through the other planets to the fiery Sol . . . Saturn has here changed from a star of ill omen into a 'domus barbae' (House of the Beard), where the 'wisest of all', Thrice-Greatest Hermes, imparts wisdom.[3]
>
> —C.G. Jung

The Wise Old Man

Philemon, whose name is invariably written in the Greek alphabet throughout the text of *Liber Novus*, is perhaps the most significant of all the figures that Jung encountered during the time he was engaged in 'the pursuit of my inner images'. Sonu Shamdasani describes Philemon as occupying 'a nodal position' in Jung's 'confrontation with the unconscious',[4] and it seems that, while other figures in *Liber Novus* faded into oblivion or were understood in the context of other symbolic frameworks such as alchemy, Philemon retained his importance as an inner potency to the end of Jung's life. Philemon's astrological significance is not the only facet of this enigmatic daimon that merits deeper investigation. But it is an important dimension that has been overlooked in the wealth of interpretive literature that has emerged since the publication of *Liber Novus* in 2009, and it can provide a connecting link between many apparently contradictory facets of this extraordinary inner figure who behaved like an autonomous power and who, according to Jung, 'gave' him most of the material in both the early part of *Liber Novus* and the section called 'Scrutinies', later known as *Septem sermones ad mortuos*.[5]

Although there are ample references to link Philemon with Saturn's web of attributes and *sunthemata*, he is more multifaceted than an obvious planetary embodiment like The Red One. That figure is unmistakably Martial, although The Red One, like many other *dramatis personae* in *Liber Novus*, displays multiple facets that appear to link him with a specific zodiacal sign (Sagittarius) as well as a specific relationship with another planet (Saturn). Philemon's role as an inner spiritual guide or *maggid*, and the way in which he combines opposites such as youth and age, rationality and magic, light and darkness, banality and profundity – and, in terms of planetary relationships, Saturn, Mercury, and the Sun – emphasises, much more than The Red One, the dynamic nature of Jung's perception of astrology and the ways in which he understood the planetary 'gods' or archetypes to develop, transform, and reveal secret affinities with other archetypal potencies through their interaction with each other and with consciousness. Ultimately these planetary daimons are absorbed into, or orchestrated by, the henotheistic image of what both Neoplatonists and Theosophists understood as the central spiritual Sun, which seems to have been interpreted in Jung's psychological framework as the expression of the Self through the individual personality. The solar centre of Jung's *Systema* diagram, discussed in Chapter 7, appears to reflect this secret underlying unity. But even the Sun in the horoscope must, according to astrological traditions from Porphyry and Iamblichus to Alan Leo, express itself through the medium of the individual's planetary ruler, which in Jung's case is Saturn.

Jung described Philemon's origin, function, and meaning with a sometimes baffling ambiguity, and it is not surprising that this figure has been the subject of so much curiosity on the part of analytical psychologists and academic commentators. Jung insisted that, psychologically, Philemon 'represented superior insight',[6] echoing Plotinus' assertion that Saturn symbolises the divine aspect of the mind, understood as Νοῦς or Intellect.[7] Philemon was named after the mythic old man who first appears in Ovid's *Metamorphoses*, and whom Goethe portrayed as the victim of Faust's evil machinations:

> Philemon (Φιλημα = kiss), the loving one, the simple old loving couple, close to the earth and aware of the Gods, the complete opposite to the Superman Faust, the product of the devil.[8]

According to Ovid's tale, Philemon and his wife Baucis spontaneously offered unconditional kindness and generosity to Zeus and Hermes, who visited the old couple disguised as poor travellers. When the deities revealed themselves and promised them that their dearest wish would be granted, Philemon declared that he and his wife desired nothing more than to spend the remainder of their days serving at Zeus' shrine, and to die at the same moment so that neither would be left grief-stricken and alone. The old couple later became the sole survivors of the great flood that Zeus sent in anger against the cruelty and stupidity of humans, and became servants at Zeus' temple, which the god created in place of the old couple's humble cottage. At the moment of their simultaneous death, they were transformed into intertwined trees, Philemon into an oak and Baucis into a linden.[9]

In Goethe's *Faust*, the magician, aided by Mephistopheles, attempted to evict the old couple from their sacred shrine, and murdered them by burning their house to the ground. It is the relationship between Philemon and Faust that forms the theme of Shamdasani's paper, 'Who Is Jung's Philemon?' Jung seems to have felt in some way responsible for this mythic and, as he viewed it, archetypal event through his German ancestry, and believed he had inherited the task of expiating Faust's crime. In a letter to Paul Schmitt, written in January 1942, Jung declared:

> All of a sudden with terror it became clear to me that I have taken over Faust as my heritage, and moreover as the advocate and avenger of Philemon and Baucis, who, unlike Faust the superman, are hosts of the gods in a ruthless and godforsaken age.[10]

In *Memories, Dreams, Reflections*, Jung reiterated this realisation:

> When Faust, in his hubris and self-inflation, caused the murder of Philemon and Baucis, I felt guilty, quite as if I myself in the past had helped commit the murder of these two old people . . . I regarded it as my responsibility to atone for this crime, or to prevent its repetition.[11]

Jung's need to 'atone' for Philemon's destruction even extended to the tower he built at Bollingen, which he called a 'representation of individuation'. On the wall, he carved the declaration: *Philemonis sacrum – Fausti poenitentia* ('Philemon's Shrine – Faust's Repentance').[12]

The stark dichotomy between the cold, arrogant rationality of Faustian modernity, which Jung believed had led to the conflagration of the Second World War,[13] and the instinctive goodness and wisdom of Ovid's mythic old couple, mirrors Jung's observations in *Liber Novus* about the 'spirit of this time' and the 'spirit of the depths'. According to Murray Stein, the mythic Philemon's 'pious receptivity to the divine strangers' is central to why Jung was drawn to this particular figure:

> This virtue is . . . precisely what Jung, as protagonist of *The Red Book*, must develop in himself . . . He [Philemon] displays the religious attitude of receptivity to the Divine, which is the basis for mystical experience.[14]

'Receptivity to the divine' echoes Iamblichus' description of επιτεδειοτες – 'fitness', 'aptitude', or 'receptivity' – which, for this Neoplatonic philosopher and magus, was believed to be the single most important requirement for a successful theurgic union with the gods.[15] Yet paradoxically, Jung's Philemon, while he embodies the receptivity of Ovid's benign mythic figure, is also Mephistopheles, Philemon's destroyer in *Faust*. In a letter to Alice Raphael discussing the alchemical significance of Philemon and his wife Baucis, Jung seems to have focused on this paradox of devil and divinity as dual aspects of the unconscious, represented in alchemy as the *prima materia* or primal substance symbolised by Saturn:

> In Alchemy Ph. [Philemon] and B. [Baucis] represented the *artifex* or *vir sapiens* and the *soror mystica* (Zosimos-Theosebeia, Nicolas Flamel-Péronelle, Mr. South and his daughter in the XIXth Cent.) and the pair in the *mutus liber* (about 1677).[16] The opus alch. tries to produce the Philosopher's stone syn. with the 'homo altus', the ανθρωπος [*anthropos*], Hermes or Christ. The risk is, that the artifex becomes identical with the goal of his opus. He becomes inflated and crazy:'multi perierunt in opere nostro!' There is a 'demon' in the prima materia, that drives people crazy.[17]

The relationship between Philemon and the benign old man of Ovid's narrative is unquestionably relevant to an understanding of how Jung might have interpreted his imaginal psychopomp. But other important facets of Philemon's multi-dimensional nature are also worthy of exploration. Jung was in the habit of linking different mythic narratives and motifs from different cultures in order to arrive at a deeper understanding of a particular archetypal pattern. In *Memories, Dreams, Reflections*, Jung stated that Philemon 'developed out of the Elijah figure',[18] who was drawn from a biblical rather than a Greco-Roman background. Philemon is the most fully developed version of that specific archetypal principle that underpins not only Elijah, but also the Old Scholar, the Anchorite, the Librarian, and the Professor, each of whom displays different and sometimes deeply unattractive but recognisably Saturnian attributes, such as rigidity of thinking, dissociation from emotional life, intractable scepticism toward the non-rational, and the compulsive need for solitude. Cary F. Baynes, who transcribed parts of *Liber Novus* for Jung, recorded in her notes that, according to Jung, Philemon and his earlier forms – Elijah in particular – 'appeared to be phases of what you thought ought to be called "the master"'.[19] Given Jung's familiarity with Neoplatonic astrological speculation, Philemon might also be called the *oikodespotes*, 'the Master of the House'.[20]

Jung called Philemon 'a pagan' who brought with him 'an Egypto–Hellenic atmosphere with a Gnostic colouration'. Philemon is thus a kind of syncretic hybrid. In him are blended Ovid's mythic old man, who is 'close to the earth and aware of the gods';[21] the biblical prophet Elijah, who was taken up to God in a chariot drawn by fiery horses; the 'Divine' Iamblichus, the Neoplatonic theurgist who knew how to invoke his personal daimon; Abraham the Jew, heir of Moses and Solomon, who could call upon his Guardian Angel to master the powers of the daimonic realms;[22] Hermes Trismegistus, the mythic teacher of astrology, alchemy, and magic; and Basilides, the third-century Alexandrian Gnostic whose name Jung used pseudepigraphically as the 'author' of *Septem sermones ad mortuos*, the published version of Part Three of *Liber Novus*.[23] As has been noted by a number of commentators, and as Jung himself stated in his letter to Alice Raphael, Philemon is the quintessential 'Wise Old Man', whose outer form is Saturnian, and who dominates the other figures in *Liber Novus* as befits a planet that Jung understood to be his horoscopic ruler. But Jung also highlighted relationships between Philemon and the Sun as well as Mercury, who in alchemy was known as Mercurius, and whose Greek name, Hermes, provided the basis for alchemy's best-known epithet, the 'Hermetic art'.

The genesis of Philemon

Philemon first appeared as a magician in the *Black Books* in January 1914. His prominent wings, portrayed in the painting in *Liber Novus* (see Plate 9), were not part of Jung's initial description, and seem to have been added after Jung's dream of the winged figure holding the keys, which he recorded in *Memories, Dreams, Reflections*. Jung painted this dream-figure in 1914, and then, perhaps with additional images and insights arising from theurgic invocation as well as astrological lore, elided Philemon's role as a magus with the winged dream-figure and with various Saturnian *sunthemata*, resulting in the portrayal given in *Liber Novus*.[24] The wings, which Jung described as being those of a kingfisher with its characteristic iridescent blue-green hues, suggest an angelic presence, linking him with the angel Raziel, the teacher of magical secrets in late antique Jewish lore.[25] The English word 'angel' comes from the Greek *angelos*, which means 'a messenger'. Philemon's angelic connotations, especially as a magician, are emphasised by Jung's pointed comment about the importance of the messenger in the practice of magic:

> But it is another thing for whoever has opened the chaos in himself. We need magic to be able to receive or invoke the messenger.[26]

Philemon's Saturnian nature is emphasised by Jung's description in *Liber Novus*:

> He has a white beard and thin white hair and a wrinkled face and there appears to be something about this face. His eyes are grey and old and something in them is strange, one would like to say alive . . . You know, Oh ΦΙΛΗΜΩΝ, the wisdom of things to come; therefore you are old, oh so very ancient, and just as you tower above me in years, so you tower above the present in futurity, and the length of your past is immeasurable.[28]

This portrayal echoes the invocation of Saturn in the eleventh-century grimoire known as *Picatrix*, in which the planetary god is 'old, ancient, wise', and has

FIGURE 5.1   Jung's first painting of Philemon, created in 1914[27]

knowledge that 'reaches far and deep'.[29] Philemon is also linked with Atmavictu, the 'old one' who 'has returned to endless history'. In the *Black Book* written in 1917, Jung made the link clear by stating that Atmavictu had transformed into Philemon.[30] Among Saturn's traditional attributes, this planetary god is a giver of form and law. According to Alan Leo, following a long line of astrologers from Ptolemy onward who related the planet to the Aristotelian contracting and crystallising qualities of coldness and dryness, Saturn is

> Judge and Lawgiver and represents the Justice of God . . . Saturn as the individualising planet makes all things permanent, binding all forms, controlling and restraining life's expressions.[31]

Jung expressed Philemon's role as a lawgiver in a letter to Constance Long, one of his patients:

> Philemon [is] that one who gives form and law . . . Philemon gives formulation to the things within elements of the collective unconscious.[32]

From a less traditional perspective, Saturn in alchemy, as the *lapis philosophorum*, is connoted by the glowing stone that Philemon holds in his hands in Jung's painting. This is the same stone that Jung placed at the centre of the Mandala in the painting following his encounters with the Librarian and the Cook. In the legend for this painting of the gem that lies behind Atmavictu's face, Jung declared that the stone 'is certainly the Lapis Philosophorum', and that 'ΦΙΛΗΜΩΝ gave the stone'.[33] According to the seventeenth-century alchemist Johann Isaac Hollandus, one of many alchemists whom Jung was fond of citing in the *Collected Works*, 'All is concealed in Saturn ... The Stone called the Philosopher's Stone, comes out of Saturn'.[34] The meticulous care with which Jung inserted these Saturnian connections into the text and paintings of *Liber Novus* suggests a very deliberate use of symbolic references layered over a genuinely spontaneous vision that he was endeavouring to understand, in large part through the hermeneutics of astrology.

Philemon may be understood as a *paredos*, the daimonic 'assistant' in Neoplatonic ritual;[35] he is also a 'mana personality', which Jung understood as a symbol of the Self, 'the most complete expression of that fateful combination we call individuality'.[36] Philemon can also be seen as a *maggid* or angelic guide in the sense that the Kabbalists understood this image of the highest dimension of the individual soul.[37] The old magician's associations with ancient Jewish magic are partly suggested by the domed building on which Philemon stands in Jung's painting. It may be meant to represent the golden temple into which Philemon's humble house is transformed in Ovid's story, and a similar temple can also be seen in Jung's paintings of the 'Caster of Holy Water' and Elijah and Salome. But its domed architecture does not resemble the temple described by Ovid,[38] and it hints at a source further to the east: the Temple of King Solomon, master of the demons, who was given a 'seal' by YHVH so that he might command the daimonic powers to help him erect his 'House of God'.[39]

The Kabbalistic Philemon

The visual details of Jung's painting of Philemon, like all symbols, are open to various interpretations, none of which alone comprises the 'right' one. But these details suggest that, like the painting of Izdubar, the finished portrayal of Philemon was intended to be magical in Iamblichus' sense of a carefully constructed talisman. It seems that Jung, following Neoplatonic ideas of theurgic practice, inserted specific *sunthemata* that were meant to invoke the daimon. Beneath the golden temple under Philemon's feet, the symbols for fire and water appear to the left and right of the symbols for the Sun (which is represented by a circle demarcated by the four cardinal points) and the Moon (which is represented by a crescent placed on its side like a receptacle). The same *sunthemata* of the conjunction of Sun and Moon, fire and water, appear at the corners of the painting and along the lower right border, and as three flower-like circles in the sky above Philemon's head and wings. The *coniunctio* of Sun and Moon can be found not only in alchemy, but in the androgynous Orphic god Phanes, whose soli-lunar attributes can be seen not only in Jung's painting of this ancient deity in *Liber Novus*, but also in a bas-relief from the classical world that Jung reproduced in *Symbols of Transformation*, which portrays the figure of the god with solar rays and a lunar crown.[40] It is also a central theme in Kabbalistic texts, in which the deity contains both male and female attributes whose *coniunctio*, magically invoked through ritual practice, can result in the reparation of the fractured godhead. It seems that Philemon, like the Saturn of alchemy, presides over, and generates from within himself, the *coniunctio* that gives birth to the *lapis philosophorum*.

Another *sunthema*, the grove of date palms at the bottom left of the painting, likewise hints, like the *Sixth and Seventh Books of Moses* – a purportedly Kabbalistic magical work that Philemon has hidden in his cupboard – at a Jewish and, more specifically, Kabbalistic link.[41] The date palm or *tamar* (*Phoenix dactylifera*) was already an important Jewish symbol of resurrection and redemption long before it was taken up by Christianity. The tree was used on coins to represent the kingdom of Judaea; its leaves provided the motif for the ornamentation of the Temple of Solomon; and its dates are still eaten on the evening of Rosh Hashanah, the Jewish New Year.[42] The Kabbalistic associations of the date palm are particularly interesting in relation to Philemon, although Jung's knowledge of Kabbalah at the time he produced the painting may not have been extensive. In the forty years of wandering, according to Exodus, the children of Israel found a desert oasis called Elim, where there were seventy date palms; they are, according to Kabbalistic teaching, the seventy elders of the tribe and the seventy 'faces' of the Torah which are revealed to those who eat of its fruit.[43] In Jung's painting, there are ten date palms, perhaps meant to correspond to the ten *sefirot* of the Kabbalistic Tree of Life. The Kabbalist Moshe Cordovero produced a work called *Pardes Rimonim* ('*Garden of the Pomegranates*') in the sixteenth century, which seems to have inspired Jung's Kabbalistic vision of the uniting of the divine male and female which he experienced after a serious heart attack in 1944.[44] *Pardes Rimonim* was included in the compilation known as *Kabbala denudata* that Jung had acquired in an original seventeenth-century edition. Cordovero also wrote a work called *Tomer Devorah* ('*The Palm Tree of Deborah*'), whose title was meant to suggest that the book itself was an oasis in which the soul could be refreshed and renewed. The date palm, according to the tradition of the *Zohar* (on which Cordovero based his text), symbolises the *tzaddik* or wise man:

> 'The *tzaddik* flourishes like the date palm; he grows like a cedar in Lebanon' (Psalms, 92:13). Why is the *tzaddik* compared to a date palm? Just as a date palm, when cut down, takes a long time for another to grow again, so too when the world loses a *tzaddik*, it takes a long time before another rises in his place . . . Just as a date palm does not grow (and bear fruit) unless the male be planted by the female, so the *tzaddik* cannot flourish save when husband and wife are united, when the male aspect of *tzaddik* is united with the female aspect of *tzaddik*, as with Avraham and Sarah.[45]

The date palm is dioecious: there are male and female trees and, as the *Zohar* states, no fruit is produced 'unless the male be planted by the female'.[46] In the *Sefer ha-Bahir*, which predated the *Zohar* by a century and which Jung cited in *Mysterium Coniunctionis*,[47] the dioecious nature of the tree is understood to be a symbol of the androgynous nature of the deity.[48] The palm tree's ability to be either male or female, according to Gershom Scholem, is symbolised in Genesis by the children of Tamar, who 'signify the moon and the sun, contained within the palm in the same way as the feminine and the masculine'.[49] Although Jung was familiar with Scholem's work,[50] the book in which this statement was made, *Origins of the Kabbalah*, was not published until 1962, over thirty years after *Liber Novus* was completed. But Jung seems to have been acquainted with some Kabbalistic themes during the time he worked on *Liber Novus*, especially through A.E. Waite's monographs. The grove of date palms that Jung painted behind Philemon may point directly to Kabbalistic works such as the *Zohar* and the *Bahir*, which contain a rich range of associations relevant to Philemon – most importantly, the symbol of the uniting of the opposites in the single image of the Wise Old Man. Among his many other roles, Philemon is a *tzaddik*. He is also a *maggid*, a spirit-guide who, according to Jewish tradition, can instruct the initiate in the knowledge of higher worlds.[51] In *Memories, Dreams, Reflections*, Jung quoted an Indian friend who, having been informed of Philemon, said to him: 'Most people have living gurus. But there are always some who have a spirit for teacher'.[52]

It may also be relevant that Saturn was perceived from antiquity onward to be the god of the Jews, and the planet's association with magic reflected late antique and medieval assumptions of Jewish expertise in the practice of the occult arts.[53] According to Frances Yates, Saturn, as the special planet of the Jews, was associated throughout the Renaissance with Kabbalistic magic as a divine science.[54] This association is also discussed by Moshe Idel, who states that a number of Jewish sources from the twelfth century onward, as well as Roman authors such as Tacitus and Cassius Dio, identified Saturn as the 'planetary genius' of the Jews, despite – or perhaps because of – the association of the planet with magic.[55] Many of the authors referring to the connection between Saturn and the Jews – including Abu Ma'shar, Plotinus, Proclus, Ficino, and Agrippa – were well known to Jung, who was familiar with this ancient and enduring association of Saturn with a specifically Jewish form of occult knowledge, magic, and prophecy. On a more personal level, it might also be reasonable to suggest that, in Philemon, Jung found a quality of inclusive wisdom and insight that he had once sought but failed to find in his Jewish mentor, Freud.

In the section of *Liber Novus* titled 'Scrutinies',[56] privately published as *Septem sermones ad mortuos*, Philemon, who appears to Jung 'dressed in the white robe of a priest' (as was the Anchorite Ammonius earlier in *Liber Novus*),[57] is the speaker of the seven 'sermons' as well as their commentator. In the published version, Jung gave the credit for the 'channelling' to Basilides, a Syrian or Egyptian Gnostic from the second century who lived in Alexandria. Basilides taught the idea of the reincarnation of the soul, and promulgated a dualist cosmology in which the highest god, Abraxas, whose name 'contains in itself the numbers amounting to three hundred and sixty-five', generated three hundred and sixty-five heavens, symbolising a complete solar revolution.[58] Jung seems to have linked Philemon and his pseudonymous counterpart, the Gnostic Basilides, with the god Abraxas, whose name was inscribed on Jung's ring and who, as a kind of *alter ego* of Phanes, symbolises Jung's 'reborn god'.[59]

The invocation of Philemon

Jung was, understandably in the context of his time and his professional milieu, not always straightforward about the origins of his images. Given his familiarity with Iamblichus' *De mysteriis* and the *Abramelin* ritual to invoke the Guardian Angel, it is likely that Philemon, and other figures in *Liber Novus*, were initially ritually invoked rather than dreamed, or invoked following a spontaneous vision or an appearance in a dream. In *Liber Novus*, when the Professor interrogates Jung about whether the hallucinatory voices he hears are following him, Jung replies: 'Oh no, Heaven forbid, I summoned them'.[60] There is an interesting similarity between Jung's description of his initial dream of Philemon, which occurred in 1914, and the occultist Dion Fortune's description, written over two decades later, of the first manifestation of her own angelic *maggid*, who appeared through a theurgic invocation based on the Kabbalistic recital of the Divine Names. According to Fortune,

> I would commence my mental rehearsal of the sacred names, and would suddenly find that I was aware of mental pictures only . . . I maintained my concentration on the images arising in consciousness, and did not allow it to wander . . . Out of the sky over the water a vast angelic figure began to form, and I saw what I felt to be an archangel bent above me in a vast curve.[61]

Fortune, who was as familiar with automatic writing as Jung was, attributed her subsequent book, *The Mystical Qabalah*, to the wisdom communicated by this imaginal figure.[62] If Jung did indeed invoke Philemon, he was drawing on a very long theurgic tradition stretching from antiquity to the present day.

According to the description he gave in *Memories, Dreams, Reflections*, Jung did not at first understand his initial dream of Philemon, so he decided to paint it. This in itself might be considered a form of invocation.

> There was a blue sky, like the sea, covered not by clouds but by flat brown clods of earth. It looked as if the clods were breaking apart and the blue water of the sea were becoming visible between them. But the water was the blue sky. Suddenly there appeared from the right a winged being sailing across the sky. I saw that it was an old man with the horns of a bull. He held a bunch of four keys, one of which he clutched as if he were about to open a lock. He had the wings of the kingfisher with its characteristic colours.[63]

The bull's horns do not appear in the painting of Philemon Jung produced for *Liber Novus*, although they were portrayed in the 1914 painting. Nor does the later version of Philemon hold a bunch of keys, although this *sunthema* belongs to the Mithraic god Aion, as Jung himself noted.[64] Philemon is a winged spirit or *daimon*, but he has, as Jung described him in *Memories, Dreams, Reflections*, a lame foot: an attribute associated with the devil ever since Goethe used the description for Mephistopheles in *Faust*,[65] and which has earlier precedents in Renaissance

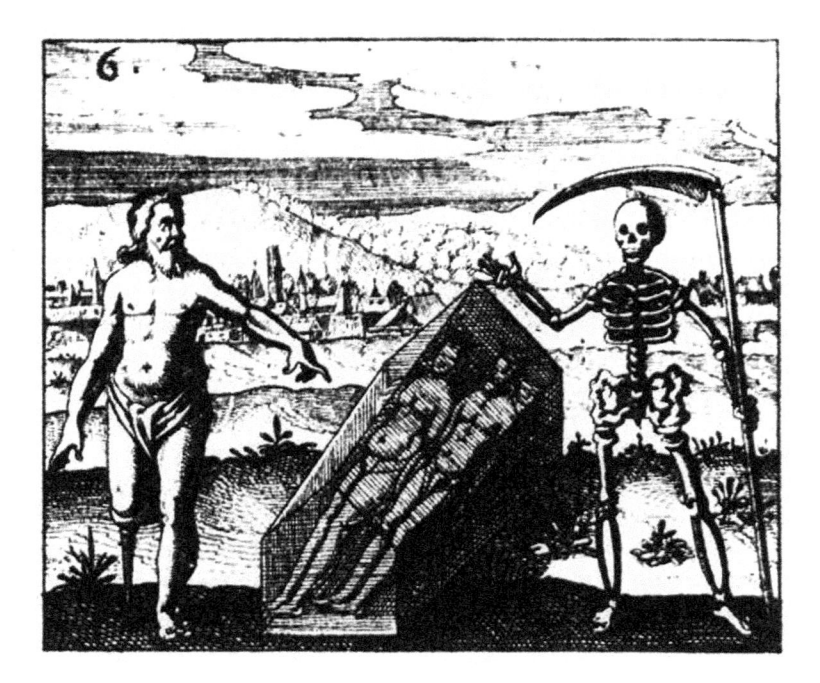

FIGURE 5.2 The one-legged Saturn presiding over the alchemical *nigredo*, in Johann Mylius, *Philosophia reformata*, Emblem 6

astro-medical descriptions of the Saturnian individual as having 'feet deformed with a cleft heel'.[66] Equally relevant is the lame Saturn of alchemy, portrayed as a one-legged bearded *senex* in Johann Mylius' work, *Philosophia reformata*, published in 1622, to which Jung made no less than one hundred and twenty-five references in the *Collected Works*. Jung possessed an original edition of this alchemical text, and the engraving of Saturn is reproduced as Plate 223 in Jung's *Psychology and Alchemy*.[67]

The Hermetic Philemon

During the time Jung worked on *Liber Novus*, he was familiar with a number of late antique alchemical texts, in particular the *Visions* of Zosimos and the various treatises in Marcelin Berthelot's *Les Alchimistes Grecs*.[68] The benignity of Saturn in Neoplatonic theurgy, and the planetary god's association with a lost Golden Age, likewise did not escape Jung's notice. The Neoplatonist Damascius, for example, referred to Kronos-Saturn as 'the liberated Demiurge' who had presided over the Golden Age,[69] and Plato himself had declared that, in the Golden Age,

> Kronos gave our communities as their kings and rulers, not men but Daimones, beings of diviner and superior kind . . . So, the god, in his kindness to man, did the same; he set over us the superior race of Daimones.[70]

The association of Saturn with the Golden Age, and thus with gold as a symbol of perfection and with Mercurius as a symbol of the alchemical gold, was not ignored by early modern alchemists such as Mylius and Khunrath. Equally relevant for Jung were the various Hermetic texts translated by Mead – the same ones described in *Liber Novus* as being hidden in Philemon's cupboard – where the source of the 'secret' knowledge is the Wise Old Man and magician known as Hermes Trismegistus.[71]

In Mead's translation of the *Hermetica*, Kronos-Saturn is equated with the Egyptian jackal-headed god Anubis, lord of the underworld, who, like the Greek Hermes, is a psychopomp who guides the souls of the dead: 'He breeds all things out of himself and conceives [all] in himself'.[72] Kronos-Saturn is also identified with the eternal young-old god Aion in some of these treatises, as well as in Mead's translation of the *Chaldean Oracles*, in which the planetary god as Aion is paradoxically 'older [than old] and younger [than young]'.[73] The youthful Aion in the *Mithras Liturgy* is likewise, according to Franz Cumont, equated with Kronos-Saturn.[74] Jung's elision of the Wise Old Man with the figure of the divine youth, Hermes-Mercury, thus drew on a number of ancient precedents.

In *Liber Novus*, Jung illustrated his perception of the hidden relationship between Saturn and Mercury by producing a mandala portraying the Saturnian *senex* at the top of the vertical axis and the Mercurial *iuvenis*, or youth, at the bottom (see Plate 10).[75] On the horizontal axis are two female figures. The figure on the left is dressed in red with long black hair, and seems to be identical with the painting of Salome that illustrates Jung's first encounter with her and Elijah; this figure portrays the erotic dimension of the feminine. The figure on the right is clothed in white and portrays what Jung or, more correctly, Philemon, called the 'Mater Coelestis' or 'Celestial Mother': a symbol of human spirituality, which 'conceives and embraces' and is therefore 'womanlike'.[76] These two female representations, according to Jung, 'can be recognized without difficulty as the two aspects of the anima'.[77] A similar polarity between 'Luna Satanas' and the 'Mater Coelistis' can be seen in the *Systema Munditotius*, discussed in Chapter 7.

There is no legend or date given with the painting, although, according to Shamdasani, Jung transcribed this section of *Liber Novus* in January 1919, and the painting probably dates from that time or the end of 1918.[78] In 1930, Jung reproduced the mandala in his 'Commentary on the Secret of the Golden Flower', stating, as was his wont, that it had been drawn by a patient 'during the course of treatment'.[79] Although intentionally misleading, this was true as far as it went: he was indeed a patient undergoing treatment, although the physician seems to have been the unconscious psyche. Jung reproduced the painting again in 1952 as Figure 28 in an essay titled 'Concerning Mandala Symbolism'. Here he called it 'Picture by a middle-aged man' – once again, no more than the truth – and referred to the Mercurial youth as 'Loki or Hephaestus with red flaming hair'.[80] Loki is a trickster-god, the Norse version of Hermes-Mercury; Hephaistos, the father of the dwarf Kabeiroi, is an artificer-god whose surpassing skill was referred to by Homer as 'trickery'.[81] In the short commentary on the painting, Jung described the secret identity between the 'old man in the attitude of contemplation' – who is dressed in a white robe, like Philemon in 'Scrutinies' – and the youth with 'flaming hair', who holds a temple in his hands. Although the temple is indistinct, it appears to have a dome, linking it with the temple in the paintings of the 'Caster of Holy Water', Elijah and Salome, and Philemon.

> The old man corresponds to the archetype of meaning, or of the spirit, and the dark chthonic figure to the opposite of the Wise Old Man, namely the magical (and sometimes destructive) Luciferian element. In alchemy it is Hermes Trismegistus versus Mercurius, the evasive 'trickster'.[82]

Hermes Trismegistus is Hermes in the guise of the Wise Old Man, but Mercurius (also associated with the ambiguous figures of Loki and Hephaistos) is likewise Hermes, in the guise of the trickster. Philemon, who contains both, is thus not only Saturnian, but also Mercurial; he is a bright angel like Raziel, but also a dark angel like Lucifer. Each is secretly contained in the other, and although they are opposites, they share a single archetypal core that Jung attempted to articulate within a psychological framework in his three volumes on alchemy, in which Saturn, the dark *prima materia* portrayed as the Old King, transforms into Mercurius, the magical alchemical agent who is also the Philosopher's Stone. Jung's ideas about Saturn had come a long way from the cold, dry malefic of Ptolemy's *Tetrabiblos*.

The third-century Christian Patrist Origen, whose work Jung possessed in an English edition, declared in his *Contra Celsum* that Saturn is 'the rational ruler of pure mind . . . and opening to the world the gate which thou didst close against thy kingdom'.[83] Philemon, like Origen's Saturn, is the daimon who opens the gate: an *angelos* or 'messenger' who serves as an intermediary between revealed and concealed worlds, the role most often assigned to Hermes-Mercury in classical myth. Jung cited the alchemist Mylius to support the idea that Saturn contains and brings forth Mercurius, the daimonic spirit that animates and brings to fruition the alchemical *opus*.[84] This idea is suggested in *Liber Novus* by Philemon's possession of the Hermetic treatises, and by Jung's stone cube at Bollingen with its figure of the youthful dwarf, Philemon/Telesphoros, crowned by the astrological glyph for Saturn and bearing the glyph for Mercury on his breast.[85] Jung also declared that 'Mercurius *senex* is identical with Saturn', that both are 'hermaphroditic', and that Saturn is 'the father and origin of Mercurius, therefore the latter is called "Saturn's child"'.[86] Jung further pointed out: 'Mercurius is closely related . . . especially to Saturn. As Mercurius he is *juvenis*, as Saturn, *senex*'.[87]

Saturn, for Jung, was thus not simply a malefic planet whose restrictive influence, as the ruler of his horoscope, he was required to bear with grace. Saturn is 'the dwelling-place of the devil himself', but the alchemical work – or, in psychological terms, individuation – can yield its ultimate fruit only 'if one conceives him [Saturn] as a process that begins with evil and ends with good'.[88] This statement is a paraphrase of a remark made by Goethe's Mephistopheles, who declares to Faust that he is 'Part of the Power that would always wish Evil, and always works the

FIGURE 5.3   The stone at Bollingen, carved in 1950

Good'.[89] According to Jung, both Saturn and Mercury are linked with 'chaos', the primal cosmogonic source:

> In Gnosticism, Saturn is the highest archon, the lion-headed Ialdabaoth, meaning 'child of chaos'. But in alchemy the child of chaos is Mercurius.[90]

Chaos, in Jung's understanding, is the dark, inchoate realm of the primordial unconscious, and any transformation of consciousness, according to *Liber Novus*, can only be accomplished 'magically', through the agency of this composite of Saturn and Mercury. For any integration of the personality to occur, the darkness of the unconscious must, however painfully and chaotically, first enter the carefully defended domain of the conscious ego:

> You open the gates of the soul to let the dark flood of chaos flow into your order and meaning. If you marry the ordered to the chaos you produce the divine child, the supreme meaning beyond meaning and meaninglessness.[91]

Philemon himself articulates this idea in 'Scrutinies', when he discloses the secret oneness of chaos and law that Jung was convinced lay in the union of opposites symbolised by Saturn:

> I teach them [the spirits of the dead] the chaos that is without measure and utterly boundless, to which justice and injustice, leniency and severity, patience and anger, love and hate, are nothing . . . Therefore you know that

the eternal law is also no law. So I cannot call it law. But how else should it be named?[92]

The secret and subtle relationship between Saturn and Mercury is entirely alien to traditional astrological texts, and seems to be one of Jung's many innovations in terms of the uniqueness of his astrological understanding. The shadowy, potentially destructive *prima materia* of the unconscious, represented by Saturn, bears a secret unity with the mysterious mediating agency in the psyche, represented by Mercury, that fosters the conscious recognition of meaning and teleology. As a power that that would 'always wish Evil, and always works the Good', Saturn is both a *maleficus* and a divine trickster. This perception seems to reflect Jung's conviction that many unfortunate, restrictive, and 'fateful' happenings secretly reflect the work of some kind of intermediary or 'magical' process. If a relationship can be developed between consciousness and the primordial world of images, events become symbols that convey profound significance and can alter the individual's understanding of, and relationship to, life.

The hidden service that one planet offers another – in Jung's descriptions, the service Mercury provides the Sun, the 'highest god', as his 'vizier', and the service Mercury offers Saturn as the agent of Saturn's transformation – reflects Iamblichus' idea of the personal daimon, the 'overseer and leader of our soul', who orchestrates and infuses the entire horoscope and all its configurations with a specific destiny:

> The daimon does not guide just one or another part of our being, but all of them at once, and it extends to us the whole administration of us, even as it has been allotted to us from all the regions of the universe.[93]

Alan Leo, echoing this Neoplatonic idea, suggested that the planetary ruler of the horoscope is the 'representative throughout the current life' of the spiritual core of the individual in the 'lower worlds'. It is the particular musical key given to each 'Divine Fragment' (or, as Jung put it, the Self, which 'might as well be called "God in us"')[94] before it enters earthly incarnation; and the other six planets, operating through 'the environment', provide the 'melody' based on that fundamental key.[95] Mercury, in Leo's view, is thus always expressed in any birth chart through the centralising power of the horoscopic ruler;[96] and Mercury's melody, along with those of all the other planets, can, in Jung's case, only be played in the key provided by Saturn.

As an astrological symbol, Mercury is conventionally related to communication and travel. In many medieval and modern astrological texts, the planet is often minimised in terms of its importance in the natal horoscope – although more sophisticated psychological and spiritual descriptions of Mercury have been offered in recent years, as well as in antiquity.[97] Alan Leo, although he made no specific connection between Saturn and Mercury, presented an interpretation of Mercury that was unusually complex for its time, emphasising the planet's role as a spiritual intermediary and highlighting its importance as ruler of the visual faculty:

> It is neither positive nor negative, but *both*. It is the planet of the adept . . . It is, in one word, the planet of *Reason*. In the physical world Mercury governs the sense of seeing . . . Mercury, accompanying the soul into Hades, represents the silver thread of memory, upon which are strung the beads which represent the personalities of its earth lives . . . At the close of each life Mercury represents the knowledge gained, as Memory, the cream of which is rendered a permanent possession of the ego as Wisdom.[98]

Max Heindel, in contrast, offered a more conventional interpretation of Mercury. Heindel acknowledged the planet's role in linking together body, soul, and spirit, but for Heindel, Mercury primarily signified 'the lower concrete mind'; it is the 'exponent of reason, the creative agency of physical progress in the world's work'.[99] It is more likely that Jung derived greater inspiration for his understanding of Mercury, not only from alchemy and from Leo's interpretations, but possibly also from Agrippa's *De occulta philosophia*, in which Mercury presides over the faculty of 'Phantasie' – the term Iamblichus used for the imagination – and is described as the 'friend' of Saturn.[100] Both planets jointly rule the domain of the angels (the 'messengers'),[101] and both planets are related to magic and prophecy. According to Agrippa, the 'ancient wise men' created a metal statue through the 'operations' of Saturn and Mercury:

> An Image of cast metall, like a beautifull man, which they promised would foretell things to come, and made it on the day of Mercury, on the third hour of Saturn, the sign of Gemini ascending, being the house of Mercury, signifying prophet, Saturn and Mercury being in conjunction in Aquarius in the ninth place of Heaven, which is also called God.[102]

Philemon, as a magician, 'Father of the Prophet', and 'father of all will-o'-the-wisps', is, in Agrippa's context as well as Jung's, both Saturnian and Mercurial.[103] His hieratic image in *Liber Novus* might even be likened to Agrippa's 'Image of cast metall', made up of Mercury, Saturn, Gemini (Mercury's zodiacal sign), and Aquarius (Saturn's zodiacal sign), which can 'foretell things to come'.

Jung had a number of ideas about Mercury that were very different from those provided by the astrologers of his own time. He understood this planetary daimon as 'a soul guide through the darkness of the mysteries', who 'plays a particularly great role in magic'; Mercury also 'embodies the *sapientia dei*', or knowledge of God.[104] Jung not only elided Mercury with Saturn; he also understood Mercury to be the servant of the Sun. In a lecture given to the ETH in 1936 on the historical background of dream interpretation, Jung expounded at length about this solar dimension of the astrological Mercury:

> In astrology he [Mercury] stands for the planet that is nearest to the sun ... The ancients call him Stilbon, the shining one ... He is, as it were, the prime minister of the sun, of *sol* or *helios*. So what we find here is, in a way, the image of the highest god, the sun, and his vizier, his closest minister ... He is nearest to the light. Therefore he is always illuminated by the divine rays of the sun.[105]

Mercury, like Philemon, is winged, and is portrayed as an aerial spirit in alchemical texts such as the fifteenth-century *Rosarium philosophorum*, which Jung used as the basis for his essay on the psychology of the transference.[106] Mercury is also fiery, an 'invisible fire, working in secret',[107] reflecting both the fiery hair of the figure of the youth in Jung's mandala painting, and the fires of hell that belong to Saturn as 'the dwelling-place of the devil himself'.[108] In Jung's view, 'ancient astrology' and Gnostic doctrines of the planetary archons formed the basis of the deeply paradoxical alchemical presentation of Mercury.[109] The 'spirit' of Mercury's metal, quicksilver, is identical with the Mercurial planetary spirit, and that planetary spirit, in turn, is also Saturn: as Jung noted, 'Saturn is simply Mercurius' and the 'father and origin of Mercurius'.[110]

The Stoics may also have contributed to Jung's understanding of Mercury as something more than mere 'concrete mind', since, as Jung pointed out, 'in Stoic conceptions, Hermes is logos or world intellect' – a role also assigned to Philemon as 'superior insight'.[111] At the end of his essay on 'The Spirit Mercurius', Jung summarised the attributes of the alchemical Mercurius, which he viewed as 'identical' with the planetary spirit. Among these are the following 'multiple aspects':

> Mercurius consists of all conceivable opposites.
> He is both material and spiritual.
> He is the process by which the lower and material is transformed into the higher and spiritual, and vice versa.
> He is the devil, a redeeming psychopomp, an evasive trickster, and God's reflection in physical nature ...
> He represents on the one hand the self and on the other the individuation process and, because of the limitless number of his names, also the collective unconscious.[112]

In this uncomfortably inclusive description, perhaps the point most relevant for Jung's use of astrology in *Liber Novus* is his understanding of a planet or, more correctly, a planetary spirit, as the symbol of a 'process'. While it might be simpler to assign the astrology of Philemon to Hermes-Mercury – after all, Philemon encompasses all the attributes Jung assigned to Mercurius – he is, nevertheless, an old man, and seems to encompass both Mercury and Saturn, youthful and aged, winged and lame at the same time.

The solar Philemon

In *Liber Novus*, Philemon is also related to the Sun. In the painting, this is suggested by the golden solar nimbus around the magician's head, found not only in Christian iconography, but also in portrayals of Mithras and many other ancient solar deities.[113] Philemon's role as *oikodespotes* or personal daimon allows him to absorb and orchestrate all the other planetary gods, even the Sun, which, for Jung as for Alan Leo, seems to have represented the chief vessel for the Self expressing through the individual personality. All alchemists knowledgeable in astrology, declared Jung, were familiar with 'the secret nature of Saturn' as the 'supreme tester'; he is the 'governor of the prison' in which the soul lies incarcerated, just as the Old Scholar in *Liber Novus* holds his blind daughter imprisoned, awaiting release through the intervention of the alchemical-psychological art.[114] But Philemon, like Saturn, contains solar light as well as Mercurial magic and trickery. Revealing his identity with the solar giant who transforms into the Sun-god earlier in *Liber Novus*, Philemon announces to Jung: 'My name was Izdubar'.[115] Philemon also declares that he will become Phanes, 'the one who brought the ☉'.[116] According to Jung,

> Saturn, in astrology the 'star of the sun', is alchemically interpreted as black; it is even called 'sol niger' and has a double nature as the arcane substance, being black outside like lead, but white inside.[117]

The image of a nocturnal sun surrounded by serpents – a Saturnian *sol niger* – was described by Jung in Book One of *Liber Novus*:

> In the deepest reach of the stream shines a red sun, radiating through the dark water. There I see – and a terror seizes me – small serpents on the dark rock walls, striving toward the depths, where the sun shines.[118]

The motif is presented again after the slaying of Siegfried, where Jung refers to 'the sun of the depths, full of riddles, a sun of the night'.[119] The image recurs several more times in *Liber Novus*, including a description of two suns – a 'lower sun' and an 'upper sun' – which maintain the creative tension between the earth–world and the world of the spirit.[120] Jung also presented a statement in *Liber Novus* that does not refer directly to Saturn but, given all the comments he made on Saturn as the dark *prima materia*, seems to point firmly toward his understanding of the paradoxical relationship between Saturn and the Sun:

> We thus fear our lowest, since that which one does not possess is forever united with the chaos and takes part in its mysterious ebb and flow. Insofar as I accept the lowest in me – precisely that red glowing sun of the depths – and thus fall victim to the confusion of chaos, the upper shining sun also rises. Therefore he who strives for the highest finds the deepest.[121]

This mirrors Alan Leo's statement about the real nature of Saturn: 'Apparently the lowest, the influence of Saturn is the highest to which mortal man may attain'.[122]

The alchemical Saturn is lead, the heaviest of the metals, but the goal of the alchemical *opus* is the transmutation of this lead into imperishable solar gold; thus the work begins with Saturn and culminates with the Sun. It was this circuitous process that Jung likened to the psychological process of individuation. The paradox of the lowest transformed into the highest was portrayed in the early third century CE by Origen in *Contra Celsum*, in which Celsus described the 'seven-gated ladder' of spiritual ascent, commencing with Saturn's lead and culminating with the Sun's gold.[123] Celsus assumed his ladder to be Mithraic, although in fact it is alchemical.[124] But Jung, who was inclined to track repeating archetypal patterns across a variety of ancient sources, had encountered in Dieterich's and Mead's translations of the *Mithras Liturgy* the idea that Mithras was born from a rock encircled by a snake;[125] his places of worship, echoing Elijah's abode in *Liber Novus*, were almost invariably subterranean caves and grottos.[126] Jung interpreted this dual aspect of Mithras – a solar deity born out of the darkness – as a 'solar myth' and sought corroboration in the *Saturnalia* of Macrobius, in which the Sun's yearly cycle ends and begins at the winter solstice when the infant Sun is born and the dying old Sun is simultaneously 'represented by the gradually diminishing form of an old man'.[127] The infant Sun as the divine child was portrayed by Waite in his Major Arcana card of The Sun:

> The card signifies . . . the transit from the manifest light of this world, represented by the glorious sun of earth, to the light of the world to come, which goes before aspiration and is typified by the heart of a child.[128]

Saturn, in Jung's view, is the golden *lapis philosophorum*, which possesses 'magical and divine properties'.[129] Saturn is also the *prima materia*, the dark and devilish raw substance of alchemy, which he equated with the dark and devilish powers of the unconscious.

> The *prima materia* is 'saturnine', and the malefic Saturn is the abode of the devil, or again it is the most despised and rejected thing, 'thrown out into the street', 'cast on the dunghill', 'found in filth'.[130]

But Saturn is also the Mithraic Helios, 'young, with golden hair, clothed in white vestments, with a golden crown'.[131] And he is Mithras himself, the 'sun-hero', who was called the 'well-beloved', just as Philemon is called 'beloved' in the image legend accompanying Jung's painting.[132] Philemon is a *coniunctio oppositorum* in a number of ways. He connects Saturn and Mercury through the mysterious and magical process of bringing to consciousness that which lies in the unknown depths; he conjoins Sun and Moon as an image of the wholeness and androgyny of the Self; he is the 'father' of the Moon and thus contains its cyclical fatality within him; and he combines Saturn and the Sun, who is in turn served by his 'vizier'

FIGURE 5.4 Waite's Tarot card of The Sun

Mercury as *sapientia dei*, as symbols of the beginning and end of the psychological process Jung understood as individuation.

The Aquarian Philemon

Given Jung's knowledge of his own horoscope and its planetary lord, it would be surprising if Philemon did not demonstrate *sunthemata* belonging to Aquarius, the zodiacal sign in which Jung's Saturn was placed at his birth. Saturn is in its 'domicile' in Aquarius, and John Thorburn, in his analysis of Jung's horoscope, emphasised the importance of this placement, stressing the 'unusual' nature of Saturn's strength and its harmonious relations with other planets – particularly Jupiter, which, according to Alan Leo, signifies 'any religious feeling in which the emotions play a prominent part'.[133] Thorburn also stressed the importance of the element of air in Jung's horoscope, as both Saturn and Jupiter are placed in signs belonging to this element, the former in Aquarius and the latter in Libra. Synthesising these various factors, Thorburn informed Jung that the benign aspect between these two planets 'is very strong evidence of life-work steadily pursued on behalf of mankind and in an unquestionable ethical and religious orientation'.[134]

One sphere in which the airy nature of Aquarius is suggested in relation to Philemon is the association Jung made with Philemon's 'superior insight'. Although Neoplatonic authors equated Saturn in any zodiacal sign with the 'higher faculties', Philemon is unquestionably a daimon of the mind, imparting an entire cosmology, philosophy, and moral and ethical framework to Jung during the course of *Liber Novus*. All of the Saturnine figures in *Liber Novus* display an acute intellect, although the Old Scholar, the Anchorite, the Librarian, and the Professor do not always utilise it in constructive ways. A more obvious link between Philemon and the Aquarian qualities of Jung's Saturn is the image of the young man dressed in black, green, and white, discussed earlier, who first appears in *Liber Novus* pouring out the 'holy' water of the 'four streams of Aquarius' to nourish the plants growing from the body of the earthly dragon below.

This figure is *iuvenis* rather than *senex*, and seems to be, as subsequent images suggest, a humanised representation of Phanes, Jung's Orphic god of the new Aquarian Aion. The temple in the heavens to the left of the figure in the painting is the same domed structure as Philemon's temple, although it is white rather than gold. The 'four streams of Aquarius' emanate from the jewel-like Philosophers' Stone in the preceding painting, and the stone, as Jung indicated, was 'brought' by Philemon and is portrayed in the old magician's hands. Describing Philemon in one of the *Black Books*, Jung related him directly to the 'four streams':

> The daimons become reconciled in the one who has found himself, who is the source of all four streams, of the source-bearing earth. From his summit waters flow in all four directions. He is the sea that bears the sun; he is the mountain that carries the sun; he is the father of all four great streams; he is the cross that binds the four great daimons.[135]

Jung further underlined the theme of the celestial water-bearer when he said of Philemon: 'You pour out living water, from which the flowers of your garden bloom, a starry water, a dew of the night'.[136] Philemon 'predicts' the advent of Phanes to Jung, thus playing the role of John the Baptist announcing the advent of a new and transformed Jesus. But Philemon also declares that he himself will become Phanes.[137] The old magician, it seems, is not only the embodiment of Jung's personal daimon, but is also the Saturnian form of the youthful god of the incoming Aquarian Aion, who is, as Shamdasani points out, 'Jung's God'.[138] This chain of associations, which emerged in the *Black Books* from 1916 onward, strongly suggests Jung's belief that his own individual destiny, and his contribution to the understanding of human psychology, were inextricably bound up with the great shift in collective consciousness symbolised by the changing of the astrological Aions, for which Phanes represented the new collective god-image, and for which Philemon was Jung's personal inner avatar.

Philemon the magician

Before Philemon makes his appearance in *Liber Novus*, Jung remarks that the ancients 'devised magic to compel fate', and then declares:

> We need it [magic] to determine inner fate and to find the way that we are unable to conceive. For a long time I considered what type of magic

this would have to be. And in the end I found nothing. Whoever cannot find it within himself should become an apprentice, and so I took myself off to a far country where a great magician lived, of whose reputation I had heard.[139]

Jung's persistent rendering of the name ΦΙΛΗΜΩΝ in Greek is unlikely to be either arbitrary or a mere affectation. He did the same with Phanes (ΦΑΝΗΣ);[140] and on the stone at Bollingen inscribed to Telesphoros (ΤΕΛΕΣΦΟΡΟΣ) – a figure related to Philemon/Phanes – the name is likewise rendered in Greek.[141] In *Liber Novus*, ostensibly a private diary that was not, at least initially, ever intended for public consumption, it seems that Jung was prepared to follow Iamblichus' instruction that a daimon or deity should be addressed in its own language, however incomprehensible:

> The symbolic character of divine similitude, which is intellectual and divine, has to be assumed in the names [of the gods] . . . For this reason we must understand that our communication with the gods should be in an appropriate tongue . . . For the names do not exactly preserve the same meaning when they are translated . . . Even if one were to translate them, this would not preserve their same power.[142]

As a Saturnian figure related to the other solitaries in *Liber Novus*, Philemon's most obvious association among the Major Arcana of the Tarot – despite the fact that in *Liber Novus*, as in Ovid's myth, he has a wife – might be assumed to be The Hermit. Although briefly mentioned, Baucis never makes an appearance in *Liber Novus*. It is possible that Jung's image of Philemon was, in part, influenced by Waite's design and interpretation of the Tarot card. Jung's own terse summary of the meaning of the card, according to Hanni Binder, was 'wisdom symbolized by the lamp . . . introversion'.[143] Waite did not include in his image *sunthemata* such as the date palms, the serpent, the domed temple, and the glowing stone in Philemon's hands; his symbolic references were almost invariably related to Rosicrucian and Masonic themes. But his Tarot image nevertheless presents the classic portrait of a wise *senex* holding the traditional magical staff and the lamp of illumination. The Hermit, according to Waite, 'blends the idea of the Ancient of Days with the Light of the World'. In philosophical language he is therefore 'the Sage' or *tzaddik*, and, despite Waite's strident antipathy to any form of what he understood as 'black' magic, he reluctantly conceded:

> It is said also that his [the Hermit's] lantern contains the light of occult science and that his staff is a magic wand.[144]

Philemon is not merely a reclusive old man. He is a magician, and Waite's illustration of the Tarot card of The Magician, the first numbered card of the Major Arcana, may also be relevant to Jung's portrayal of Philemon. The symbolism in Waite's figure, whose youthful countenance is more Mercurial than Saturnine, accords with a number of Jung's references to Philemon.

> About his waist is a serpent-cincture, the serpent appearing to devour its own tail ... In the Magician's right hand is a wand raised toward heaven ... This card signifies the divine motive in man, reflecting God ... It is also the unity of individual being on all planes, and in a very high sense it is thought.[145]

All four astrological elements in the form of the Tarot suits are present in this image – the wand (fire), the pentacle (earth), the cup (water), and the sword (air) – and the manner in which the Magician points upward with one hand and downward with the other appears to be a pictorial representation of the ancient axiom attributed to Hermes Trismegistus, 'As above, so below'.[146] The various references in Waite's description closely mirror several attributes Jung associated with Philemon: the serpent, the magic wand, the 'divine motive in man', higher 'thought', and the 'unity of individual being' encapsulated in Jung's idea of the Self. The serpent-cincture also echoes the serpent lying at Philemon's feet in Jung's painting, as well as late antique sculptures of the Mithraic god Aion and the Roman bas-relief of the Orphic god Phanes that Jung reproduced in *Symbols of Transformation*. And

FIGURE 5.5   Waite's Tarot card of The Magician

Waite's pictorial reference to the ancient axiom of the so-called Emerald Tablet of Hermes Trismegistus is reflected in Philemon's possession of the *Hermetica*, locked away in his cupboard. Waite also emphasised the 'garden flowers' at the bottom of the card, intended 'to shew the culture of aspiration'; these flowers seem to find an echo in Philemon's conscientious cultivation of his own garden, as well as in the Kabeiroi-flowers that spring from the green dragon in Jung's painting of the 'Caster of Holy Water'. Waite designed two Tarot cards with a direct relationship to magic: the Hermit and the Magician. He presented the old Hermit as a Saturnian figure, but his Magician is unmistakably the youthful Hermes-Mercury, who controls the four 'elements of natural life'. Philemon likewise 'binds the four great daimons' of the elements. Waite's design for the Magician evidently presented themes that Jung found highly relevant for the Mercurial dimension of his own Saturnian magician.

The astrological Saturn has been associated with magic for two millennia. In the Orphic doctrines that inspired Plato and the Neoplatonists of late antiquity and the Renaissance, this planetary god was regarded as a seer (προμαντις).[147] Although Philemon first appears in *Liber Novus* as a feeble old man, tranquilly pottering among his beds of tulips, he is also a powerful magus. Even his garden reflects the alchemical magic of the planetary daimon: as Jung himself noted, 'In alchemy, Saturn is the gardener, while the black earth and *prima materia* is lead'.[148] The Arab astrologer and Islamic philosopher Abu Ma'shar, writing at the end of the eighth century CE, declared that the planet Saturn presides over magic; so too did the tenth-century Arab astrologer and astronomer Al-Qabisi (Alcabitius), who stated that Saturn is the lord of magicians.[149] Marsilio Ficino's description of Saturn, cited at the beginning of Chapter 4, combines peaceful agriculture with magic, solitude, and 'esoteric theology', and displays numerous resonances with Jung's Philemon.

> By withdrawal from earthly things, by leisure, solitude, constancy, esoteric theology and philosophy, by superstition, magic, agriculture, and grief, we come under the influence of Saturn.[150]

Jung, speaking of that magical power to bring things forth from the 'black earth' of the psyche, says of Philemon:

> You are wise, Oh ΦΙΛΗΜΩΝ, you do not give. You want your garden to bloom, and for everything to grow from within itself.[151]

According to Ficino, if a magician wishes to create a magical talisman for long life, he or she should choose the hour of Saturn to engrave on a sapphire a picture of an old man with his head covered.[152] The word 'sapphire' (Greek *sappheiros*) comes from the Sanskrit *sánipriya*, meaning 'dear to Saturn', the planet associated with this precious stone in Vedic astrology.[153] It is an interesting coincidence that Ficino, who considered himself a melancholic as well as an astrologer-magician, and whom Jung cited regularly in the *Collected Works*, attributed his melancholy and need for solitude to the fact that Saturn, at the moment of his birth, was rising close to the Ascendant in Aquarius – the same placement that is found in Jung's natal horoscope.[154] Saturn, for Ficino as for Jung, was the *oikodespotes*, the Master of the House.

Among the gifts of Saturn to the 'melancholic' (or, as Jung might have understood it, the 'introverted thinking') temperament of his children are the 'numbering and measuring studies' – mathematics, astronomy, astrology, Kabbalistic numerology – cultivated as 'the highest kind of learning which brought man nearest to the divine'.[155] Saturn endows those whom he rules with 'an exceptional propensity toward metaphysical contemplation'.[156] Melancholy also serves to help the soul separate from the body, bestowing the gifts of clairvoyance and prophecy.[157] According to Agrippa, the melancholic individual ruled by Saturn is by nature a prophet, because his soul

> becomes a receptacle of divine spirits, and learns of them the secrets of divine things … It foretells things which are appointed by God's special predestination, as future prodigies, or miracles, the prophet to come, the changing of the Law.[158]

Alan Leo, echoing these earlier sources, referred to this planet as 'the god of Contemplation, Regeneration and Perfection',[159] and asserted that Saturn is

> the great Bridge … the bridge of self-consciousness leading first from simple consciousness to self-consciousness, and then from self-consciousness to the threshold of super, or cosmic consciousness.[160]

Although Leo did not use the word 'magic' – which was as unwelcome in many early twentieth-century Theosophical circles as it is today in many psychological circles – it is implied in the idea that Saturn facilitates the leap from ordinary human awareness to 'cosmic consciousness' or, in Iamblichus' terms, the direct communion with the gods that can be achieved only through theurgy.

When Jung wrote his two essays on synchronicity, he discussed the idea of magic in relation to synchronistic phenomena. These essays were based on the astrological experiment he conducted with the assistance of the astrologer and analytical psychologist Liliane Frey-Rohn.[161] Jung also engaged in a lengthy correspondence about the idea of synchronicity with the Swiss physicist Professor Markus Fierz, attempting to persuade this entrenched rationalist that 'divinatory events actually produce synchronistic phenomena … These seem to me most clearly discernible in astrology'.[162] Jung's papers on synchronicity are now frequently cited by astrologers to provide sceptics like Fierz with a rational explanation of how astrology works. The papers are unquestionably important in terms of Jung's efforts to make sense of astrology within an acceptable scientific and linguistic framework. But they are edited and published works that present the workings of 'mantic procedures' such as astrology, alchemy, and Tarot to a rationally minded public predisposed against anything that appears to trail clouds of mysticism behind it.[163] These papers do not reveal what Jung really felt about his astrological work, or what it meant to him during the period he worked on *Liber Novus*. Citing the usual suspects – Zosimos, Paracelsus, Agrippa – Jung referred to 'the theory of *correspondentia*' and the 'classical idea of the *sympathy of all things*' as forerunners of his own idea of synchronicity, underlining his belief that astrology 'works' on the same basis as other mantic arts.[164] An innate *sumpatheia* exists between a planetary god as an image of a particular quality of time, and a particular dynamism within the human unconscious psyche, because they share an underlying archetypal principle.

> Synchronicity therefore consists of two factors: a) An unconscious image comes into consciousness either directly (i.e. literally) or indirectly (symbolized or suggested) in the form of a dream, idea, or premonition. b) An objective situation coincides with this content.[165]

Synchronicity, as the basis for the workings of astrology, needs to be viewed, according to Jung, 'partly as a universal factor existing from all eternity, and partly as the sum of countless individual acts of creation occurring in time'.[166] The deliberate practice of magic, in turn, is an effort to make conscious use of the *sumpatheia* between apparently disparate objects, events, and psychic states through the symbols or *sunthemata* that unify them. Magic, like astrology, is thus a partnership between an 'individual act of creation' and those 'universal factors existing from all eternity' which Jung understood as the archetypes. The individual act of creation, in turn, relies on a particular kind of emotional receptivity, resulting in events that are both synchronistic and magical.

Referring to Goethe's belief that synchronistic events arise from a 'magical faculty of the soul' and are triggered by unexpressed emotions and passions, Jung observed: 'Synchronistic ("magical") happenings are regarded as being dependent on affects'.[167] They are also dependent on the right astrological moment.[168] Astrological 'timing', like magic, works because there is sympathy between *kairos* – the 'right moment' – and the unconscious emotional state of the individual, who, as Jung insisted, knows innately the qualitative nature of a particular moment in time, and whose unconscious psyche at that moment reflects these qualities. Jung's various observations on the unconscious activation of synchronistic events echo Philemon's statement that magic 'will never be lost to humanity, since magic is reborn with each and every one of us'.[169] Magic is not limited to those who practice rituals; it is inherent in the unconscious itself. It is highly likely that Jung engaged in the theurgic use of astrology to invoke Philemon, once he had made the connection between the initial visionary figure and the planetary potency that most resembled it. As he stated in *Liber Novus*,

> We need magic to be able to receive or invoke the messenger and the communication of the incomprehensible.[170]

Whatever technical approaches Jung adopted for his invocation, this theurgic application of astrology is itself an aspect of the knowledge possessed by the old magician and the ancient wisdom he personifies.

Not surprisingly, Jung's 'I', after his encounter with the old magician, states that he 'learned magic from ΦΙΛΗΜΩΝ'.[171] Jung's understanding of the term 'magic', as we have seen, rests on the idea of *sumpatheia* working through the unconscious and its meaningful intervention in conscious life. The initial dialogue between Jung and Philemon concerns the nature of magic, which Philemon ultimately defines as 'everything that eludes comprehension'.[172] What Jung learns about magic from Philemon is encapsulated in a realisation that is entirely Mercurial in its provocative circuitousness:

> It is an error to believe that there are magical practices that one can learn. One cannot understand magic. One can only understand what accords with reason. Magic accords with unreason, which one cannot understand . . . Magical understanding is what one calls noncomprehension. Everything that works magically is incomprehensible, and the incomprehensible often works magically . . . The practice of magic consists in making what is not understood understandable in an incomprehensible manner.[173]

Earlier in *Liber Novus*, during a dialogue with his Soul about magic, Jung is given a magical black rod formed like a serpent, reminiscent of the rod which Moses and Aaron used to defeat Pharoah's magicians.[174]

> It is cold and heavy, like iron. The pearl eyes of the serpent look at me blindly and dazzlingly. What do you want, mysterious gift? . . . Are you time and fate? The essence of nature, hard and eternally inconsolable, yet the sum of all creative force? Primordial magic words seem to emanate from you, mysterious effects weave around you, and what powerful arts slumber in you?'[175]

Iron, as we have seen, is the metal of Mars; pearls, drawn from the depths of the sea, traditionally belong to the Moon. Jung associated both planetary symbols with the world of the unconscious, which exhibits a 'magical faculty of the soul'.[176] Philemon likewise has a magic rod, but it is hidden in his cupboard along with the *Hermetica* and *Moses*, leading Jung to assume that Philemon has retired from full-time magical practice and is now content to murmur 'a few magical spells for the well-being of bewitched cattle'.[177] However, it slowly becomes apparent that Philemon no longer needs these material aids because he is himself an embodiment of magic.

Planets and processes

Philemon, in his appearance, his nature, and his words, draws together the threads of a number of ancient disciplines, cosmologies, symbolic systems, and religious formulations, allowing Jung to build a fragile but workable bridge between the conflicting 'pagan' and Christian dimensions of his own complex world-view. It is unlikely that Jung meant Philemon to be reducible to a single astrological symbol, nor can the old magician be 'explained' through astrology alone. He probably cannot be 'explained' at all, in any strictly rational sense. Nor is it possible to know with any certainty just how Jung understood the workings of his ruling planet, other than what is suggested by his comment to the American writer Upton Sinclair, made in 1955:

> The ruler of my birth, old Saturnus, slowed down my maturation process to such an extent that I became aware of my own ideas only at the beginning of the second half of life, i.e. exactly with 36 years.[178]

'Thirty-six years' from his birth refers to 1911–1912, when Jung began his studies in astrology and its late antique philosophical, mythic, and theurgic framework, initiated the parting of the ways with Freud, and entered that period of psychic suffering that is sometimes viewed as a time of mental 'breakdown'. From Jung's perspective, the *oikodespotes*, acting, as personal daimons tend to do, as the orchestrator of the individual's destiny, evidently held Jung's ultimate path in check until it was ready to be revealed at the optimum moment, through the breaking down of rigid conscious structures and the emergence of a new creative vision. Although Jung enlisted a number of astrologers to explain his birth chart to him, he did not provide a written interpretation of his own horoscope or, if he did produce one, it has not yet come to light. But the role Philemon plays in *Liber Novus* suggests that Jung understood his planetary ruler, Saturn, as a mythic potency, an archetypal dominant representing both a facet of the collective psyche and a dimension of his own personality: the voice of the Self as it expressed itself through the unique path of his daimon and his individuation process.

Philemon provided Jung with his wisdom, his insight, his understanding of the workings of the psyche, and, ultimately, his cosmology, translated into psychological terms. Philemon also appears to have provided the foundation for the idea of synchronicity, which Jung coupled with the workings of magic. Philemon as a Saturnian figure is the mouthpiece for, and orchestrator of, all the other planetary potencies; he is a process unfolding as personal fate. As the archetype of the 'Wise Old Man', he is universal in the sense that everyone, and not just Jung, is born with Saturn somewhere in the natal horoscope. But Philemon was especially important to Jung because he seems to personify Jung's 'Master of the House', the particular daimon standing behind his own soul-journey. Philemon appeared as an inner 'guru' or transpersonal guide, a 'mana personality' who spoke directly to Jung about his role and his destiny, and a repository for the entire unfoldment of human psychological history – or what Blavatsky called the *akasha* or 'memory of nature' – made available first through a dream, and then through Jung's deliberate invocation of him.

The approach to astrology suggested by the figure of Philemon was unique to Jung at the time, although it seems that Zosimos, Iamblichus, Plotinus, Proclus, the authors of the Greek Magical Papyri, and medieval and early modern magi such as Ficino, Paracelsus, and Agrippa, had got there before him and provided comprehensible precedents. Although Jung was entirely capable of articulating a classical Ptolemaic description of the characterological attributes of zodiacal signs and planets, during the time he worked on the second layer of *Liber Novus* he not only used astrological symbols as a hermeneutic device; he also seems to have developed a form of astral magic or, more correctly, astral theurgy, which involved a deliberate use of the imaginal faculty to enter and participate in the world of the planetary daimons, which he understood as psychological potencies. This is precisely the goal of Iamblichus' theurgy, and the fully developed Philemon is perhaps the most potent result of Jung's efforts. During a period when much of his life was chaotic, painful, and distressing, this figure appears to have provided Jung with the connecting thread of meaning that made sense of what he was experiencing, and inspired him to formulate a psychology rooted as much in astrological symbolism as in the myths he believed were based on it.

Jung never wrote a work on astrological interpretation, and it is easy enough to see why. The reluctance with which he allowed others to glimpse the depth of his astrological interests would alone have precluded it. And even if he had been so inclined, he could not have reduced the nature of his perceptions and experiences to a list of 'cookbook' delineations like those provided by the astrologers of his time. No textbook description of the nature and function of the 'ruling planet' can approach the depth, complexity, subtlety, and extraordinary potency of what Jung created in Philemon – or, viewed from another perspective, what Philemon created in Jung.

Notes

1 Johann Isaac Hollandus, *Opus Saturni*, in Basilius Valentinus, *Of Natural and Supernatural Things*, trans. Daniel Cable (London: Moses Pitt, 1670), pp. 184–85.
2 *Tractatus aureus*, in *Theatrum chemicum* (Strasbourg, 1613), Vol. IV, p. 718, cited in Jung, CW9i, p. 4, n. 8.
3 Jung, CW14, ¶303.
4 Sonu Shamdasani, 'Who Is Jung's Philemon?', *Jung History* 2:2 (2011), <www.philemon foundation.org/resources/jung_history/volume_2_issue_2>.
5 Jung, *Liber Novus*, p. 339: 'Probably the greater part of what I have written in the earlier part of this book was given to me by ΦΙΛΗΜΩΝ'.
6 Jung, *MDR*, p. 208.
7 Plotinus, Ennead 5, 8.13. The word Νοῦς does not imply intellect in the sense of rational thinking as we might understand it in the twenty-first century, but suggests the Platonic idea of 'reason', or truthful insight inspired by an intuitive comprehension of the unity of the cosmos and the hidden links forming the chains of symbolic interconnections. Νοῦς can also imply the Platonic idea of the Divine Mind.
8 Jung, Letter to Alice Raphael, cited in Sonu Shamdasani, 'Who Is Jung's Philemon?' Unpublished Letter to Alice', *Jung History* 2:2 (2011), <www.philemonfoundation.org/resources/jung_history/volume_2_issue_2>.
9 Ovid, *Metamorphoses*, Book VIII, at Internet Classics Archive, <http://classics.mit.edu//Ovid/metam.html>.
10 C.G. Jung, Letter to Paul Schmitt, 5 January 1942, in *Jung Letters*, Vol. 1, pp. 309–10.
11 Jung, *MDR*, p. 260.

12 See Shamdasani, 'Introduction', in Jung, *Liber Novus*, p. 216. Shamdasani has suggested that the tower 'may be regarded as a three-dimensional continuation of *Liber Novus*: its *'Liber Quartus'* (*Liber Novus*, p. 216).

13 See C.G. Jung, letter to Alice Raphael, 7 June 1955, cited in Shamdasani, 'Who Is Jung's Philemon?', in which Jung declares that due to inflation, the 'demon' in the *prima materia* would overwhelm the German nation.

14 Murray Stein, 'What Is *The Red Book* for Analytical Psychology?', *Journal of Analytical Psychology* 56 (2011), 590–606, on p. 600.

15 For Iamblichus' 'receptivity', see Greene, *Jung's Studies in Astrology*, chapter 4.

16 'Mr. South' is Thomas South, an esoterically inclined scholar and the father of Mary Ann Atwood, who wrote a seminal work on the spiritual dimensions of alchemy titled *Hermetic Philosophy and Alchemy* (London: Trelawney Saunders, 1850). This work, originally published anonymously, exercised enormous influence on the burgeoning of occultism in England at the end of the nineteenth century, and was included in Jung's private library. Nicholas Flamel (1330–1418) was a French scrivener and manuscript-seller who posthumously acquired the reputation of an alchemist in the seventeenth century through a work called *Le Livre des figures hiéroglyphiques* (Paris: Veuve Guillemot, 1612). For Jung's references to this work, see Jung, CW8, ¶394; CW9i, ¶246; CW14, ¶45. Flamel's wife was called Péronelle. *Mutus Liber* ('The Silent Book') by 'Altus', published in 1677, is an alchemical work with images but no text (hence its title); the alchemical process is portrayed through a couple or syzygy (husband and wife, brother and sister, Sol and Luna) working together on the alchemical *opus*. For *Mutus Liber*, see Jung, CW14, ¶181 n. 317. For a complete set of the plates for *Mutus Liber*, see Stanislas Klossowski de Rola, *The Golden Game* (London: Thames and Hudson, 1988), pp. 266–84.

17 Jung, letter to Alice Raphael, cited in Shamdasani, 'Who Is Jung's Philemon?'

18 Jung, *MDR*, p. 207.

19 Shamdasani, 'Introduction', in Jung, *Liber Novus*, p. 213.

20 See Greene, *Jung's Studies in Astrology*, chapter 4.

21 C.G. Jung, Letter to Alice Raphael, 7 June 1955, cited in Shamdasani, 'Who is Jung's Philemon?'

22 For Abraham the Jew and his grimoire, see Greene, *Jung's Studies in Astrology*, chapter 4.

23 C.G. Jung, *Septem Sermones ad Mortuos*, trans. Stephan A. Hoeller, in Stephan A. Hoeller, *The Gnostic Jung and the Seven Sermons to the Dead* (Wheaton, IL: Theosophical Publishing House, 1982), pp. 44–58. The *Septem sermones* is also reprinted in English in Robert A. Segal (ed.), *The Gnostic Jung* (Princeton, NJ: Princeton University Press, 1992), 181–93, and the text is available at <www.gnosis.org/library/7Sermons.htm>. For the history of the publication of the work, see Hoeller, *The Gnostic Jung*, xxiii–xxiv, 8–9, 219–20.

24 There are in fact four extant paintings of Philemon. Two of them seem to have vanished into private collections, although they have appeared in various papers about Jung's work. The first painting, which Jung created in 1914, was reproduced in the first edition of Gerhard Wehr, *An Illustrated Biography of Jung*, trans. M. Kohn (Boston: Shambhala, 1989), p. 72. This painting reflects the dream Jung described in *MDF*. The image was reproduced in a paper by Jay Sherry, 'A Pictorial Guide to the Red Book', *ARAS Connections: Image and Archetype* 1 (2010). The present location of the original is unknown. The second painting is the version presented in *Liber Novus*. The third was painted at Bollingen, and replicates the image from *Liber Novus* as a huge mural in one of the bedrooms in the tower. The fourth painting, which presents Philemon as a giant standing behind and enclosing or emanating five smaller figures (perhaps planetary images) with a solar disk below, was shown at an exhibition on *The Red Book* at the Musée nationale des arts asiatiques Guimet in Paris in the autumn of 2011, but its provenance is noted as 'Collecton particulière: droits réservés' – in other words, a private collection whose owner prefers anonymity. This painting also appeared in a paper by Sylvester Wojtkowski titled 'Jung's "Art Complex"', published in *ARAS* 3 (2009), but no reference is given there for its source or location.

25 For the reference to the kingfisher's wings, see Jung, *MDF*, p. 207. For the angel Raziel, whom Jung mentioned in CW14, ¶572, see Rachel Elior, 'The Concept of God in Hekhalot Mysticism', in Joseph Dan (ed.), *Binah*, Vol. 2 (New York: Praeger, 1989), pp. 97–120, esp. pp. 101 and 112. Raziel might be considered the divine Jewish equivalent of Hermes Trismegistus. For the *Sefer ha-Raziel* ('Book of Raziel'), see Jung, CW14, ¶572; Joseph Dan, 'Book of Raziel', in *Encyclopaedia Judaica*, 13 volumes, pp. 1591–593; François Secret, 'Sur quelques traductions du Sefer Raziel', *REJ* 128 (1969), pp. 223–45. For an English translation of the *Sefer ha-Raziel,* see Steve Savedow, *Sepher Rezial Hemelach* (York Beach, ME: Weiser Books, 2001). Another English translation, Sloane MS 3826, can be found in the British Museum, titled *Liber Salomonis*; see Savedow's Appendix of *Sefer ha-Raziel* manuscripts in Savedow (trans.), *Sepher Rezial Hemelach*, pp. 280–86. See also Chapter 2.
26 Jung, *Liber Novus*, p. 314.
27 Wehr, *An Illustrated Biography of C.G. Jung*, p. 72, © 2007 Foundation of the Works of C.G. Jung, Zürich.
28 Jung, *Liber Novus*, pp. 312–16.
29 *Picatrix*, pp. 159–60; see the full quote and references at the beginning of this chapter.
30 See Chapter 4.
31 Leo, *Esoteric Astrology*, pp. 25–26.
32 C.G. Jung, letter to Constance Long, cited by Shamdasani in Jung, *Liber Novus*, p. 232, n. 306.
33 See Jung, *Liber Novus*, p. 121.
34 Johann Isaac Hollandus, *Opus Saturni*, in Basilius Valentinus, *Of Natural and Supernatural Things*, trans. Daniel Cable (London: Moses Pitt, 1670), pp. 184–85, available at <www. levity.com/alchemy/hollandus_saturn.html>. The text is found in Latin in Valentinus' compilation in Jung's library: *Opera mineralis, sive de lapide philosophico* (Middleburgi, 1600), *C.G. Jung Bibliothek* CE39.
35 See Henry Corbin, *The Man of Light in Iranian Sufism* (Green Oaks, IL: Omega, 1994), pp. 13–37, for the *paredos* or 'heavenly twin'. See also Porphyry, *Life of Plotinus* 10.14–30 for a description of Plotinus' divine 'attending daimon'.
36 Jung, CW7, ¶405. See also CW7, ¶399 on the 'mana personality', and Shamdasani, 'Introduction', in Jung, *Liber Novus*, p. 218.
37 For the *maggid*, see below.
38 The temple described in Ovid's *Metamorphoses* has a gold roof and marble columns; the columns do not appear in the painting of Philemon. In some pictorial presentations of Solomon's Temple from the fifteenth to the early twentieth centuries, the mosque known as the Dome of the Rock, which now stands on the site of the Second Temple, was used as a model; an example is a view of the Temple from the *Nuremberg Chronicle* by Hartmann Schedel, c. 1493. See Pamela Berger, 'Ways of Knowing Through Iconography: The Temple of Solomon and the Dome of the Rock', paper given at Boston College, BOISI Center for Religion and American Public Life, 8 April 2009. Jung describes the temple of Philemon as 'a golden temple' in Jung, *Liber Novus*, p. 315.
39 For Solomon as a great magician, see Pablo A. Torijano, *Solomon the Esoteric King* (Leiden: Brill, 2002).
40 See Chapter 6 for this bas-relief.
41 Moses himself was perceived as a great magician by ancient and medieval authors; see Andreas Kilcher, 'The Moses of Sinai and the Moses of Egypt', *Aries* 4:2 (2004), pp. 148–70; John G. Gager, *Moses in Greco-Roman Paganism* (New York: Abingdon Press, 1972); Jan Assman, *Moses the Egyptian* (Cambridge, MA: Harvard University Press, 1998). A connection between Moses and Philemon is suggested by the magical black rod which is also the black serpent that accompanies both Elijah and Philemon in *Liber Novus*; for the rod, see Jung, *Liber Novus*, pp. 307–308. Jung made his own connection between Moses and Elijah: see Jung, *Liber Novus*, p. 248, n. 187, citing *Black Book* 2, p. 84, where Jung stated that Elijah resembled Michelangelo's 'sitting Moses'.
42 See Leviticus 22:40; Nehemiah 8:15; 1 Kings 6:29.

43 Exodus 15:27.
44 Jung, *MDR*, p. 325. Jung encountered Cordovero later, in the eighteenth-century Kabbalistic compendium by Christian Knorr von Rosenroth, translated into Latin and known as *Kabbala denudata*. This work was in Jung's library in an original edition: Christian Knorr von Rosenroth, *Kabbala denudata*, 3 volumes (Sulzbach/Frankfurt: Abraham Lichtental, 1677–84). The *Kabbala denudata* is regularly cited in Jung, CW5, the revised version of *Psychology of the Unconscious*. However, he does not mention it in the original publication.
45 *Zohar, Bereshit* 82a.
46 Jung was familiar with the *Zohar*, the great seminal work of Kabbalistic thought, written in the late thirteenth century. He possessed copies of the work in German and English translations: Ernst Müller (trans.), *Der Sohar* (Düsseldorf: Diederich, 1932) and Harry Sperling and Maurice Simon (trans.), *The Zohar*, 5 volumes (London: Soncino Press, 1931–34). Jung also had a copy of A.E. Waite, *The Doctrine and Literature of the Kabbalah* (London: Theosophical Publishing Society, 1902), as well as A.E. Waite, *The Secret Doctrine of Israel* (London: William Rider & So, 1912), and A.E. Waite, *The Holy Kabbalah* (London: Williams & Norgate, 1929). All these works by Waite include lengthy expositions of the *Zohar*. Other works on the Kabbalah in Jung's library that were published before, during, or soon after the period in which Jung worked on *Liber Novus* are: Gershom Scholem, *Die Geheimnisse der Schöpfung* (Berlin: Schocken, 1935); Oswald Erich Bischoff, *Die Elemente der Kabbalah*, 2 volumes (Berlin: Hermann Barsdorf, 1913–20); Knut Stenring (trans.), *The Book of Formation (Sepher Yetzirah) by Rabbi Akiba ben Joseph* (New York: Ktav Publishing House, 1923), with an introduction by A. E Waite; Chajim Bloch, *Lebenserinnerungen des Kabbalisten Vital* (Vienna: Vernay-Verlag, 1927). This last work may be particularly relevant for an early date for Jung's knowledge of Kabbalah because Rabbi Bloch, an historian and Kabbalistic scholar who had frequent contact with Freud, stated in an interview that Freud possessed a number of Kabbalistic works in his library. For this reference, see Bakan, *Sigmund Freud and the Jewish Mystical Tradition*, p. xviii. G.R.S. Mead, although he did not publish any work on the Kabbalah, was entirely familiar with it through his long, close friendship with Rabbi Moses Gaster; see Greene, *Magi and Maggidim*, pp. 291–92.
47 Jung, CW14, ¶625.
48 *Sefer ha-Bahir*, 117 and 139.
49 Genesis 38:28–30. See Gershom Scholem, *Origins of the Kabbalah*, ed. R.J. Zwi Werblowsky, trans. Allan Arkush (Princeton, NJ: Princeton University Press, 1987; originally published in German as *Ursprung und Anfänge der Kabbala*, Berlin: Walter de Gruyter, 1962), p. 173.
50 Jung possessed several of Scholem's works on the Kabbalah, the earliest (*Das Geheimnisse der Schöpfung: Ein Kapitel aus dem Sohar*) of which was published in 1935.
51 For the definition of a *maggid*, see Joseph Dan, 'Maggid', in *Encyclopaedia Judaica*, 16 volumes (Jerusalem: Keter, 1971), 11:698–701. For seventeenth-century instructions on how to invoke a *maggid*, see the revelation of Rabbi Joseph Taitazak in Joseph Dan (ed. and trans.), *The Heart and the Fountain* (Oxford: Oxford University Press, 2002), pp. 175–80. For examples of Kabbalists who believed their writings were 'dictated' by a *maggid*, see, among others, Werblowsky, *Joseph Karo*, pp. 257–86; Moshe Idel, *Absorbing Perfections* (Leiden: Brill, 2002), pp. 143–45; Louis Jacobs, 'The Maggid of Rabbi Moses Hayyim Luzzato', in Louis Jacobs (ed. and trans.), *The Jewish Mystics* (London: Kyle Cathie, 1990), pp. 136–47; Fine, *Physician of the Soul*, pp. 96–9. Isaac Luria, the subject of the last-mentioned book, believed his *maggid* was none other than the prophet Elijah. The late nineteenth-century British occultist Anna Bonus Kingsford, whose work seems to have been of interest to Jung, also had an angelic *maggid*, and Blavatsky's 'Masters' appear to be based on the prototype of the Jewish Kabbalistic tradition. For further scholarly discussions on the *maggid*, see Wolfson, 'Beyond the Spoken Word'; Moshe Idel, 'Transmission in Thirteenth-Century Kabbalah', in Elmon and Gershoni (eds.), *Transmitting Jewish Traditions*, pp. 138–65. For the use of *maggidim* and angelic guides in the occult revival of the late nineteenth and early twentieth centuries, see Greene, *Magi and Maggidim*.

52 Jung, *MDR*, pp. 208–9.
53 For Jung's references to Saturn as the 'star of the Jews', see Jung, CW5, ¶421, n. 5; Jung, CW9ii, ¶128; Jung, CW11, ¶¶350 and 403. For a full exposition of this historical tradition, see Moshe Idel, *Saturn's Jews* (London: Continuum, 2011). See also Joshua Trachtenberg, *The Devil and the Jews* (New Haven, CT: Yale University Press, 1943); Greene, *Magi and Maggidim*, pp. 125–26.
54 Frances A. Yates, *The Occult Philosophy in the Elizabethan Age* (London: Routledge & Kegan Paul, 1979), pp. 23, 33–34.
55 Idel, *Saturn's Jews*, p. xiii. For a comprehensive list of references on the relationship between Saturn and the Jews, see Idel, *Saturn's Jews*, p. 120, n. 1.
56 This section of *Liber Novus*, which begins on p. 333, was not originally part of *Liber Novus*. It was written in 1917, and consisted of Jung's fantasies from April 1913 to June 1916. Shamdasani notes that 'Scrutinies', although written separately from the main body of the work, was produced in the same time period, and 'effectively forms *Liber Tertius* of *Liber Novus*'. See Shamdasani, 'Introduction', in Jung, *Liber Novus*, p. 207.
57 Jung, *Liber Novus*, p. 346. This garb links him directly to the priest in Zosimos' *Visions*.
58 Irenaeus, *Against Heresies* I.24.3–7. For Jung's reference to Abraxas as 'a made-up name meaning three hundred and sixty-five', see Jung, *Visions Seminars*, Vol. 2, pp. 806–7. All of Basilides' works have perished, but they are described by Christian apologists and heresiologists such as Irenaeus; Clement, *Stromateis* 4–5; Hippolytus, *Philosophumena* VII; and Epiphanius, *Adversus Haeresias* 7:20–27. Jung was familiar with, and frequently cited, all of these authors. For further references on Basilides, see Gilles Quispel, 'Gnostic Man: The Gospel of Basilides', in *The Mystic Vision* (Princeton, NJ: Princeton University Press, 1968), pp. 210–46; Paul Allan Mirecki, 'Basilides', in *The Anchor Bible Dictionary*, Vol. 1, p. 624.
59 See Shamdasani, 'Introduction', in Jung, *Liber Novus*, p. 207. The attributes of Abraxas are presented in Jung, *Liber Novus*, p. 349. For more on Abraxas, see Chapter 6.
60 Jung, *Liber Novus*, p. 295.
61 Cited in Gareth Knight, *Dion Fortune and the Inner Light* (Loughborough: Thoth, 2000), pp. 213–14. Fortune was deeply impressed by Jung's work and adopted it to her particular brand of occultism, although it is unlikely that she had access to any of the materials of *The Red Book*. She did, however, have access to Jung's discussions of active imagination, as well as to Iamblichus' *De mysteriis* and Samuel Liddell MacGregor Mathers' translation of *The Sacred Magic of Abramelin the Mage*. For more on Fortune and her sources, see Greene, *Magi and Maggidim*, pp. 377–440.
62 See Knight, *Dion Fortune*, p. 212.
63 Jung, *MDR*, p. 207.
64 Jung, *Psychology of the Unconscious*, p. 314.
65 Johann Wolfgang von Goethe, *Faust: Der Tragödie erster Teil* (Tübingen: J.G. Cotta'schen, 1808), IV:2184. *Schleppfuss*, a word taken up by Thomas Mann for the name of his Mephistophelian character, Dr. Schleppfuss, in *Doktor Faustus* (Frankfurt: S. Fischer, 1947), means 'drag-foot'. For the use of the epithet in Goethe and Mann, see E.M. Butler, *The Fortunes of Faust* (Cambridge: Cambridge University Press, 1952), 326; Harry Redner, *In the Beginning Was the Deed* (Berkeley: University of California Press, 1982), 226–27; John P. Anderson, *Mann's Doctor Faustus* (Boca Raton, FL: Universal, 2007), 157; Caroline Joan S. Picart, *Thomas Mann and Friedrich Nietzsche* (Amsterdam: Editions Rodopi, 1999), 45.
66 See, for example, Johannes of Hasfurt, *De cognoscendis et medendis morbis ex corporum coelestium positione*, fol. 22v, cited in Ioan P. Couliano, *Eros and Magic in the Renaissance* (Chicago: University of Chicago Press, 1987), p. 47.
67 Jung, CW12, p. 410. The image, from Johann Daniel Mylius, *Philosophia reformata* (Frankfurt: Jennis, 1622), Emblem 6, is reproduced with the kind permission of Adam McLean, at www.alchemywebsite.com/Emblems_Mylius_Rosarium_1622.html. See also Michael Maier's engraving of the one-legged alchemical Saturn as a gardener in Maier, *Symbola aureae mensae* (1617).

68 See, for example, the references to Zosimos in Jung, *Psychology of the Unconscious*, pp. 351 and 416. Jung refers to Berthelot's work on p. 511, n. 36, and to 'the original meaning of alchemy' on p. 511, n. 37. Jung's copy of Marcelin Berthelot's *Collection des anciens alchimistes grecs* was published in 1887–88, as well as Berthelot's *Les origines de l'alchimie*, published in 1885.

69 Damascius, *Dubitationes et solutiones de primis principiis in Platonis Parmenidem*, 2 volumes (Paris: Ruelle, 1889), II:214, 222, cited in Shaw, Theurgy and the Soul, p. 137.

70 Plato, *Laws* 713c–d.

71 Mead, *Thrice-Greatest Hermes*. I.417.

72 Mead, *Thrice-Greatest Hermes*, I. 322.

73 G.R.S. Mead, *The Chaldaean Oracles*, published as Volume 8 of *Echoes from the Gnosis* (Theosophical Publishing Society, 1908), p. 22, n. 2. See also Lewy, *Chaldean Oracles and Theurgy*, p. 152 and p. 406, n. 25, where Lewy refers to the same equation of Aion and Kronos in Proclus and in the Mithraic cult; Copenhaver, *Hermetica*, p. 167.

74 Cumont, *Textes et monuments*, Vol. 1, p. 76.

75 Jung, *Liber Novus*, p. 105. See Shamdasani's comments in *Liber Novus*, p. 297, n. 186.

76 Jung, *Liber Novus*, p. 352.

77 Jung, *Liber Novus*, p. 297, n. 186.

78 Jung, CW9i, ¶682. This reference is also given by Shamdasani in Jung, *Liber Novus*, p. 296, n. 179.

79 Jung, CW13, p. 56.

80 Jung, CW9i, ¶682.

81 See Margery L. Brown, 'Hephaestus, Hermes, and Prometheus: Jesters to the Gods', in Vicki K. Janik (ed.), *Fools and Jesters in Literature, Art, and History* (Westport, CT: Greenwood Press, 1998), pp 237–45; Esther Clinton, 'The Trickster', in Jane Garry and Hasan El-Shamy (eds.), *Archetypes and Motifs in Folklore and Literature* (Armonk, NY: M.E. Sharpe, 2005), pp. 472–81; Norman Oliver Brown, *Hermes the Thief* (Madison: University of Wisconsin Press, 1947), pp. 21–22, 48, and 64; (Joseph Russo, 'A Jungian Analysis of Homer's Odysseus', in Polly Young-Eisendrath and Terence Dawson (eds.), *The Cambridge Companion to Jung* (Cambridge: Cambridge University Press, 2008), pp. 253–68.

82 Jung, CW9i, ¶682.

83 Origen, *Contra Celsum*, XXXI. Jung's edition of this work was published in two volumes: Frederick Crombie (ed. and trans.), *The Writings of Origen* (Edinburgh: 1910–11).

84 Jung, CW9ii, ¶215.

85 The four main planetary glyphs on the stone, apart from Mercury at the centre, are those of the Sun and Moon, along with Saturn and Mars. Jupiter's glyph is smaller and appears to be subsidiary to the Sun, and Venus' glyph is likewise smaller and appears to be subsidiary to the Moon. The symbolism of Jupiter and Venus does not figure prominently in *Liber Novus*.

86 Jung, CW13, ¶274.

87 Jung, CW13, ¶250. See also Jung, CW13, ¶269; Jung, CW14, ¶298.

88 Jung, CW13, ¶276.

89 Goethe, *Faust*, Part One, Scene 3.

90 Jung, CW13, ¶275.

91 Jung, *Liber Novus*, trans. p. 235.

92 Jung, *Liber Novus*, trans. p. 350–51.

93 Iamblichus, *De mysteriis*, IX.7.

94 Jung, CW7, ¶299.

95 Leo, *Esoteric Astrology*, p. 149.

96 Mercury may, of course, be the chart ruler, if either of its zodiacal signs – Gemini or Virgo – was rising at birth. In this case, all the other planets, including Saturn, are expressed through Mercury.

97 For contemporary works focusing on Mercury's importance, see, for example, Freda Edis, *The God Between* (London: Penguin, 1996); Per Henrik Gullfoss, *The Complete Book of Spiritual Astrology* (Woodbury, MN: Llewellyn, 2008), pp. 107–19. For ancient

definitions of Mercury that Jung was acquainted with, see, among others, Ptolemy, *Tetrabiblos* II.3; Vettius Valens, *Anthologies*, I.1.

98 Leo, *How to Judge a Nativity*, p. 36.
99 Heindel, *Simplified Scientific Astrology*, p. 149; Heindel, *Message of the Stars*, p. 35.
100 Agrippa, *De occulta philosophia*, II:xxvii; I.xvii. It is unclear when Jung first encountered *De occulta philosophia*; he reproduced an image from it in CW5, the revised version of *Psychology of the Unconscious*, but the image does not appear in the original publication. All citations from Agrippa in the *Collected Works* were written long after the completion of *Liber Novus*. However, given Jung's early familiarity with grimoires such as *Sixth and Seventh Books of Moses*, and given Agrippa's fame as a great German magus on whom Goethe based many aspects of Faust – an observation well known by the end of the nineteenth century – it is unlikely that Jung would have been ignorant of *De occulta philosophia* during the time the figure of Philemon was developing. For an early discussion of Goethe's Faust and Agrippa, see Anton Reichl, 'Goethes Faust und Agrippa von Nettesheim', *Euphorion* 4 (1897), pp. 287–301. For more recent discussions, see J.M. van der Laan, *Seeking Meaning for Goethe's Faust* (London: Continuum, 2007), pp. 8, 11, 54–56; Paola Zambelli, *White Magic, Black Magic in the European Renaissance* (Leiden: Brill, 2007), pp. 115–16.
101 Agrippa, *De occulta philosophia*, II.1.
102 Agrippa, *De occulta philosophia*, II.xxxvii.
103 Jung, *Liber Novus*, p. 317. See also Jung, *Liber Novus*, p. 154; the text in the image of Philemon states, 'Father of the Prophet, Beloved Philemon'.
104 Jung, *Dream Interpretation, Ancient and Modern*, p. 165.
105 Jung, *Dream Interpretation, Ancient and Modern*, p. 165.
106 Jung, CW13, ¶261. For 'Psychology of the Transference', see Jung, CW16, ¶¶353–539.
107 Jung, CW13, ¶256.
108 Jung, CW13, ¶276.
109 Jung, CW13, ¶273.
110 Jung, CW13, ¶274, referring to the work of the alchemist Heinrich Khunrath.
111 Jung, *Psychology of the Unconscious*, p. 547, n. 61.
112 Jung, CW13, ¶284.
113 For the halo as a solar symbol in both Christian and pre-Christian iconography, see, among others, Jonathan Bardill, *Constantine, Divine Emperor of the Christian Golden Age* (Cambridge: Cambridge University Press, 2012), pp. 97–99; John M. Rosenfield, *The Dynastic Art of the Kushans* (Berkeley: University of California Press, 1967), pp. 196–98; David Ulansey, 'Mithras and the Hypercosmic Sun', in John R. Hinnells (ed.), *Studies in Mithraism* (Rome: L'Erma' di Brettschneider, 1994), pp. 257–64; Steven Hijmans, *Sol: The Sun in the Art and Religions of Rome* (unpublished PhD dissertation, University of Groningen, 2009).
114 Jung, CW14, ¶140.
115 See Jung, *Liber Novus*, p. 305, n. 232.
116 See Jung, *Liber Novus*, p. 301, n. 211.
117 Jung, CW9ii, ¶215. Jung also points out in this paragraph that Saturn is referred to as 'the sacred lead of the wise'.
118 Jung, *Liber Novus*, p. 237.
119 Jung, *Liber Novus*, p. 239.
120 Jung, *Liber Novus*, p. 292, n. 157, citing an entry from *Black Book* 7, written in October 1917.
121 Jung, *Liber Novus*, p. 300.
122 Leo, *Esoteric Astrology*, p. 26.
123 Origen, *Contra Celsum*, 6:22.
124 The planetary order for the Mithraic ascent of the soul is different, beginning with Mercury and culminating with Saturn; see Beck, *Planetary Gods*, p. 8.
125 Jung, *Psychology of the Unconscious*, p. 293.
126 Jung, *Psychology of the Unconscious*, pp. 407 and 550, n. 89.

127 Jung, *Psychology of the Unconscious*, citing Macrobius, *Saturnalia*, 1:18, p. 226.

128 Waite, *Pictorial Key to the Tarot*, p. 144.

129 Jung, CW9ii, ¶215.

130 Jung, CW13, ¶209.

131 Jung, *Psychology of the Unconscious*, citing the *Mithras Liturgy*, p. 111.

132 For Mithras as 'well-beloved', see Jung, *Psychology of the Unconscious*, pp. 104–5. For the translation of the image legend for Philemon, see Jung, *Liber Novus*, p. 317, n. 282.

133 Leo, *Esoteric Astrology*, p. 28.

134 Thorburn, 'Natus for C.G. Jung', p. 1.

135 See Shamdasani's comments in Jung, *Liber Novus*, p. 305, n. 230; the quotation is from *Black Book* 7, p. 61.

136 Jung, *Liber Novus*, p. 316.

137 Jung, *Liber Novus*, p. 301, n. 211. The statement is from *Black Book* 6, p. 195.

138 Jung, *Liber Novus*, p. 301, n. 211.

139 Jung, *Liber Novus*, p. 311.

140 See, for example, Jung, *Liber Novus*, p. 301, n. 211.

141 See Jung, *Liber Novus*, p. 303, n. 222.

142 Iamblichus, *De mysteriis*, VII.4–5.

143 <http://marygreer.wordpress.com/2008/04/18/carl-jung-on-the-major-arcana/>.

144 Waite, *The Pictorial Key to the Tarot*, p. 17.

145 Waite, *Pictorial Key to the Tarot*, pp. 72–75, illustration on p. 73.

146 The full text reads: '*Quod est inferius est sicut quod est superius; et quod est superius est sicunt quod est inferiorius ad perpetranda miracula rei unius*' ('That which is below is like that which is above; and that which is above is like that which is below, to perform the miracle of the one thing'). Text from Heinrich Khunrath, *Amphiteatrum sapientiae aeternae* (Hanau, 1609).

147 See Klibansky *et al.*, *Saturn and Melancholy*, p. 154.

148 Jung, *On Psychological and Visionary Art*, p. 64. Although this reference to Saturn was made in a lecture given in 1945, Saturn as lord of agriculture is described in Virgil's *Georgics*, and it is likely that Jung had seen, if not entirely comprehended the full significance of, engravings in the alchemical authors of the seventeenth century, such as Michael Maier and Michael Sendivogius, portraying the lame Saturn tilling the soil with his scythe and watering the Tree of the Philosophers.

149 Abu Ma'shar, Leiden Codex or. 47; Alcabitius, Bodleian Marsh 663; both cited in Klibansky *et al.*, *Saturn and Melancholy*, pp. 130–31. For Jung's references to Abu Ma'shar, see Jung, CW9ii, ¶¶128, 131, 133, 153–54.

150 Marsilio Ficino, *De vita triplici,* III.2.

151 Jung, *Liber Novus*, p. 316.

152 Ficino, *De vita triplici*, III.18. Waite's Hermit has a covered head, although Philemon's head, in Jung's painting, is uncovered.

153 See Eric Partridge, *Origins: A Short Etymological Dictionary of Modern English* (London: Routledge, 2006), p. 588.

154 Marsilio Ficino, Letter to Filippo Valori, 7 November 1492, in Marsilio Ficino, *Opera*, p. 888, cited in Couliano, *Eros and Magic*, p. 46. Ficino was born on 19 October 1433 at 1.26 pm LMT in Figline Valdamo, Italy. In his natal chart, Saturn in Aquarius conjuncts the Ascendant within 6°, in the first house. In Jung's chart Saturn in Aquarius is further away, 22° from the Ascendant, but in the same sign and house.

155 Yates, *The Occult Philosophy*, p. 51.

156 Couliano, *Eros and Magic*, p. 48.

157 Couliano, *Eros and Magic*, p. 49.

158 Agrippa, *De occulta philosophia*, I:60.

159 Leo, *Saturn*, p. iv.

160 Leo, *Saturn*, p. 25.

161 C.G. Jung, 'Synchronicity', in Jung, CW8, pp. 417–519; C.G. Jung, 'On Synchronicity', in Jung, CW8, pp. 520–32. For Frey-Rohn, see Greene, *Jung's Studies in Astrology*, chapter 2.

162 Jung, CW18, ¶1198. The collection, 'Letters on Synchronicity' (CW18, ¶¶1193–212), also includes a letter to Michael Fordham in which he discusses the 'psychoid' nature of the unconscious archetype. For more on Fordham, see Greene, *Jung's Studies in Astrology*, chapter 1. See also Jung, CW18, ¶¶1174–192, a condensed version of the longer essay, 'Synchronicity: An Acausal Connecting Principle'.

163 Astrology, for Jung, possesses a 'mantic character'; see Jung, CW8, ¶994. The adjective 'mantic' is derived from the Greek *mantikos*, meaning prophetic or oracular, from *mantis*, a seer. See Plato's use of the word *mantikos* in *Phaedrus*, 265b and 275b.

164 Jung, CW8, ¶965.

165 Jung, CW8, ¶858.

166 Jung, CW8, ¶967.

167 Jung, CW8, ¶860.

168 See Jung's citation of Albertus Magnus in Chapter 3.

169 Jung, *Liber Novus*, p. 313.

170 Jung, *Liber Novus*, p. 314.

171 Jung, *Liber Novus*, p. 317.

172 Jung, *Liber Novus*, p. 313.

173 Jung, *Liber Novus*, p. 314.

174 Jung, *Liber Novus*, p. 307. For the magical powers of the rods carried by Moses and Aaron, see Exodus 7:17, 8:5, 8:16–17, 9:23, and 10:13.

175 Jung, *Liber Novus*, p. 307.

176 The pearl, according to Jung (CW5, ¶510), is a symbol of 'the mystery': the treasure that lies hidden in the darkness of the unconscious. In ancient Greek lapidaries, the pearl was associated with Mercury, as well as with the Moon. See Damigeron, *De Virtutibus Lapidum*, p. 4; Diane Morgan, *Gemlore: Ancient Secrets and Modern Myths from the Stone Age to the Rock Age* (Westport, CT: Greenwood Press, 2008), pp. 137–40.

177 Jung, *Liber Novus*, p. 312.

178 Jung, Letter to Upton Sinclair, 25 February 1955, in *C. G. Jung Letters*, Vol. 2, pp. 230–32.

PLATE 1 The planetary angels of Mars, from *Liber iuratus*

Liber iuratus, Royal MS 17 A XLII, ff. 68v–69, British Library, reproduced in Sophie Page, *Magic in Medieval Manuscripts* (London: British Library, 2004), p. 46.

PLATE 2 The giant Izdubar

Image in Jung, *Liber Novus*, p. 36, © 2007 Foundation of the Works of C. G. Jung, Zürich, used by permission of W. W. Norton & Co., Inc.

PLATE 3 The solar apotheosis of Izdubar

Image in Jung, *Liber Novus*, p. 64, © 2007 Foundation of the Works of C. G. Jung, Zürich, used by permission of W. W. Norton & Co., Inc.

PLATE 4 Salome, Elijah, the black serpent, and, on the left, Jung's 'I'

Image in Jung, *Liber Novus,* fol. vi, © 2007 Foundation of the Work of C. G. Jung, used by permission of W. W. Norton & Co., Inc.

PLATE 5 The Anima

Image in Jung, *Liber Novus,* p. 155, © 2007 Foundation of the Works of C. G. Jung, used by permission of W. W. Norton & Co., Inc.

PLATE 6 The castle in the forest under the crescent Moon

Image in Jung, *Liber Novus*, p. 5, © 2007 Foundation of the Work of C. G. Jung, used by permission of W. W. Norton & Co., Inc.

PLATE 7 Atmavictu

Image in Jung, *Liber Novus*, p. 122, © 2007 Foundation of the Works of C. G. Jung, used by permission of W. W. Norton & Co., Inc.

PLATE 8   Jung's 'Caster of Holy Water'

Image in Jung, *Liber Novus*, p. 123, © 2007 Foundation of the Works of C. G. Jung, used by permission of W. W. Norton & Co., Inc.

PLATE 9   Philemon

Image in Jung, *Liber Novus*, p. 154, © Foundation of the Works of C. G. Jung, Zürich, used by permission of W. W. Norton & Co.

PLATE 10   Mandala portraying the Wise Old Man (top) and Mercurius (bottom)

Image in Jung, *Liber Novus*, p. 105, © Foundation of the Works of C. G. Jung, Zürich, used by permission of W. W. Norton & Co.

PLATE 11 Phanes receiving fire from the Sun

PLATE 12 Jung's *Systema Munditotius* in its final form

6

ΦΑΝΗΣ, THE 'ONE WHO BROUGHT THE SUN'

This Chronos unaging, of immortal resource, begot
Aither and a great Chasm, vast this way and that, no limit below it, no base, no
place to settle . . .
Then great Chronos fashioned from divine Aither a bright white egg.[1]

—*Orphic Rhapsodies*

He [Phanes] is foresight. He is the end of fear. He is the sprouting seed, the opening bud . . . He is the spring and the desert. He is the safe haven and the stormy night. He is the certainty in desperation. He is the solid in dissolution. He is the liberation from imprisonment. He is counsel and strength in advancement. He is the friend of man, the light emanating from man, the bright glow that man beholds on his path.[2]

—C.G. Jung

The divine child

In 1919, Jung painted a childlike figure whose body is composed of spherical shapes, wearing a harlequin costume patterned in black and white against a gold ground. Above the image, Jung wrote:

This is the image of the divine child. It means the completion of a long path. Just as the image was finished in April 1919, and work on the next image had already begun, the one who brought the ☉ [Sun] came, as ΦΙΛΗΜΩΝ [Philemon] had predicted to me. I called him ΦΑΝΗΣ [Phanes] because he is the newly appearing God.[3]

Phanes is the great primal androgynous deity of Orphic cosmogonic myth,[5] identified by Aristophanes as identical with Eros,[6] whom Plato called 'unbegotten'

FIGURE 6.1   Phanes, the 'newly appearing God'[4]

and the oldest of gods.[7] In Jung's *Black Book 7*, Phanes recites a long poetic monologue about his own attributes and powers, but he does not make an appearance
in *Liber Novus* as a character with whom Jung engages in dialogue.[8] Instead, he
is the divinity toward whom the entire movement of *Liber Novus* is directed: the
'Way of What Is to Come'. Abraxas, whose name, interestingly, is *not* written in
Greek in *Liber Novus*, is his personification within the fabric of the corruptible
physical world. Although Jung remarked in *Black Book 6* that Phanes was the
messenger of Abraxas,[9] it is clear from many references in *Liber Novus* that Jung
ultimately viewed Abraxas as the embodiment of Phanes in the corporeal realm,
generating the life-cycles of all living things.

In Orphic literature, Phanes has a number of solar attributes, and there are direct
parallels between this deity and the giant Izdubar. They share not only typical solar
motifs, but also the theme of emergence from the cosmic egg. After his healing,
Izdubar rises from an egg, surrounded by flames and transformed into the Sun-
god. Phanes, the 'shining one', likewise emerges from an egg in Orphic texts and
iconography, surrounded by flames. Before his encounter with Izdubar, Jung had

already written a good deal in *Liber Novus* about the 'divine child' as an image of both the solar source of life and the nascent form of the Self, declaring: 'My God is a child'.[10] Once this mysterious centre of being intrudes on individual consciousness, it is remorseless in its daimonic purpose:

> The primordial force is the radiance of the sun . . . But if the soul dips into radiance she becomes as remorseless as the God himself, since the life of the divine child, which you have eaten, will feel like glowing coals in you. It will burn inside you like a terrible, inextinguishable fire . . . From this you will understand that your God is alive and that your soul has begun wandering on remorseless paths. You feel that the fire of the sun has erupted in you.[11]

The divine child 'which you have eaten' refers to Phanes, who is eaten twice in the Orphic cosmogony: first by his grandson Zeus, who swallows him in order to absorb the life-creating power of his progenitor, and then, a second time, when Phanes has been reborn as Phanes-Dionysus and is torn to pieces and devoured by the earth-bound Titans. From the ashes of the Titans, whom Zeus destroys with a lightning-bolt, rise human beings: earthy, greedy, and savage like their Titanic progenitors, but containing within them a tiny spark of the primal deity of light and revelation,[12] which, for Jung, burned inside 'like a terrible inextinguishable fire'.

The cosmic egg is given different antecedents in various renderings of the Phanes myth. Sometimes the egg is described as the progeny of Chaos and Night, but the Neoplatonists insisted that Chronos (Time), imaged as a winged serpent and later elided with the planetary Kronos-Saturn,[13] had engendered the world-egg:[14]

> Chronos . . . generated a huge egg, which, being filled full, by the force of its engenderer was broken in two from friction. Its crown became Ouranos [Heaven], and what had sunk downwards, Gaia [Earth]. There also came forth an incorporeal god [Phanes].[15]

The Greek name Phanes is derived from the verb *phaino* ('to show' or 'to reveal'). It has given the English language words such as 'theophany' (the visible appearance of a god), 'epiphany' (a sudden appearance or revelation), 'diaphanous' (transparent), and 'phenomenon' (an object visible to human perception). Mead cited Clement of Alexandria's exegesis of the name as 'shining forth' (αυτου φανεντος) because, when Phanes emerges from the egg, 'the universe shines forth from him, through the lustre of Fire, most glorious of elements'.[16] Jung referred to Phanes as the 'shining one',[17] and understood the Orphic god as a libido-symbol, a 'creative impulse' equivalent to Eros (an equation that had already been made, as Jung noted, by Hesiod and Plato):[18]

> I am reminded here of the cosmogenic meaning of Eros in Plato and Hesiod, and also of the orphic figure of Phanes, the 'shining one', the first-created, the 'father of Eros'. Phanes has also orphically the significance of Priapus; he is a god of love, bisexual and similar to the Theban Dionysus Lysios.[19]

In the Orphic Hymns, Phanes is called Erikepaios, a word that, according to mid-twentieth-century Orphic scholars, is 'un-Greek' and seems to have no agreed interpretation.[20] In more current views, the name may be derived from a composite word with the paradoxical meaning of 'an adult male child'.[21] Perhaps not coincidentally, the beautiful, youthful Phanes, as he was described by the Christian heresiologist Hippolytus, can also appear as a grey-headed, winged old man: a precise description of Jung's Philemon.[22] Jung encountered the name Erikepaios in Thomas Taylor's translation of the Orphic Hymn to the god,[23] and used it as an epithet for Phanes in the cosmological painting he titled *Systema Munditotius*, produced in 1916, three years before he produced the painting of Phanes in *Liber Novus*.[24] In the legend for this painting, Jung used the astrological glyph for the Sun, rather than the word itself. In this extraordinary visual image, the androgynous figure is both child and adult, rounded as though composed of spheres (which, for Jung, connoted wholeness),[25] floating among golden clouds, and dressed in a striped costume similar to that of the Aquarian 'Caster of Holy Water', who bears a solar disc behind his head.

Jung painted Phanes again, this time portraying his rotund form facing a crouching tiger. Although the god's image is identical with that in the earlier painting, his name has changed, and he is now called ΤΕΛΕΣΦΟΡΟΣ. Phanes-Telesphoros shares the painting with Atmavictu, who is portrayed as a huge multi-legged crocodile, its jaws open, either to swallow the solar disk above it or, more likely, having just given birth to it, as Saturn in alchemy gives birth to the solar gold. According to Alan Leo, the crocodile is 'the pre-planetary form of Saturn' and 'the true Saturnian symbol for Capricorn';[26] this comment highlights the relationship between Jung's Atmavictu and the alchemical stone that he conceals, and the polarity (and secret identity) between Saturn and the Sun, already suggested by the Saturnian Elijah with his Temple of the Sun, by the Saturnian Anchorite Ammonius and his longing for the light of the Sun, and by the crocodiles that adorn the painting of Izdubar the solar hero. To the crocodile-Atmavictu's right in the Telesphoros painting, the figure of a young man kneels in homage, dressed in the harlequin garb of Phanes and with the same black hair in a rounded, quasi-Egyptian cut; but the white in this young man's gown is replaced by Martial red. The legend under the youthful figure states, '*Iuvenis adiutor*' ('a youthful supporter'). In contrast, the tiger crouches in a pose of genuflection before the diminutive form of Phanes-Telesphoros, the divine child. The colours Jung chose for this painting, and the differences in who is worshipping whom, seem to imply that the youth driven by Martial instinct will worship God as the crocodile-Atmavictu, while the instinctual world that Atmavictu rules in his tiger-shape will bow before the recognition of the divine child within. The name Telesphoros means 'bringer of completion'. Beneath the tiger, Jung wrote: '*Spiritus malus in hominibus quibusdam*': 'The evil spirit in some men'. Even this 'evil spirit' will do homage to that which brings completion: Phanes, the god of the new Aion.

Telesphoros is one of the dwarf Kabeiroi, sometimes associated in myth with the healer-god Asklepios as a daimon of healing and bringer of dreams.[28] Jung was intrigued by the Kabeiroi, who usually appear in ancient narratives as a group; he

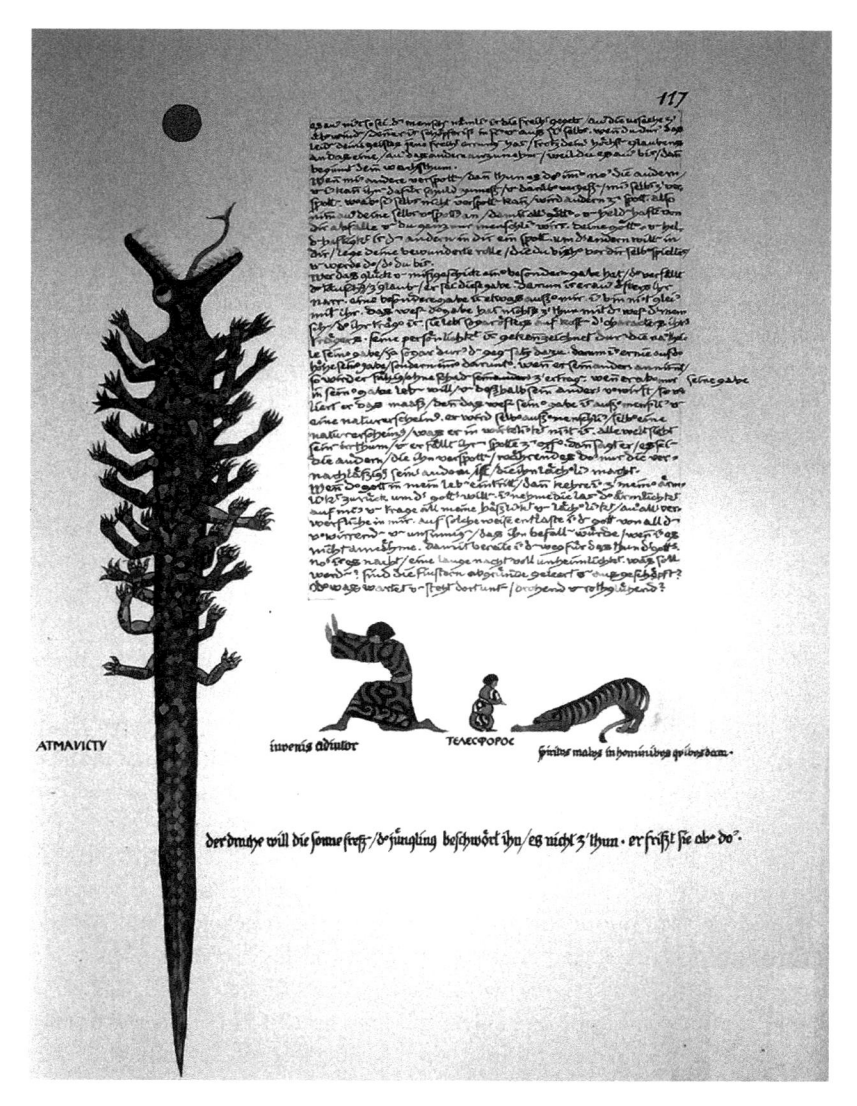

FIGURE 6.2   Phanes–Telesphoros[27]

associated them with the phallic aspect of the libido as the 'visible expression of the creative strength incarnate in man'.[29] He seems to have perceived the diminutive size of the Kabeiroi as a representation of the microcosm of divinity within the instinctual realm. The Sun, on the other hand, represents the microcosm of divinity within the human soul.[30] On Jung's carving of Phanes-Telesphoros at Bollingen, all seven planets are represented on and around him by their traditional glyphs: the dwarf-god, who is also both Phanes and Philemon, contains or orchestrates the entire planetary pantheon. He stands within a small circle that is quartered and, in turn, enclosed within another, larger circle: the traditional astrological glyph for the Sun, which also provides the form of the Temple of the Sun that Jung described in *Liber Novus* during his encounter with the prophet Elijah.

Phanes as cosmocrator

Jung painted Phanes a third time, clearly portraying the Orphic primal deity as 'the one who brought the Sun' (see Plate 11). Seated in the sky on a floating cushion beneath the solar disc, Phanes wears the same striped garb, and the same bowl-shaped black hair, as does the figure of the 'Caster of Holy Water', with whom he seems to be closely related.[31] But the jug that the water-bearer uses to pour his bounty onto the earth in the earlier image is now held over the head of Phanes as a receptacle for the solar life-force. The disc of the Sun is, as usual, quartered, to designate its equinoxes and solstices at the four cardinal points, the 'turnings' of its yearly cycle. Jung left no legend to help explicate this painting, but perhaps none is needed.

Among his many sources for Orphic materials, Jung drew on the work of Mead's friend and colleague, the art historian and biblical scholar Robert Eisler, whom Mead had recommended in a letter he wrote to Jung in 1919.[32] In 1910, Eisler had published a two-volume work in German titled *Weltenmantel und Himmelszelt*, in which a photograph was included of a Roman bas-relief of Phanes from the second century CE.[33] Eisler argued that this figure was not the Mithraic Aion, as Franz Cumont had suggested four years earlier, but was in fact the Orphic Phanes.[34] Jung reproduced the image in *Symbols of Transformation*, titled it 'Phanes in the egg', and referred to it as an 'Orphic relief'. The identification of it as Orphic rather than Mithraic is based on Eisler's argument.[35]

In the bas-relief, Phanes is shown emerging from a cosmic egg filled with flames, like the egg from which Izdubar rises after his deification. Phanes is winged and surrounded by the ring of the zodiac, and bears the heads of a bull (Taurus), a lion (Leo), a ram (Aries), and a goat (Capricorn) on his body. He is encircled by a serpent, as are the Mithraic images of Aion, Waite's figure of The Magician, the sculpture of Atmavictu in Jung's garden, and Jung himself in *Liber Novus* during his 'crucifixion'.[37] But unlike the Mithraic Aion or Jung's Leontocephalus, the figure in the bas-relief bears the head of a beautiful youth rather than a lion. Phanes' feet are cloven like those of a goat, suggesting Pan, the god of primal nature, who is mirrored in the goat-face of Jung's painting of Atmavictu.[38] He bears a rayed solar crown on his head, like the solar crown in Jung's painting of Izdubar and the solar halo of Philemon; the horns of a lunar crescent rise behind the god's shoulders, echoing the lunar crescent in Jung's painting of the Anima. In his left hand Phanes holds a staff whose unknown length extends beyond the bas-relief, interpreted by David Ulansey as the cosmic pole around which the stars and planets circle.[39] In this late antique representation, Phanes appears as a *coniunctio* of Sun and Moon, male and female, day and night, light and darkness, heaven and earth. He is also cosmocrator

FIGURE 6.3 The Orphic primal god Phanes[36]

of the solar cycle through the zodiacal round, and is thus the 'central spiritual Sun' as the noetic life-force.

According to Proclus, Phanes 'the Father' was the creator of the astrological cosmos, generating the constellations, the planets, the Moon, and the Sun, and appointing the Sun as a 'guardian' to have 'lordship over all'.[40] Jung linked Phanes – also known as Protogonos, the 'firstborn'[41] – with the Saturnian Philemon, as well as with the astrological symbol of the Sun, and viewed this androgynous, all-encompassing cosmic principle as the symbol of a new God-image arising in the collective psyche, for which Philemon, the winged *senex*, was his own personal embodiment. Phanes in Orphic literature was never a planetary deity, although in late antiquity he came to be associated with the 'intelligible' or spiritual Sun, as distinct from the physical Sun in the heavens.[42] According to the late antique Greek epic poet Nonnus, Phanes, because he created everything, could also foresee everything, and engraved on a set of sacred tablets those great events he had 'ordained' for the world according to 'the house [zodiacal constellation] proper for each'.[43]

Although he is not strictly a planetary daimon, Phanes stands at the centre of an astrological cosmology, reflected in the writings of the Neoplatonists and in the zodiacal band surrounding his figure in the Modena bas-relief. That Jung associated all the planetary gods with Phanes is evident both in his diagram of the *Systema Munditotius*, discussed in the next chapter, and in his equation of Phanes with Telesphoros, who is surrounded on the Bollingen stone by the glyphs of the seven planets. Jung's identification of Phanes with Aquarius the water-bearer in the paintings in *Liber Novus* points to a specific zodiacal association. But the iconography and attributes of Aquarius, in Jung's view, provide the imaginal form in which humans will envisage the life-force only in the incoming new astrological Aion. In other Aions, this life-force was evidently envisaged in other forms, each appropriate to the symbolism of the zodiacal constellation of the particular Aion: the fertility of the earth-goddess in Taurus, the rule of the patriarchs and heroes in Aries, and the sacrificial messiah in Pisces.

Just as Izdubar rises transformed out of the fiery cosmic egg in *Liber Novus*, so too does Phanes in the Orphic 'Hymn to Protogonos':

> O Mighty first-begotten, hear my pray'r,
> Twofold, egg-born, and wand'ring thro' the air;
> Bull-roarer, glorying in thy golden wings,
> From whom the race of Gods and mortal springs.
> Ericapaeus, celebrated pow'r,
> Ineffable, occult, all-shining flow'r.
> 'Tis thine from darksome mists to purge the sight,
> All-spreading, splendour, pure and holy light.[44]

In 1917, Jung, through the 'voice' of Philemon, wrote his own hymn to Phanes, recorded in *Black Book* 7. While it is more intensely personal than the Orphic 'Hymn to Protogonos', it was clearly inspired by some of the Hymn's motifs, which Jung read in Thomas Taylor's English translation. A particular characteristic that marks all the Orphic Hymns – strings of nouns or epithets used as a form of invocation of the deity – is repeated precisely in Jung's own hymn.[45]

> Phanes is the god who rises agleam from the waters.
> Phanes is the smile of dawn.
> Phanes is the resplendent day.
> He is the immortal present . . .
> He is the light that illuminates every darkness.
> He is the eternal day.

He is the silver light of the moon.
He is the flickering stars.
He is the shooting star that flashes and falls and lapses.[46]

Jung's hymn continues for many lines, and is followed by another, similar invocation to Phanes, written in 1918.[47] Jung created his own liturgy for the god, but his familiarity with the Orphic Hymn appears in his description of Phanes as 'the light that illuminates every darkness', echoing the Hymn's declaration that it is the work of Phanes 'to purge the sight from dark mists'.[48] Jung referred to Phanes as a 'golden bird',[49] echoing the Hymn's reference to Phanes' 'golden wings'. Jung was also familiar with the equation of Phanes with Eros presented by Blavatsky, who declared that Phanes, the 'revealed' god who is the first-born primal light, is also symbolised by the serpent as a symbol of the 'hidden, or unrevealed deity' from which he emerged: Kronos-Saturn.[50] Blavatsky herself, like Jung, relied on Taylor for her translations of the Orphic texts, declaring that he was 'one of the very few commentators on old Greek and Latin authors, who have given their just dues to the ancients for their mental development'.[51]

Phanes and Abraxas

Jung related Phanes to the invisible source of life: a symbol of the libido or life-force, which is also the world-soul and the union of all opposites. While Philemon seems to represent the 'spark' of this divinity in the guise of Jung's own individual daimon, Phanes is the universal creative force, portrayed in *Liber Novus*, like Waite's Tarot card of The Sun, as a divine child. This god is mirrored by another god in whom Jung was deeply interested, especially in the latter part of *Liber Novus*: the so-called Gnostic deity Abraxas. On late antique gemstone amulets, the name Abraxas usually connotes solar power, but it seems to symbolise the solar life-force as it manifests in the world rather than in the heavens. The image most often associated with this god on magical amulets is that of a snake-legged being (anguipede) with a cock's head, dressed in the garb of a charioteer and holding a whip.[52] But this figure may be accompanied by names other than Abraxas, such as IAO, the Greek rendition of the Hebrew YHVH; and the word Abraxas is often coupled on the amulets with other images, such as Chnoumis, who, like Abraxas, is often portrayed in serpentine form.[53]

In Part Three of *Liber Novus*, Philemon instructs the dead on the nature of Abraxas:

> Fullness and emptiness, generation and destruction, are what distinguish God and the devil. Effectiveness is common to both . . . Effectiveness, therefore, stands above both, and is a God above God, since it unites fullness and emptiness through its effectuality. This is a God you knew nothing about, because mankind forgot him. We call him by his name ABRAXAS . . . To distinguish him from God, we call God HELIOS or sun. Abraxas is effect . . . He is force, duration, change.[54]

Whereas Phanes is eternal and exists before time, Jung referred to Abraxas as a 'time-god', reflected in the numerological significance of the name as the 365-day solar cycle. Abraxas is 'life and death' because he is 'the life of vegetation in the course of one year, the spring and the autumn, the summer and the winter, the yea and nay of nature'.[55] He is solar like Phanes, but he is a 'dark' sun, like the *sol niger* of alchemy and of *Liber Novus*: the animating power in the world of nature and the instinctual force behind the physical life of human beings. The closest counterpart to Abraxas in terms of Jung's philosophical sources is probably Nieztsche's idea of Dionysus as the god of chaos, instinct, and the irrational.[56] Jung illustrated his perception of Abraxas by placing the god at the base or root of the mandala of the *Systema Munditotius*, portraying him as a black serpent and calling him 'Dominus mundi' ('Lord of the World'), a title once given to medieval Holy Roman emperors, and 'Vita' ('Life').[57] Abraxas also seems to be the earthly serpent-dragon whose body generates the seven flowers watered by the Aquarian water-bearer in Jung's painting.

In the third Sermon to the Dead in 'Scrutinies', Philemon delivers a hymn-like address to Abraxas, echoing Jung's earlier hymn to Phanes and replicating once again the hieratic tone of the Orphic Hymns. In Philemon's recital, 'terrible Abraxas' is called Priapos, a god of fertility whom Kerényi described as the son of Pan,[58] and who is equated with Phanes in the Orphic 'Hymn to Protogonos'. Abraxas is also the 'hermaphrodite of the earliest beginning', which is equally a description of the primal, androgynous Phanes. But Abraxas, as a 'created being', does not possess the parthenogenic power of Phanes.[59] He is not so much a daimon as an image of the quality of power expressed by the daimon in the world. Perhaps this is why Jung, in *Liber Novus*, never rendered his name in the Greek alphabet. While Abraxas is 'effectiveness', this is only possible within the context of time and matter, and not in the timeless, eternal realm of the 'shining one'.

Abraxas bears a close affinity with the Saturnian Atmavictu, and both the crocodile-shape of Atmavictu and the tiger in Jung's painting of Phanes–Telesphoros might also be understood as Abraxas. Philemon, in his third Sermon, declares: 'In this world, man is Abraxas, the creator and destroyer of his own world'.[60] If Phanes embodies the entire celestial chorus of planetary gods as archetypal potencies within the psyche, then Abraxas, as Phanes in the world of form, is likewise the entire celestial chorus, but in its earthly, instinctual expressions. As Jung stated, Abraxas 'is the life of the earth'.[61] In Jung's view, the horoscope, and astrology in general, can evidently be understood at two levels: macrocosmic and microcosmic in the universal sense, and psychological and physical in the individual. For Jung, there was no essential contradiction between understanding the planets as universal archetypal patterns expressed within the psyche, and those same planets as specific significators of the individual's earthly character and circumstances.

This duality of levels also reflects Jung's perception of the dual nature of alchemical texts, which describe the divine planetary spirits and interpret their material embodiments as the planetary metals trapped in the earth, awaiting transformation and release through the efforts of the individual alchemist. In the context of astrology, it seems that Jung viewed Phanes as a symbol of the spiritual principle that animates all the planetary 'gods', and stands behind the drive toward individuation: in other words, the Self, which is not indicated by the time and space constrictions of the natal horoscope. Phanes is the power that unites the opposites, including planetary antimonies such as Mercury and Saturn, Sun and Saturn, and Sun and Moon. Abraxas, on the other hand, apparently reflects the biological and instinctual *durée créatrice*, as Henri Bergson put it, that animates the corporeal manifestations of the planetary 'gods'. He is 'terrible Abraxas' because these manifestations are so often accompanied by suffering and conflict, experienced by the individual as 'bad fate'. Jung believed Abraxas to be a 'Gnostic' god who reflected the Gnostics' deeply pessimistic view of *Heimarmene*. But ultimately Phanes and Abraxas, the twin gods of *Liber Novus* whom Jung placed at the apex and the root of his 'System of All Worlds', mirror each other, become each other, and form a hidden unity 'whose roots reach into Hell and whose top touches Heaven'.[62]

Notes

1 *Orphic Rhapsodies*, Fragments 66 and 70, translated by and cited in M.L. West, *The Orphic Poems* (Oxford: Oxford University Press, 1983), p. 198.
2 Jung, *Black Book* 7, pp. 16–19, cited in Jung, *Liber Novus*, p. 301, n. 211.
3 Jung, *Liber Novus*, p. 301.
4 Image in Jung, *Liber Novus*, p. 113, © 2007 Foundation of the Works of C.G. Jung, Zürich, used by permission of W.W. Norton & Co.
5 For more on the Orphic Phanes, see Alberto Bernabé and Ana Isabel Jiménez San Cristóbal, *Instructions for the Netherworld: The Orphic Gold Tablets* (Leiden: Brill, 2008), pp. 142–54; Walter Wili, 'The Orphic Mysteries and the Greek Spirit', in Joseph Campbell (ed.), *The Mysteries* (Princeton, NJ: Princeton University Press, 1955), pp. 64–92; Apostolos N. Athanassakis and Benjamin M. Wolkow (trans.), *The Orphic Hymns* (Baltimore, MD: Johns Hopkins University Press, 2013), 'Notes', pp. 69–220; Arthur Bernard Cook, *Zeus*, Vol. 2, Part 2 (Cambridge: Cambridge University Press, 1925), p. 1051. For Phanes-Eros, see Barbara Breitenberger, *Aphrodite and Eros* (London: Routledge, 2013), pp. 160–65; Daniel E. Anderson, *The Masks of Dionysos* (Albany: SUNY Press, 1993), pp. 153–54.
6 Aristophanes, *Birds*, 694b–697.
7 Plato, *Symposium*, 178b.
8 For Phanes' monologue in *Black Book* 7, see Jung, *Liber Novus*, pp. 301–2, n. 211.
9 Jung, *Black Book* 6, p. 167, cited in Jung, *Liber Novus*, p. 301, n. 211.
10 Jung, *Liber Novus*, p. 234. For Jung's later work on the archetypal motif of the divine child as a symbol of the union of opposites, see Jung, CW9i, ¶¶259–305.
11 Jung, *Liber Novus*, p. 291.
12 For the general themes of the Orphic cosmology, see W.K.C. Guthrie, *Orpheus and Greek Religion* (London: Methuen, 1952), pp. 69–147, and the various references given above in n. 5.
13 See West, *The Orphic Poems*, p. 178, pp. 190–99.
14 See, for example, Damascius in Otto Kern (ed.), *Orphicorum fragmenta* (Berlin: Weidmann, 1922), Frag. 66–75, cited in Guthrie, *Orpheus and Greek Religion*, p. 137.
15 Athenogoras, *Theogonies*, Orphic Fragment 57, cited in West, *The Orphic Poems*, p. 180.
16 Mead, *Thrice-Great Hermes*, Vol. 1, p. 391. The citation is from Clement, *Homilies*, VI:iii.
17 See Shamdasani's reference in Jung, *Liber Novus*, p. 301, n. 211, for Jung's use of the Orphic cosmogony presented in Isaac Preston Cory's impossibly titled work, *Ancient*

Fragments of the Phoenician, Chaldean, Egyptian, Tyrian, Carthaginian, Indian, Persian, and Other Writers (London: Reeves and Turner, 1876). Equally relevant were Jung's editions of Mead's *Orpheus*, Roscher's *Lexikon*, Thomas Taylor's English translations of *The Hymns of Orpheus* (London: T. Payne, 1792), and Erwin Rohde's *Seelencult und Unsterlichkeitsglaube der Griechen*, 2 volumes (Tübingen: Mohr, 1903).

18 See Hesiod, *Theogony*, 116–25; Plato, *Symposium*, 187b–188d.

19 Jung, *Psychology of the Unconscious*, p. 147.

20 West, in *The Orphic Poems*, p. 205, states that Erikepaios is 'beyond doubt a non-Greek name'. Guthrie, writing in 1952, stated that the epithet does not appear in older Orphic materials, but only emerged in the late antique *Rhapsodies*; see Guthrie, *Orpheus and Greek Religion*, pp. 97–98. However, the name appears on the fifth century BCE Orphic gold funerary tablet from Pherai, discovered in 1904, as well as in the Gurôb Papyrus from c. 275 BCE, where it seems to describe both Phanes and Dionysus. For the Gurôb Papyrus, see James Hordern, 'Notes on the Orphic Papyrus from Gurob', *Zeitschrift für Papyrologie und Epigraphik* 129 (2000), pp. 131–40; H.S. Smith and H.M. Stewart, 'The Gurob Shrine Papyrus', *Journal of Egyptian Archaeology* 70 (1984), pp. 54–64; Miguel Herrero de Jáuregui, *Orphism and Christianity in Late Antiquity* (Berlin: Walter de Gruyter, 2010), p. 54. For the Pherai tablet, see Alberto Bernabé, 'Some Thoughts about the "New" Gold Tablet from Pherae', *Zeitschrift für Papyrologie und Epigraphik* 166 (2008), 53–58; A. Chaniotis, T. Corsten, R.S. Stroud, and R.A. Tybout, 'Pherae. Inscribed gold lamella of an initiate into the cult of Demeter Chthonia, Meter Oreia (and Dionysos?), late 4th/early 3rd cent. BC (55–612)', *Supplementum Epigraphicum Graecum*, Brill Online, 2012, available at <http://referenceworks.brillonline.com/entries/supplementum-epigraphicum-graecum/pherai-inscribed-gold-lamella-of-an-initiate-into-the-cult-of-demeter-chthonia-meter-oreia-and-dionysos-late-4th-early-3rd-cent-b-c-55-612-a55_612>. For the name Erikepaios, see also Bernabé and San Cristóbal, *Instructions for the Netherworld*, pp. 152–54; Fritz Graf and Sarah Iles Johnston, *Ritual Texts for the Afterlife: Orpheus and the Bacchic Gold Tablets* (London: Routledge, 2007), pp. 188–89.

21 Bernabé and San Cristóbal, *Instructions for the Netherworld*, p. 155.

22 See Miroslav Marcovich, *Studies in Graeco-Roman Religions and Gnosticism* (Leiden: Brill, 1988), p. 90. Hippolytus, in his *Elenchos* (a work which Jung utilised for much of his knowledge of the Gnostics), cites a fragment from Plutarch's *Moralia* in which Phanes takes the form of a winged *senex*.

23 Jung's edition was Thomas Taylor (trans.), *The Mystical Hymns of Orpheus* (London: Dobell, 1896); 'Hymn to Protogonos [Phanes]' is on pp. 18–20. 'Protogonos' means 'firstborn', another of Phanes' epithets. Taylor equated Phanes-Protogonos with Erikepaios on pp. xv, 108, n. 87, and 110, n. 89. That Jung relied on Taylor's translations of the Orphic hymns is clear from numerous references in the *Collected Works*, e.g. CW14, ¶5, n. 23 and ¶19, n. 128.

24 See Chapter 7. According to Shamdasani, Phanes first appeared in *Black Book* 6 in 1916, although he was discussed in *Psychology of the Unconscious* in 1912; see Jung, *Liber Novus*, p. 301, n. 211.

25 See, for example, Jung, CW11, ¶246.

26 Leo, *Saturn*, pp. 8–9.

27 Image in Jung, *Liber Novus*, p. 117, © 2007 Foundation of the Works of C.G. Jung, Zürich, used by permission of W.W. Norton & Co.

28 For scholarly works on Telesphoros contemporaneous with *Liber Novus*, see Jane Ellen Harrison, *Themis* (Cambridge: Cambridge University Press, 1927), pp. 381–83; Warwick William Wroth, 'A Statue of the Youthful Asklepios', *Journal of Hellenic Studies* 3 (1882), pp. 283–300; Arthur Bernard Cook, *Zeus: A Study in Ancient Religion*, 3 volumes (Cambridge: Cambridge University Press, 1925), Vol. 3, Part 2, pp. 1182–83. For later discussions, see, among others, C.A. Meier, 'Ancient Incubation and Modern Psychotherapy', in Louise Carus Mahdi, Steven Foster, and Meredith Little (eds.), *Betwixt and Between* (Peru, IL: Open Court, 1987), pp. 415–27; Edward Tick, *The Practice of Dream Healing*

(Wheaton, IL: Theosophical Publishing House, 2001), pp. 121–23. Numerous discussions have recently appeared on Jung's relationship with Telesphoros: see, for example, Thomas Barrie, *The Sacred In-Between* (London: Routledge, 2013), pp. 72–74; Robert C. Smith, *The Wounded Jung* (Evanston, IL: Northwestern University Press, 1997), pp. 36–37; Mathew Mather, *The Alchemical Mercurius* (London: Routledge, 2014), pp. 86–87.

29 Jung, *Psychology of the Unconscious*, p. 72.

30 According to Jung, the name 'Kabeiroi' signifies 'powerful', and these dwarf-gods were also paradoxically known as μεγαλοι θεοι: 'great gods'. See Jung, *Psychology of the Unconscious*, p. 73.

31 The only differences between them lie in the colours of their garments and their respective ages. Phanes is shown in black, white, and gold stripes, while the water-bearer wears black, white, and green. As Jung associated green with the earth-dragon in the painting of the 'Caster of Holy Water', the green stripes may designate Phanes in the earthly realm (Abraxas), while the gold may designate Phanes in the spiritual realm. The water-bearer is more mature than Phanes, a slender youth rather than a spherical child, and thus closer to the adult human world.

32 See Greene, *Jung's Studies in Astrology*, chapter 4.

33 Robert Eisler, *Weltenmantel und Himmelszelt: Religionsgeschichtliche Untersuchungen zur Urgeschichte des Antiken Weltbildes*, 2 volumes (Munich: Oskar Beck, 1910), Vol. 2, Fig. 47, pp. 399–400.

34 Eisler's discussion of the bas-relief appeared later in Robert Eisler, *Orpheus the Fisher* (London: J.M. Watkins, 1921), Plate IV, p. 6. The photograph was reproduced in Franz Cumont, *The Mysteries of Mithra*, trans. Thomas J. McCormack (Chicago, IL: Open Court, 1903), Fig. 49, p. 223. Cumont called the figure 'Mithraic Kronos, or Personification of Infinite Time', and stated that this 'glorious youth' is 'a Roman beautification of the horrific features of the Oriental god'.

35 Jung, CW5, Plate XII.

36 Roman bas-relief, second century CE, Galleria e Museo Estense, Modena, Italy/Bridgeman Images.

37 See Jung, *Liber Novus*, p. 252.

38 The link between Phanes' goat-feet and Pan was made by Cook, *Zeus*, Vol. 2, Part 2, p. 1051.

39 See David Ulansey, *The Origins of the Mithraic Mysteries* (Oxford: Oxford University Press, 1991), pp. 86–107.

40 Proclus, in Kern, *Orphicorum fragmentum* 89–97, cited in Guthrie, *Orpheus and Greek Religion*, p. 138.

41 For the name Protogonos as an epithet for Phanes, see Athanassakis and Wolkow (trans.), *The Orphic Hymns*, pp. 81–83. The Orphic Hymns consist of seventy-eight poems dedicated to the various deities of the Orphic cosmology, and Phanes is addressed as Protogonos.

42 See, for example, Macrobius, who declared that the Orphics called Phanes 'Sun'. See Kern, *Orphicorum fragmentum* 540, and Cook, *Zeus*, Vol. 2, Part 2, p. 1051.

43 Nonnus, *Dionysiaca*, 3 volumes, trans. W.H.D. Rouse (Cambridge, MA: Harvard University Press, 1940), Books 1–15, 12:29–41. According to Nonnus, the 'fruitage of wine' was discovered 'where is the Lion and the Virgin', while the 'Prince of Grapes' (Dionysus) will arrive 'where Ganymedes [associated in the Roman world with Aquarius] draws the delicious nectar, and lifts cup in hand'. The significance of these attributions is unclear, but it is possible that Nonnus was referring to a precessional cycle of astrological Aions, in which case he is the first recorded author in history to do so.

44 Orphic Hymn VI to Protogonos, in Taylor (trans.), *The Hymns of Orpheus*, pp. 118–21. This work was reissued in a number of later editions; Jung's edition was Thomas Taylor (trans.), *The Mystical Hymns of Orpheus* (London: B. Dobell, 1896). The work has been recently republished as Thomas Taylor (trans.), *Hymns and Initiations* (Frome: Prometheus Trust, 1994). 'Bull-roarer' was one of the epithets for the Sumerian solar hero

Gilgamesh. Bulls are also associated in the Orphic Hymns with Dionysus, who is also Phanes; in Hymn XLV, the god is called 'bull-faced' (Taylor, p. 103). Izdubar's bull-horns and the bull-horns of Philemon in Jung's first painting of him are also relevant.

45 For this characteristic of the Hymns, see the translators' Introduction in Athanassakis and Wolkow (trans.), *The Orphic Hymns*, p. xix. See also Jung's invocations to the Sun-god during the emergence of Izdubar from the egg, in *Liber Novus*, pp. 284–85.

46 Jung, *The Black Book*, 7, pp. 16–19, cited in *Liber Novus*, p. 301, n. 211.

47 Jung, *The Black Book*, 7, pp. 76–80, quoted in Jung, *Liber Novus*, p. 301, n. 211.

48 Taylor, *The Mystical Hymns of Orpheus*, p. 37.

49 Jung, *Liber Novus*, p. 354, n. 125, and p. 301, n. 211.

50 H. P. Blavatsky, *Isis Unveiled*, 2 volumes (London: Theosophical Publishing, 1877), I.146–7.

51 H. P. Blavatsky, *The Secret Doctrine,* 2 volumes (London: Theosophical Publishing, 1888), I.425. See also Blavatsky, *Isis Unveiled*, I.284; II.108–109; Blavatsky, *The Secret Doctrine*, II.104, II.599.

52 See, for example, Amulet 163 at the Taubman Health Sciences Medical Library, University of Michigan, portraying a cock-headed anguipede with three stars and a crescent Moon, with the name IAO inscribed below him; see Campbell Bonner, *Studies in Magical Amulets* (Ann Arbor: University of Michigan Press, 1950), p. 280.

53 A gemstone amulet in the British Museum, for example, portrays a leaping ram with a lunar crescent and star, accompanied by the name 'Abraxas'; for more on this amulet, see Simone Michel-von-Dungern, 'Studies on Magical Amulets in the British Museum', in Chris Entwistle and Noel Adams (eds.), *Gems of Heaven* (London: British Museum, 2011), pp. 82–83. Another late antique amulet of rock crystal, held at the Kelsey Museum of Archaeology in Michigan and portraying a lion and a star, bears the names Abraxas and IAO. See also Christopher Faraone, 'Text, Image, and Medium', in Entwistle and Adams (eds.), *Gems of Heaven*, pp. 50–61; Attilio Mastrocinque, 'The Colours of Magical Gems', in Entwistle and Adams (eds.), *Gems of Heaven*, pp. 62–68. For the figure of Chnoumis, which Jung described as the 'Agathodaimon serpent', see Michel-von-Dungern, 'Studies on Magical Amulets'. For IAO and the use of the name in magical texts, see Hans Dieter Betz (ed. and trans.), *The Greek Magical Papyri in Translation* (Chicago: University of Chicago Press, 1986), p. 335.

54 Jung, *Liber Novus*, p. 349.

55 Jung, *Visions Seminars*, Vol. 2, pp. 806–7.

56 For Nietzsche's polarity of 'Apollonian' and 'Dionysian' as opposing forces in artistic creation, see Friedrich Nietzsche, *The Birth of Tragedy,* trans. Shaun Whiteside (London: Penguin, 1993); original German, *Die Geburt der Tragödie aus dem Geiste der Musik* (Leipzig: W. Fritzch, 1872). For Jung's references to this work during the period he worked on *Liber Novus*, see Jung, CW6, ¶¶223, 225–26, 232, 242, 876–77.

57 For a fuller exploration of the *Systema Munditotius*, see Chapter 7.

58 Karl Kerényi, *The Gods of the Greeks*, trans. John N. Cameron (London: Thames and Hudson, 1951), p. 175.

59 Jung, *Liber Novus*, p. 350.

60 Jung, *Liber Novus*, p. 354. This statement is given in *Black Book* 5, which, according to Shamdasani (*Liber Novus*, Appendix C, p. 370), gives a 'preliminary sketch' of the cosmology of the *Septem sermones*.

61 Jung, *Liber Novus*, p. 371.

62 Jung, *Liber Novus*, p. 301.

7

THE *SYSTEMA MUNDITOTIUS* AND JUNG'S NATAL HOROSCOPE

It [the soul] is an essence eternally unvaried; it is common to all that follows upon it: it is like the circle's centre to which all the radii are attached while leaving it unbroken in possession of itself, the starting-point of their course and of their essential being, the ground in which they all participate.[1]

—Plotinus

Mandala means 'circle' . . . Their basic motif is the premonition of a centre of personality, a kind of central point within the psyche, to which everything is related, by which everything is arranged, and which is itself a source of energy. The energy of the central point is manifested in the almost irresistible compulsion and urge to *become what one is* . . . This centre is not felt or thought of as the ego but, if one may so express it, as the *self*.[2]

—C.G. Jung

The structure of the *Systema*

A richly coloured painting titled 'Mandala of a Modern Man' appears as the frontispiece to the second English edition of Jung's work, *The Archetypes and the Collective Unconscious* (CW9i), published in 1968 (see Plate 12). In *Memories, Dreams, Reflections*, Jung described this image as his 'first mandala', which he had painted in January 1916 before writing 'Scrutinies', the third part of *Liber Novus*.[3] But this date indicates the first draft of the mandala; the final version has no precise dating, and does not appear in *Liber Novus*. In April 1955, the painting was published in a special edition of the Swiss journal *Du*, dedicated to the Eranos Conferences, but Jung specifically requested that it be published anonymously,[4] and did not acknowledge that it was his own work until *Memories, Dreams, Reflections* appeared in 1961.[5] The title inscribed on the painting is *Systema Munditotius*: 'System of All Worlds'.

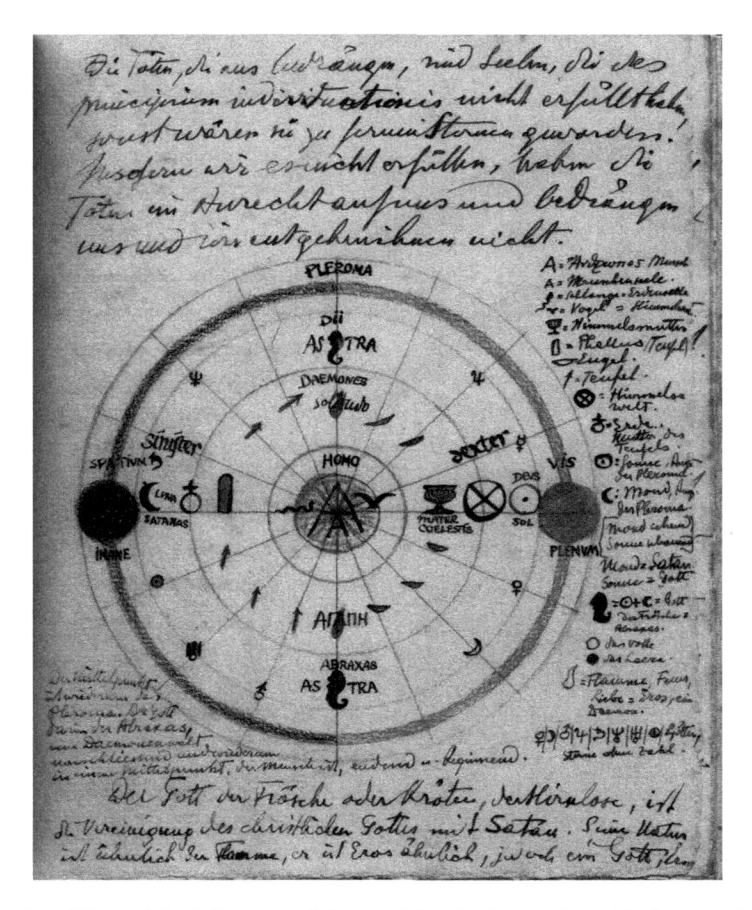

FIGURE 7.1 The original diagram of *Systema Munditotius*, produced in January 1916[6]

The *Systema* might best be understood as a cosmological map. There is a long tradition of such pictorial representations of the cosmos in both Eastern and Western traditions, stretching back into antiquity. All of them portray, through a particular cultural lens and a particular religious or philosophical world-view, the place of the human microcosm within the greater macrocosm. Jung was thoroughly familiar with these maps, which provided him with ample precedents for his *Systema*. The images in these cosmological presentations are sometimes literal as well as symbolic, as in the late thirteenth-century *Mappa Mundi* at Hereford Cathedral, which presents, within a Christian framework, an historical, geographical, and spiritual journey with an imaginal as well as a physical Jerusalem at its centre.[8] Some cosmological maps make use of astrological and alchemical themes to connote the *sumpatheia* between the planetary spheres and human life, such as Robert Fludd's portrayal of the World Soul (the Kabbalistic *Shekhinah*) as a female figure mediating between the deity and the highest angelic realms, the planetary spheres, and, at the centre, the physical world with its division into the four elements and their expressions through the kingdoms of Nature and the arts created by humans.[9] The Tibetan mandalas which Jung discussed in his essay, 'Concerning Mandala Symbolism', first published in 1950,[10] are 'instruments of contemplation' that Jung understood to 'represent the world': they are both cosmological maps of the universe and psychological portrayals of the journey inward to the 'central point within the psyche', the Self.[11]

In a letter to the Swiss philosopher and publicist Walter Robert Corti (1910–1990), who was the editor of *Du* at the time the *Systema* painting was published, Jung elaborated on the cosmology of his image.[12] He explained to Corti that it represented 'the antimonies of the microcosm within the macrocosmic world and its antimonies'. Although Jung offered numerous insights into the symbolism of the painting, he did not mention astrology in his letter to Corti, nor are there any overt astrological references in the painting. However, there are covert ones, and the elaborate diagram that constituted the original version of the *Systema* is very different from the beautifully polished image that was published in *Du*. This diagram appeared in *Black Book 5*, and was not included in Jung's final version of *Liber Novus*,[13] although it is reproduced in an Appendix in the published edition of the work. It is profoundly relevant for an understanding of Jung's astrology, because the entire diagram is punctuated with astrological symbols and notations that do not appear in the finished painting. In a web-based seminar given at the Asheville Jung Center, Murray Stein referred to this original diagram as a 'doodle'.[14] The diagram is certainly a rough draft or prototype. But it appears to have considerably more significance than the word 'doodle' might suggest.

The way in which Jung concealed, but did not remove, the astrological dimensions of the *Systema*'s cosmology is a remarkable reflection of his understanding of the nature of symbols. On a pragmatic level, he may have felt, perhaps with considerable justification, that obvious astrological indicators would provoke animosity in anyone viewing the *Systema*; this, in turn, suggests that, although initially the recording of his visions was an entirely private matter, he later expected that his work would eventually be viewed and discussed, and this expectation can be discerned in the immense care with which he executed the final calligraphic version of *Liber Novus*. However, the kind of astrological hermeneutics that Jung applied throughout the text and images of *Liber Novus* reflects an interrelationship of symbols that has a broader base than horoscopic astrology and its unique glyphic language. Jung's images link astrology directly to myth, alchemy, Tarot, Kabbalah, numerology, and the physical *sunthemata* of the celestial gods and daimons of the ancient world. He was not averse to throwing in the occasional Jewish or Christian symbol as well. Like the alchemists, who referred to their planetary metals through oblique images such as the green lion, the salamander, the unicorn, the peacock's tail, and the erotic *coniunctio* of solar and lunar figures, Jung seems to have applied a particular aesthetic sensitivity to his paintings. Although the astrological material is there to be explored, it does not club the viewer over the head with one specific language. The apparent concealment of astrological references in the *Systema* – and, indeed, in the whole of *Liber Novus* – is not really concealment at all, but reflects Jung's understanding of the analogic manner in which the unconscious psyche portrays itself.

In his introduction to *Liber Novus*, Sonu Shamdasani describes the *Systema* as 'a pictorial cosmology of the *Sermones*'.[15] Barry Jeromson, in a paper discussing the *Systema*, likewise points out that the painting is 'a psychocosmological model of *Sermons*, while *Sermons* is a poetic elaboration of the symbolism of *Systema*'.[16] In a second paper on the *Systema*, Jeromson notes that it has been largely ignored by writers on Jung's symbolism.[17] Discussing the painting in the context of the Gnostic currents that might have influenced the cosmology of 'Scrutinies', Jeromson suggests that the basis for the *Systema* lies in specific Gnostic concepts, such as the dualism of a corruptible body and an immortal spirit – a perspective on Jung which is shared by a number of scholars who view him as a 'modern Gnostic', and also a perspective which Jung himself seemed to support in his explanatory letter to Walter Corti.[18] Jeromson's discussions on the sources of the *Systema* – from Gnostic texts to the works of Boehme and Goethe – are comprehensive and incisive. However, he does not discuss the astrological underpinnings, not only of Gnostic ideas about *Heimarmene* and the descent and ascent of the soul through the planetary spheres, but also of the *Systema* itself. As it was the first of the many mandalas that Jung produced for *Liber Novus*, it is important to recognise that the diagram displays a distinctive astrological cosmology, which appears to have provided one of the primary models for Jung's passionate commitment to the cyclical, circular, and centrifugal 'shapes' of psychic processes.

The first polarity: spirit and matter

The astrological information in the original diagram of the *Systema* is highly complex. No attempt will be made here to provide an exhaustive interpretation of the symbolism of either the diagram or the painting; this would merit a book in itself and, in the end, would provide only one of many possible interpretations. The *Systema* is filled with symbols and is itself a symbol, and thus tends to inspire a multiplicity of approaches and connections. Three features of the diagram will be explored below, with specific reference to Jung's astrology: the horoscopic structure of the diagram, Jung's use of the planetary glyphs, and the relationship between the diagram and Jung's natal horoscope.

The cosmology presented in the diagram is consistent, not only with the cosmology provided by Philemon in 'Scrutinies', as Shamdasani and Jeromson have noted, but also with the astro-cosmological models offered by Hermetic and Neoplatonic texts. Although obvious astrological symbols are absent from the final painting of the *Systema*, these symbols in the original diagram reveal the thinking behind the finished mandala. Astral symbolism apparently provided Jung with a valuable hermeneutic lens through which to order and comprehend the cosmology of the seven 'sermons' that appear in 'Scrutinies'. Both the diagram and the painting appear to be based on the structure of the horoscope, which is, in turn, based on the ecliptic – the apparent path of the Sun around the earth. As in a horoscope, the four cardinal points of the *Systema* are apparently reversed from those in a normal map. The east point is on the left, the west point on the right, the south point at the top, and the north point at the bottom.

There is no specific indication in either the diagram or the painting of which end of the horizontal axis is the west point, and which is the east. But Jung, in his dialogue with Izdubar, speaks of the 'Western land' as being the place of immortality 'where the sun goes to be reborn', and 'where the sun and the maternal sea are united in an eternally rejuvenating embrace'. In turn, he placed the chief solar symbol (*Deus Sol*) in both the painting and the diagram of the *Systema*, together with the symbol of lunar spirituality (*Mater Coelistis*), at the right end of this axis rather than the left. From these indications, it seems clear that the right side of the axis represents the west point, as it does in the traditional structure of a horoscope.

Although the diagram of the *Systema* is arranged like a horoscope, it differs from the usual horoscopic structure because the four quadrants, generated by the axes of the horizon and the meridian, are each divided into four sectors each rather than three, giving sixteen 'houses' or *loci* rather than the traditional twelve. This is not as unusual as it might seem to those versed in modern astrology; divisions of the heavenly sphere based on multiples of four were known in antiquity. For example, an anonymously authored Hermetic text attributed to Asclepius, dated to the

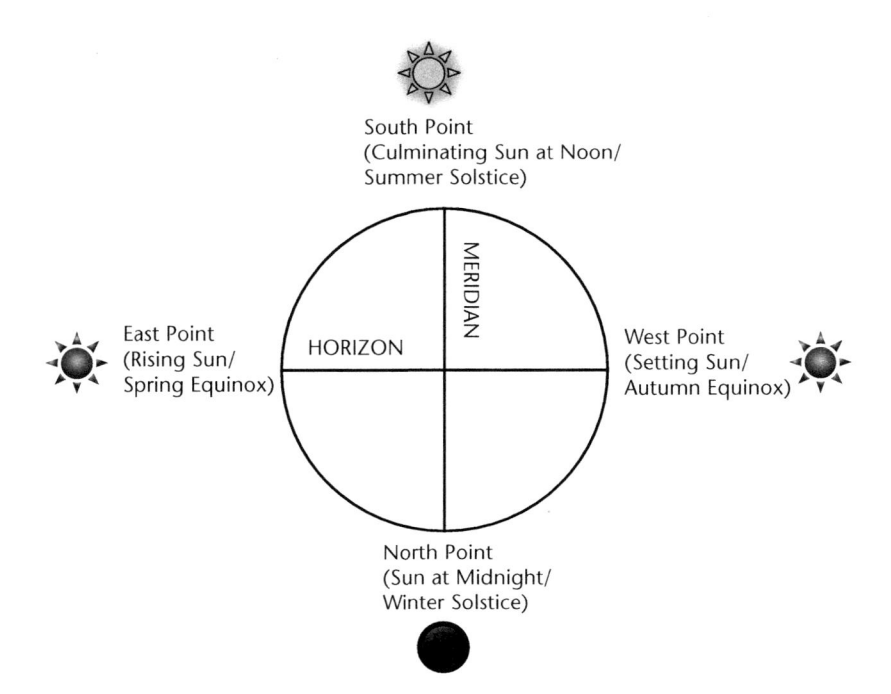

FIGURE 7.2   The cardinal points of the *Systema*

second century CE, describes a system of eight *loci*.[19] Firmicus Maternus, writing in the fourth century CE, described eight *loci* in the *Matheseos*, a work well known to Jung;[20] and the French historian of ancient religions, Auguste Bouché-Leclercq (1842–1923), whose definitive text on Hellenistic astrology was cited many times by Jung in the *Collected Works*, suggested that the *oktotopos* (eight *loci*) is a much more ancient system that predates the *dodekatopos* (twelve *loci*) most familiar to astrologers.[21] The idea of eight 'heavens' also appears in both the Hermetic *Poimandres* and the *Adversus haereses* of Irenaeus of Lyon:

> They maintain, then, that first of all the four elements, Fire, Water, Earth and Air, were produced after the image of the primary Tetrad above, and that then, when we add their operations, *viz.*, heat, cold, dryness, and humidity, an exact likeness of the Ogdoad is presented.[22]

It is possible that Jung, who would have encountered the eight *loci* in these late antique sources as well as in Bouché-Leclercq's analysis, felt that he wished to present his *Systema* in a form more ancient than that of the conventional horoscopes of his time, and more related to Hermetic and Neoplatonic astral cosmologies. However, Jung created sixteen *loci* rather than eight. These sixteen *loci* may be related to his perception of the symbolism of the number sixteen as a higher multiple of four, the 'quaternity' that forms the underlying structure of the psychic functions as Jung portrayed them in *Psychological Types*, which he was researching at the time he created the *Systema* diagram.[23] Later, Jung understood the horoscope to be a type of mandala,[24] and sixteen, as well as eight, reflected an increasingly conscious expression of the unfolding of the basic quaternity:

> We know from experience that the quaternity found at the centre of a mandala often becomes 8, 16, 32, or more when extended to the periphery.[25]

Jung also suggested that sixteen, as a multiple of four, describes the process through which the unconscious quaternity gradually emerges into awareness through the discriminating lenses of the four functions of consciousness, resulting in 'an unfolding of totality into four parts four times' which constitutes 'nothing less than its becoming conscious'.[26] But this statement was made many years after the *Systema* diagram. Whatever the reasons for sixteen *loci*, Jung apparently felt justified in interpolating his own cosmological perceptions into the traditional horoscopic wheel; the *Systema* is not, after all, a horoscope in any ordinary sense. In the finished *Systema* painting, the *loci* have disappeared, and only the four cardinal points remain.

In the *Systema* diagram, the outermost, 'macrocosmic' or universal zone of the circle is designated as *Pleroma*, a Greek term used in Platonic and Gnostic as well as early Christian texts to connote the totality of the divine powers.[27] Mead, citing the heresiologist Hippolytus, understood the Pleroma as a 'boundary', a liminal zone separating the realms of the planetary archons from the abode of the higher, unknown God.[28] Jung described the Pleroma as 'the upper world of fullness',[29] and stated that it is 'nothingness or fullness . . . the eternal and endless possess no qualities'.[30] In Platonic language, it is the World Soul, the realm of eternal being; in Jung's language, it might be understood as the 'objective psyche' or collective unconscious.[31] Although the Pleroma is often indicated in cosmological maps such as Fludd's 'Mirror of the Whole of Nature',[32] it is not generally designated in any horoscope, even those drawn by spiritually inclined astrologers such as Alan Leo,[33] because it lies beyond the spheres of the planets and thus beyond the dominion of astral fate and temporal change. It is out of this 'nothing and everything' that the Gnostic and Neoplatonic planetary spirits emanate. For Jung, it was also the source of the individual Self, which emerges like 'a shining star . . . a heavenly body in the making, comparable to a small sun'.[34] The Pleroma surrounds the entire cosmos of the *Systema*. As Jung put it, the collective unconscious is 'unafflicted by Christian splitting', and is the source and reconciliation of all apparent opposites. This suggests that the *Systema* does not portray a dualist cosmology, but rather, a series of apparent 'antimonies' experienced in incarnate life; these antimonies emerge only when the unity of the Pleroma is 'split' by the human perception of opposites.

The circle of the *Systema*, in both the diagram and the painting, is quartered by two axes, the meridian (north and south) and the horizon (east and west). In the same way, horoscopes are quartered to designate the rising, culmination, setting, and nadir of the Sun in its apparent daily journey around the earth, and to likewise symbolise the cardinal points – spring equinox, summer solstice, autumn equinox, and winter solstice – of the solar year. This quartering, which produces the four 'angles' of the horoscope, divides the *Systema* into two pairs of hemispheres: the north/south polarity of hemispheres based on the horizon axis, and the east/west polarity of hemispheres based on the meridian axis. In the *Systema* diagram, the hemisphere above the horizon axis comprises the domain of the spirit; its centre is the south point of the meridian axis, at the top of the circle. Jung designated this hemisphere as the realm of the *dii astra* or 'star-gods': the planetary archetypes in their unmanifest form.

The 'star-gods' are also indicated in the diagram by the astrological glyphs for the planets, discussed in greater detail below. Although these beings emanate from the higher realms of the Pleroma, Jung placed their planetary glyphs in various positions around the diagram, depending on the particular dimension of life through which he understood them to operate. In the finished painting of the *Systema*, the phrase *dii astra* has been replaced by the words ΗΡΙΚΑΠΑΙΟΣ ΦΑΝΗΣ ('Erikepaios Phanes'), inscribed beneath an image of the golden-winged god within the cosmic egg.[35] Phanes, whom Jung blandly described in his letter to Walter Corti as 'a spiritual figure of the Orphic Gods', is flanked by six golden stars, three to his left and three to his right. These, including Phanes as the seventh, comprise the celestial spirits that stand behind the seven visible planets, the 'star-gods' of the original diagram, with Phanes occupying the central position of the noetic Sun.[36] The arrangement of seven planetary 'stars', with the solar potency as either the centre of

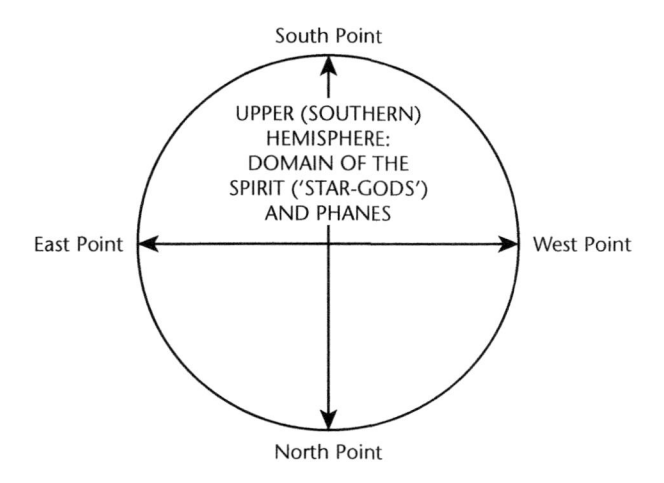

FIGURE 7.3 The upper hemisphere of the *Systema*

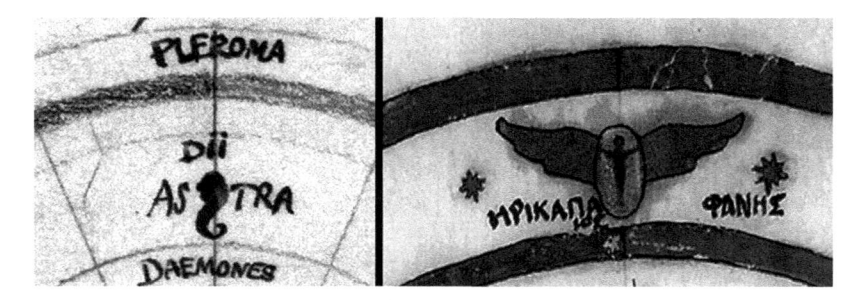

FIGURE 7.4 Left, the south point of the *Systema* diagram, the realm of the 'star-gods'. Right, the south point of the *Systema* painting, the realm of the winged Erikepaios Phanes, flanked by three stars on each side.

the heptad or represented as an additional image (such as Helios or Chnoumis), is common among the late antique magical amulets once thought of as 'Gnostic', as well as on the coins of Sun-worshipping Roman emperors.[37]

In the *Systema* diagram, the hemisphere below the horizon, in contrast to the upper hemisphere of the 'star-gods', belongs to corporeal life. Its centre is the north point of the meridian axis, at the bottom of the circle. In the diagram, Jung wrote *Abraxas astra* or 'stars of Abraxas' at this north point. As we have seen, Jung referred to Abraxas as 'the life of the earth'. In the painting, he inscribed '*Abraxas dominus mundi*' ('Abraxas Lord of the World') beneath an image of that black serpent who makes such frequent and ambiguous appearances in *Liber Novus*. The seven 'star-gods' that preside over the south point, portrayed as Phanes flanked by his six golden stars, are repeated at the north point; but Phanes as the central deity is replaced in the painting by a strange nimbate creature, wolf-like and lion-like at the same time, who appears to be disgorging the serpent from its mouth: Ialdabaoth wearing a solar crown.

The association of the south point of the ecliptic with the immortal spirit, and the north point with mortal life, has ancient antecedents with which Jung was familiar when he produced the diagram of the *Systema*. The motif appears in Porphyry's *De antro nympharum*, a Neoplatonic exegesis of the symbolism of the Mithraic 'cave' or *mithraeum*. In this third-century CE text, which Jung, using Thomas Taylor's English translation, cited in *Psychology of the Unconscious*,[38] Porphyry declared that souls incarnate in mortal form through the north 'gate' of Cancer, governed by the Moon, and depart for the realm of the spirit through the south 'gate' of Capricorn, governed by Saturn.

> Theologists therefore assert, that these two gates are Cancer and Capricorn; but Plato calls them entrances. And of these, theologists say, that Cancer is the gate through which souls descend; but Capricorn that through which they ascend.[39]

The theme of the soul-gates appears later, in the fifth century CE in Macrobius' commentary on Cicero's *Dream of Scipio*;[40] Jung cited this work in 1936 in his lecture on the historical background of dream interpretation, but he probably encountered it much earlier. According to Jung's interpretation of Macrobius' text,

> The soul wanders on the Milky Way from heaven to earth. The Milky Way intersects the astrological zodiac in Cancer and Capricorn, the two gates of the sun. The first gate, Cancer, is the gate of man while the second gate, Capricorn, is the gate of the gods. Through the first gate souls descend to earth, through the second they return.[41]

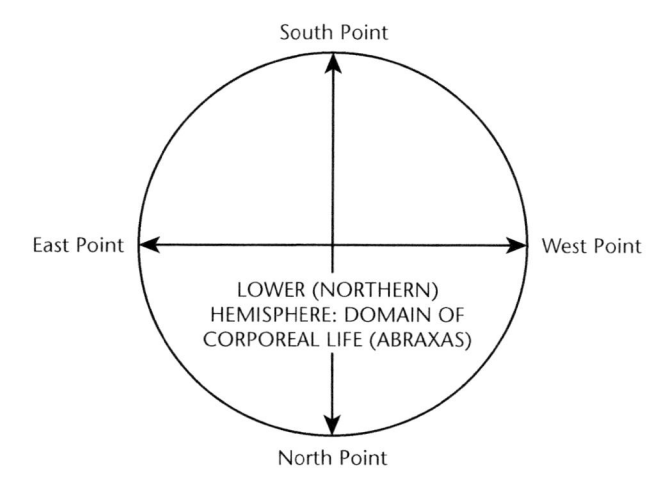

FIGURE 7.5   The lower hemisphere of the *Systema*

FIGURE 7.6 Left, the north point of the diagram of the '*Systema*', the realm of the 'stars of Abraxas'. Right, the north point of the painting of the '*Systema*', the realm of Abraxas 'Lord of the World'.

In the *Systema* diagram, Saturn's gate, the 'gate of the gods', is occupied by the *dii astra* and, in the painting, by the solar Phanes and his attendant six stars. In both the diagram and the painting of the *Systema*, the Moon's gate, the 'gate of man', is occupied by Abraxas, Lord of the World, flanked by his own six stars. This visual recreation of Porphyry's and Macrobius' soul-gates confirms that the *Systema* is constructed like a horoscope, with the south point or *medium coeli*, associated with the sign of Capricorn, at the top. To the right of the diagram, Jung provided annotations for the various symbols he employed, including a reference to a curious silhouette, identical to the lion-headed serpent of so-called Gnostic gems, which appears in both the southern and northern hemispheres of the diagram at the centre of the two groups of stars. This symbol, according to Jung, is '☉ + ☽ (Sun + Moon) = God of the Frogs = Abraxas', the *coniunctio* of the solar and lunar principles in the domains of both spirit and matter.

Although Jung designated the silhouette as Abraxas in the lower hemisphere of the *Systema* drawing, the crowned lion-headed serpent of late antiquity is neither Abraxas nor an exclusively Gnostic symbol, as Jung himself would have been aware. He later referred to it as the 'Agathodaimon Serpent', probably drawing on descriptions provided in King's work, *The Gnostics and Their Remains*.[43] King described this leontocephalic serpent as 'the undoubted emblem of the Solar god'.[44] The crowned lion-headed serpent also appears in the frontispiece engraving of Schultz' *Dokumente der Gnosis*.[45] Its golden crown is an attribute of Helios-Mithras in the *Mithras Liturgy*, as Jung noted in *Psychology of the Unconscious*, emphasising its solar nature. It seems that Jung used the name Abraxas to describe his own unique synthesis, based on a variety of ancient testimonies and modern interpretations, to connote the immortal spirit or solar life-force that incarnates in the world of matter.

On late antique magical amulets, this figure is usually called Chnoumis or Chnoubis, a syncretic deity who represents the cosmocratic solar power in both spiritual and corporeal manifestations.[46] Sometimes the figure is accompanied by the name IAO, the Greek equivalent of the Hebrew sacred Name of God, YHVH.

On amulets, the god is usually portrayed facing left, as is Jung's figure, whose presence in both hemispheres of the *Systema* diagram, as a symbol of the conjunction of solar and lunar principles, suggests a secret unity between spiritual and corporeal worlds. The symbolism of the upper and lower hemispheres of the *Systema* is not exclusively, nor even primarily, Gnostic, but borrows equally freely from a Neoplatonic astrological, solar-centred cosmology that Porphyry, like Jung, believed to be Mithraic. This cosmology embraces the idea of the descent and ascent of the soul into and out of incarnation through the northern lunar gate of mortal birth and the southern Saturnian gate of immortality. The pairing of Elijah and Salome, the Saturnian *senex* and the lunar anima, assumes a new significance in the light of Jung's *Systema* diagram, and the vision of his transformation into the lion-headed deity may be deeply relevant to these two great soul-gates that are personified in *Liber Novus* and unified in the image of Chnoumis.

Jung incorporated other symbols in the *Systema* diagram to clarify his understanding of the hemispheres of 'above' and 'below'. Beneath the *dii astra* are the *daimones*, the intermediaries in Orphic and Neoplatonic cosmologies; Philemon, as Jung's 'personal daimon', might be accounted the chief of these in the context of his own life. In the diagram, the daimons only appear in the upper, spiritual hemisphere, but in the painting they appear only in the lower, corporeal hemisphere. Perhaps Jung eventually concluded that the daimons are happy to mediate both Phanes and Abraxas, who only seem to be opposites from the viewpoint of human consciousness. This is certainly the case with the daimon signified by the flame-shaped symbol in the diagram, which Jung's annotation designates as *Flamme, Feuer, Liebe = Eros, ein Daemon*.[47] This symbol, like the lion-headed serpent, appears in both the upper and lower hemispheres. In the fourth sermon of 'Scrutinies', Philemon elaborates on the nature of this daimon, the 'Burning One', who 'binds two together and spreads himself out in brightness'.[48] In an essay titled 'The Eros Theory', written in 1917, Jung specifically indicated the capacity of Eros to bridge spiritual and instinctual realms:

> The Erotic . . . belongs on the one hand to the original drive nature of man . . . On the other hand it is related to the highest forms of the spirit.[49]

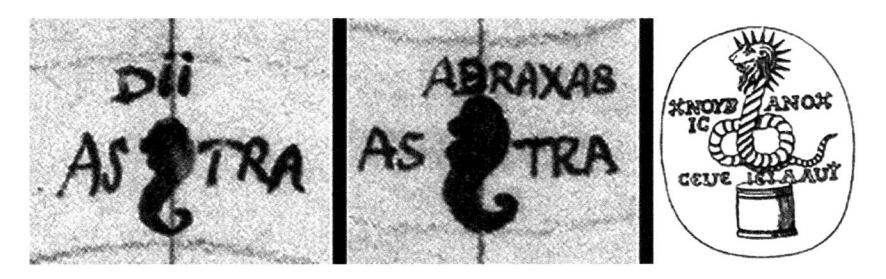

FIGURE 7.7   Left and centre, the silhouette in Jung's diagram of the *Systema*; right, the lion-headed serpent on a late antique magical amulet[41]

As Diotima eloquently articulates in Plato's *Symposium*, Eros, as a 'great daimon', can manifest on both spiritual and corporeal levels.[50] Jung referred to Eros as the principle that 'unites humanity with the transcendental', which is presumably why the daimon's flame appears in both hemispheres.[51] Eros is the microcosmic equivalent of the macrocosmic Agathodaimon Serpent, animating the world with his fiery libido. Behind the flame of Eros in the upper hemisphere, Jung wrote the word *Solitudo*. Behind the flame in the lower hemisphere, Jung inscribed a Greek word which could be either ΑΓΑΠΕ – the expression of unconditional divine love – or ΑΠΑΠΗ, the Greek word for 'dandelion'. It is unclear which interpretation is correct, as the second and third letters of the word appear to be amalgamated. It is possible that he intended it to be read as both. Jung did not refer to the dandelion in any published work, and therefore only speculation is possible on what he might have meant by associating this flower with Abraxas/Eros. The dandelion (*Taraxacum officinale*) is a prolific plant, reproducing itself asexually without pollination, and spreading its seeds everywhere. It may be these qualities which Jung linked with the earthy, fertile, promiscuous nature of Abraxas as the life-force within matter and the dark face of the Sun-god. It is more difficult to understand why he would have associated the essentially spiritual quality of ΑΓΑΠΕ, unconditional divine love, with Abraxas. Whether ΑΓΑΠΕ or ΑΠΑΠΕ is meant, it is the counterpart of *Solitudo*, which can refer not only to solitude in the usual sense, but to singularity or individuality, the opposite of both unconditional love and the dandelion's indiscriminate and prolific reproductive habits. In German the dandelion is *Löwenzahn*, meaning 'lion's tooth', relating it to the lion-headed serpent in the painting.

In the *Systema* painting, the images are more elaborate. Beneath Phanes is a seven-branched lit candelabrum, its central arm marked by a larger flame and the phrase *ignis eros*, the 'fire of love'. The seven-branched candelabrum is also known as the *menorah*, understood to be a symbol of Judaism since ancient times. Philo of Alexandria, a Jewish Platonic philosopher of the first century CE whose work Jung cited in *Psychology of the Unconscious* as well as in later volumes of the *Collected Works*, interpreted the *menorah* as a symbol of the planetary system, with the central light symbolising the Sun:[52]

> The candlestick . . . intimates, in a figurative manner, the motions of the stars which give light; for the sun, and the moon, and the rest of the stars, being all at a great distance from the northern parts of the universe, make all their revolutions in the south. And from this candlestick there proceeded six branches, three on each side, projecting from the candlestick in the centre, so as altogether to complete the number of seven . . . being symbols of those seven stars which are called planets by those men who are versed in natural philosophy; for the sun, like the candlestick, being placed in the middle of the other six . . . gives light to the three planets which are above him, and to those of equal number which are below him.[53]

Although Jung did not mention the *menorah* in the lengthy explanation he gave of the candlestick in his letter to Corti, he was clearly aware of its astral symbolism, and his use of it in the *Systema* painting provides an excellent example of a symbol that conceals its astrological nature while revealing it at the same time.

In Kabbalistic texts, the *menorah* was also understood to represent the 'Tree of Life', which symbolises the ten *sefirot* or divine emanations. Only the lower seven emanations are portrayed by the *menorah*, as the upper three *sefirot* are considered transcendent and belong to what the Gnostics understood as the realm of the unknown, ineffable godhead.[54] The central light of the Tree is related to the *sefira* called *Tiferet*, translated as 'glory' or 'beauty', who unites the upper realms with the lower and is symbolised by the light of the Sun.[55] It seems that Jung was fully aware of this relationship between the *menorah* and Kabbalistic lore: in the *Systema* painting, he mirrored his *menorah* in the lower realm of Abraxas with the image of a tree, which he called the 'Tree of Life'. This symbol unites good and evil, as does Eros, and 'grows with slow and constant increase through measureless periods of time'.[56] Jung informed Corti that the candelabrum 'points to the spiritual world of the divine child', thus linking it with Phanes. He also insisted to Corti that the numerology of the candelabrum was based on 'the principle of the spiritual number three (twice-three flames with one large flame in the middle)'. As Jung assiduously removed all traces of overt astrological symbolism from the painting of the *Systema*, this explanation is characteristic of the kind of evasion he employed when presenting astrological themes to those unsympathetic to the subject. As he was well aware, the number seven in antiquity was almost invariably associated, in Jewish as well as pagan circles, with the heptad of the planetary spirits, and not with the Christian trinity.[57]

The seven planetary gods in the upper, macrocosmic sphere of the *Systema* painting also express themselves in ways more accessible to human consciousness. To the left of the candelabrum is a winged mouse, designated *scientia*. Jung explained to Corti that the mouse was included because of its 'hole-digging activity'; he neglected to mention that the Greeks considered the mouse sacred to Apollo the Sun-god.[58] To the right of the candelabrum is the same golden-winged salamander-serpent that forms the background of Jung's painting of the solar hero Izdubar, designated *ars* in the *Systema* painting. Jung informed Corti that these salamanders 'also belong to this spiritual realm', although he failed to tell Corti this creature's alchemical epithet, 'Salamander of the Wise', and its role as the daimon of the element of fire. Below the candelabrum, at an increasingly microcosmic level, is a rayed Sun-symbol, again flanked by six stars: the manifestation of Phanes and his attendant planetary gods as the seven planets of the horoscope. At the centre of the painting, the Sun appears again, this time, as Jung informed Corti, 'an inner Sun', which contains both upper and lower hemispheres within it: the individual Self.

At the northern, Abraxas-ruled end of the meridian axis in the painting, just above the black serpent, Jung portrayed the head of that same solar-rayed, lion-headed serpent that appears in silhouette in the original diagram, although the face of this creature has a wolf-like quality as well. The six stars that accompany Phanes in the realm of the spirit reappear in the realm of Abraxas, flanking the head of the Agathodaimon on either side, and designated as *dii Abraxas*: the life-force of the 'star-gods' expressed in the manifest world. They appear yet again on the microcosmic level as seven stars. From the Agathodaimon sprouts the 'Tree of Life'. To the left of the tree is an image that Jung painted in a larger version in *Liber Novus*: a threatening caterpillar-like monster with sharp teeth.[59] In *Liber Novus*, it emerges upright from a blood-red underworld Sun. There is no caption for the image in *Liber Novus*, but it accompanies the description of a multitude of dead souls dissolving in a sea of blood, from which 'a new sun escapes from the bloody sea'.[60]

To the right of this monster in the *Systema* painting is a larva-like creature. Above the larva, Jung wrote: 'The human body and the solitary god and the microcosmic inner worlds. Death and future life'.[61] Jung described these two creatures to Corti as 'death and rebirth'. The appearance of the seven 'star-gods' in both upper and lower hemispheres points to a cosmology in which the divine life-force or, as Jung understood it, the libido, symbolised in the realm of spirit by Phanes and in the realm of matter by Abraxas, is expressed through the symbols of the planetary gods on all levels, macrocosmic to microcosmic, collective to individual, spiritual to earthly. These 'star-gods' are the 'Seven Spirits burning before the Throne' described in the *Apocalypse of John*.[62] In *Pistis Sophia* they are the seven angels of light who emanate from the unknown transcendent God, as well as their dark counterparts, the seven planetary archons who preside over the Great Fate. They are served by their intermediaries, the daimons, and manifest as archetypal principles in both the eternal, timeless realm and the cyclical, time-bound experiences of human birth, life, and death. Although Jung seems to have avoided any astrological explanations of the *Systema* painting in his letter to Corti, the entire structure of the map reflects a cosmology firmly rooted in astrological symbolism.

The second polarity: darkness and light

The east and west hemispheres of the diagram, demarcated by the vertical axis of the meridian, comprise another polarity: that of light and darkness. The vertical axis in a horoscope has as its apex the *medium coeli* ('middle of the sky'), or place of the culminating Sun at noon, and as its nadir, the *imum coeli* ('bottom of the sky'), or place of the hidden Sun at midnight. In the *Systema* diagram, this axis divides the eastern realm of darkness, centred on the east point, from the western realm of light, centred on the west point. Light, for Jung, is evidently not necessarily spiritual, nor is darkness necessarily corporeal; there can be darkness in Phanes' domain, as there can be light in the domain of Abraxas. At the east point of the diagram, Jung wrote, 'Left: the zone of emptiness'. At the west point, he wrote: 'Right: the power of fullness'. In the annotations, he indicated that the black disc at the east point was 'The Emptiness', while the white disc at the west point was 'The Fullness'. Jung also made clear the attributes he associated with these two hemispheres: the left or eastern hemisphere is marked with arrows that he designated as 'devil', while the right or western hemisphere is marked with crescent-shaped symbols which he designated as 'Angel'.

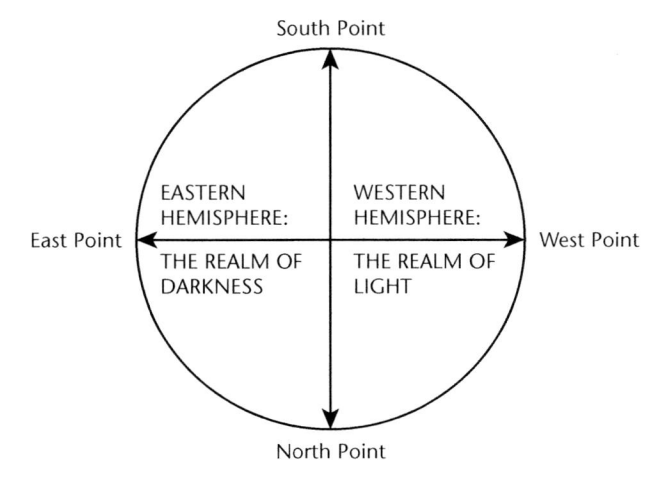

FIGURE 7.8 The east and west hemispheres of the *Systema*

At the east point of the *Systema* diagram, the apex of the realm of darkness, Jung placed the symbol of a black Moon, which he called *Luna Satanas*. In the painting, her divinity is acknowledged: *Dea Luna Satanas*, equivalent to the underworld goddess Hecate. In the fourth sermon of 'Scrutinies', Philemon informs Jung: 'The Sun God is the highest good, the devil the opposite'.[63] In the annotations, Jung noted: 'Moon = Satan, Sun = God'. However, both Sun and Moon, according to Jung's notes, are the 'Eyes of the Pleroma'; the Sun is 'the God's eye of fullness' while the Moon is 'the God's eye of emptiness'.[64] The 'antimony' is only an apparent one and, as Philemon declares, 'Good and evil unite in the flame. Good and evil unite in the growth of the tree'.

To the right of the lunar crescent in the diagram is the inverted astrological glyph for Venus, which Jung noted as 'Earth: Mother of Devils'. This symbol is also the alchemical glyph for the metalloid known as antimony. In alchemy this substance was called 'The Grey Wolf' because, when molten, it adapts to, amalgamates with, and apparently 'swallows up' other metals such as copper and tin, forming various alloys. Jung considered antimony to be associated with 'blackness',[65] but noted that it was also 'the secret transformative substance, which fell from the highest place into the darkest depths of matter where it awaits deliverance'.[66] This description suggests that the dark Venusian 'anima' is a destructive erotic principle that 'swallows up' yet ultimately transforms that which it devours: a paradox entirely in keeping, not only with Jung's portrayal of Salome in *Liber Novus*, but with Goethe's Mephistopheles, who 'would always wish Evil, and always works the Good'.

This presentation of a devouring, Satanic Venus, who is secretly also a transformative substance, is unusual in terms of traditional astrology. This planet is usually described as a 'benefic', although anyone familiar with the mythic narratives involving Venus-Aphrodite, as Jung himself was, might be inclined to be somewhat more suspicious; and no doubt his own experiences taught him that Venus can be even trickier than Mercury. Jung's interpretation also seems to draw on Plato's less judgemental division of the goddess of love into two equally radiant forms: Aphrodite Ourania, the 'heavenly' Venus, and Aphrodite Pandemos, the 'earthly' Venus, reflected in astrology by the planet's rulership of two zodiacal signs: earthy Taurus and airy Libra.

> If, then, there were only one goddess of that name [Aphrodite], we might suppose that there was only one kind of Love, but since in fact there are two such goddesses there must also be two kinds of Love . . . One, the elder . . . we call the Uranian, the heavenly Aphrodite, while the younger . . . we call Pandemos, the earthly Aphrodite. It follows, then, that Love should be known as earthly or as heavenly according to the goddess in whose company his work is done.[67]

Next to the 'earthly' Venus in the *Systema* diagram is a phallus, which Jung's notes identify as 'devil'. Sexuality, represented by the inverted Venus and the phallus, evidently belongs to the realm of darkness, because it is driven by unconscious instinct; the east point of the diagram seems to be firmly entrenched in Freud's world of the *id*. But all opposites, as Jung insisted, are contained in the Pleroma, and the counterparts of these symbols in the realm of light are found at the west point of the diagram, the place of the setting Sun that Izdubar pursues in his quest for immortality. Here Jung inserted the astrological glyph for the Sun, designated as *Deus Sol*, the Sun-god, along with a chalice resembling the Grail, which is designated *Mater Coelestis*, the Celestial Mother. In the *Systema* painting, the chalice remains, now turned on its side and accompanied by the white wings of the *Spiritus Sanctus*. The astrological glyph for the Sun, inevitably, has been replaced by a simple gold disc. The astrological glyph for the dark Venus has likewise been removed, replaced by a green disc.

The planetary opposites that delineate the hemispheres of darkness and light in the diagram, arranged in concentric circles from macrocosmic to microcosmic levels of reality, can briefly be summarised as follows: Luna Satanas, represented in the east by the astrological glyph for the Moon, is mirrored in the west by Deus Sol, represented by the astrological glyph for the Sun. This is the classic alchemical pairing of Sol and Luna, sulphur and salt: in psychological terms, the *coniunctio* of the dark instinctual unconscious and the solar light of consciousness. The 'earthly' eastern Venus, who might be compared with Plato's Aphrodite Pandemos and whom Jung described in the finished *Systema* painting as *Mater natura et terra* ('Mother Nature and Earth'), is mirrored in the west by the female chalice of the Celestial Mother, linking the *Systema* with the dark and light female 'anima' figures, dressed respectively in red and white robes, that Jung painted in the mandala in Part One of *Liber Novus*. The phallus in the east is mirrored by a diagonally quartered circle described in Jung's notes as the 'Heavenly World'. This latter symbol, unlike the circle quartered by horizontal and vertical axes, is not part of either astrological or alchemical iconography. However, Plato, in the *Timaeus*, explained that the two parts of the World Soul are 'joined to one another at the centre [of the circle] like the letter χ' (the Greek letter *chi*).[68] Finally, on the individual, microcosmic level, the serpent at the east point of the *Systema* diagram, described by Jung as the 'Earthly soul', is mirrored at the west point by a bird, described as the 'Heavenly soul'.

The planetary glyphs

Within the astrological framework of the *Systema* diagram, Jung distributed the traditional planetary glyphs, placing them in particular hemispheres and quadrants according to his individual understanding of their meanings and expressions. It is not possible to know to what extent Jung's perception of these meanings was based on the astrological texts he was reading at the time, or to what degree his interpretation of the planetary 'gods' was rooted in his observations of astrological workings in his own and his patients' lives. The glyphs, which appear in the diagram but are, not surprisingly, missing from the painting, reveal Jung's incorporation of astrological symbols at the very foundation of the cosmology depicted in the *Systema* and explained by Philemon in the seven sermons of 'Scrutinies'. In the annotations to the diagram, Jung described the planets, represented by their glyphs, as 'Gods, stars without numbers'. In an entry in *Black Book 5*, Jung stated explicitly his understanding of the planets as divinities:

> Sun and moon, that is, their symbols, are Gods. There are still other Gods; their symbols are the planets . . . The Gods are favorable and unfavorable, impersonal, the souls of stars, influences, forces, grandfathers of souls, rulers in the heavenly world, both in space and in force. They are neither dangerous nor kind, strong yet humble, clarifications of the Pleroma and of the eternal emptiness, configurations of the eternal qualities.[69]

Although they are not included in the starry heptad that dominates both the upper and lower hemispheres of the *Systema*, Jung added to his diagram the glyphs for two planets known only in modern times: Uranus and Neptune. Uranus was discovered in 1781 and Neptune in 1846, and the astrological texts written since the sighting of these 'new' planets have offered various and often contradictory interpretations of their meanings. Alan Leo favoured Uranus as the planet of 'advanced thinkers', but also associated it with 'sudden and unexpected events' that can prove destructive to order and stability.[70] He did not refer to Uranus as a malefic, but he was clearly uneasy about its nature, preferring to believe that it was too distant to have any relevance except for especially evolved souls with many incarnations behind them. Leo was even more ambivalent about Neptune, pointing out its relationship with obsession, a weak will, mediumistic tendencies, impressionability, and 'exceptional immorality'; only those who are 'very highly advanced psychically' can avail themselves of its spiritual dimension without suffering from the more treacherous aspects of its nature.[71] Max Heindel, like Alan Leo, believed that only the spiritually evolved could respond to Uranus and Neptune, but his view of these planets was essentially positive: Heindel understood Uranus to be the 'higher octave' of Venus, concerned with universal rather than personal love, and embracing 'all humankind regardless of sex or any other distinction'.[72] Neptune, in turn, represents 'cosmic consciousness'.[73] Jung's placing of both planets in the hemisphere of darkness suggests a less optimistic interpretation.

John Thorburn, in his interpretation of Jung's natal horoscope, associated Neptune with mysticism, and informed Jung that the tense angle between the Sun and Neptune in Jung's natal horoscope indicated a 'mystical complex'.[74] In the *Systema* diagram, Jung placed the glyph for Neptune in the upper quadrant of darkness, which, because of its proximity to the south point, partakes of both the 'emptiness' of the darkness and the spiritual essence of the 'star-gods'. Jung appears to have associated Neptune with the ambiguous receptivity of the trance medium, which he understood to reflect a dangerous but potentially immensely creative porousness to the collective unconscious.[75] Receptivity to the light is matched by an equal receptivity to the darkness, and often without the discriminating faculties to distinguish the difference. This accords not only with Leo's similar, albeit less psychological, understanding of the planet's disturbing attributes, but also with Jung's own experience at the time he was writing 'Scrutinies', when he found himself acting as a kind of helpless medium for Philemon.[76] The glyph for Uranus in the *Systema* diagram is placed in the lower quadrant of darkness, which partakes of the earthy realm of Abraxas. Jung apparently associated Uranus with those sudden and unexpected material events described by Leo, which can disrupt and even shatter the individual's stability and equilibrium.

In the 'Special Chart' that Johan van Ophuijsen prepared for Jung, Uranus is indicated as forming a tense 90° or quadrate angle to the Moon. According to Alan Leo's accompanying paragraph, this configuration is reflected in 'sudden troubles or difficulties', a 'tendency towards eccentricity', and an inclination to 'do things that you may afterwards regret'. Moreover, Leo admonished, 'you will be considered a crank in your peculiar way',[77] echoing Freud's warning when Jung informed him that he was studying astrology:'You will be accused of mysticism'.[78] Leo also had a good deal to say about Uranian marital proclivities, as Uranus in Jung's natal horoscope is placed in the *locus* or 'house' concerned with marriage:

> This mystical planet [Uranus] will bring some very peculiar experiences into the marriage state, and it is very probable that it may bring you disappointment, or estrangement . . . Sudden and very unexpected events occur in all regions that Uranus governs, and there are more divorce cases under his dominance than any other planet; therefore see that your partner is original and fond of metaphysical subjects.[79]

Jung did not divorce, perhaps because Emma was indeed 'original' and 'fond of metaphysical subjects'; she participated in Jung's astrological as well as psychological research, and produced two highly respected books of her own.[80] Toni Wolff was likewise 'original' and 'fond of metaphysical subjects', and was a competent astrologer.[81] But Jung's domestic life could certainly be said to reflect the kind of 'peculiar experiences' that Leo described, particularly during the period when Jung produced the *Systema* diagram. His placement of the glyph for Uranus in the hemisphere of darkness in the domain of Abraxas might be viewed as based, at least in part, on his own experience.

The glyph for the Sun lies, appropriately enough, at the west point of the diagram, the 'heavenly' world, where it is designated *Deus Sol*. But on the microcosmic level, the solar glyph appears again in the hemisphere of darkness, just below the east point in the quadrant belonging to the realm of Abraxas. This unusual association of the Sun with darkness and the earth-world suggests the *sol niger* of alchemy and the 'lower' or underworld sun that Jung described several times in *Liber Novus*. It is a surprising interpretation of the astrological Sun, given Jung's focus on the significance of the Sun as a spiritual life-source; and it contradicts traditional interpretations of the beneficent 'Great Light', although Apollo, in myth, was a god of plague, disease, and death as well as of life and healing. Jung's dark solar glyph is deliberately shaded, as though he specifically intended to represent that dark Sun, shining in the depths, which radiates its hidden light through the density, vulnerability, and mortality of the physical body, the instinctual realm, and the world of nature. This is the Sun as the great cosmic sperm-maker, an association known since the earliest Orphic texts and which Jung emphasised in *Psychology of the Unconscious*.[82] It is also the Sun as the secret face of Saturn, who presides over the alchemical *nigredo*.

Not surprisingly, the glyphs for Saturn and Mars are also found in the hemisphere of darkness, with Saturn close to the east point above *Luna Satanas*, and Mars near the north point in proximity to Abraxas himself. This is entirely in accord with ancient perceptions of Saturn and Mars as malefic planets, and with Jung's association of Saturn with the *nigredo* or 'blackening' stage of the alchemical work. It also reflects his understanding of Mars, the devilish Red One, as a disruptive and often destructive agent that precipitates the individuation process in highly uncomfortable ways. The entire group of planetary glyphs in the eastern hemisphere – the black Moon, the inverted Venus, Neptune, Uranus, Saturn, Mars, and the dark Sun – appear to describe Jung's understanding of the expressions of these planetary archetypes in the domain of instinct, passion, sexuality, compulsion, and corporeal birth and death.

The Moon's glyph, like the Sun's, is represented twice. At the east point, the place of the void, the black lunar crescent is called *Luna Satanas*. But a white lunar crescent, facing in the opposite direction to the black Moon, appears in the hemisphere of light, although it is in the quadrant ruled by Abraxas. This Moon is not the pure spiritual force of the Celestial Mother, but suggests a perception of the Moon in the horoscope as a symbol of light and fullness working through the instincts. It is the 'good mother' who, like the Cook in *Liber Novus*, provides physical nourishment, affection, and protection for her child, while at the same time holding the keys to the doors of the underworld. The glyph for Venus also appears twice. At the east point it is shown inverted: Aphrodite Pandemos as the 'Mother of Devils', or the 'Grey Wolf' of antimony in alchemical lore. But the normal glyph for Venus appears in the zone of light, just below the west point and, like the Moon, in the quadrant related to the realm of body and instinct. Although Jung seems to have viewed Aphrodite Pandemos as a dangerous potency, perhaps with some justification in terms of his own personal experience, this 'other' Venus, who has more in common with Plato's more spiritual Aphrodite Ourania, expresses herself through erotic love and physical beauty, but ultimately serves the heavenly realm of the Celestial Mother.

The glyph for Mercury appears above that of the Sun in the upper quadrant related to the spirit. This Mercury, unlike the tricky, devilish youth with fiery hair whom Jung associated with Loke and Hephaistos, seems here to fulfil his role in alchemy as Mercurius, the agent of transformation, and his mythic role as psycho-pomp and messenger of the 'star-gods'. Jupiter's glyph likewise appears in the upper quadrant in the hemisphere of light, perhaps reflecting John Thorburn's associa-tion of this 'benefic' planet in Jung's horoscope with a religious and humanitarian disposition, and Alan Leo's statement that Jupiter, linked in Jung's horoscope with 'money coming from others' and 'occult affairs', would bring him 'good fortune through other persons' and a 'natural and easy death'.[83]

Jung's understanding of the planets, as portrayed in the diagram of the *Systema*, was unique. Some features, such as Jupiter's beneficent nature and the unpleasant attributes of Saturn and Mars, are described in astrological texts from Ptolemy to the present day. But Jung's use of the glyph for the dark Sun, his presentation of an inverted Venus who mothers Devils, and his portrayal of *Luna Satanas*, are strik-ingly original and do not follow any astrological system, ancient or modern. Jung's distribution of the glyphs is derived from neither Gnostic texts (in which all the planets are entirely evil) nor Neoplatonic ones (in which all the planets are entirely good). His perception of the 'new' planets, Uranus and Neptune, is more or less in accord with Alan Leo's descriptions, but reflects a greater depth and subtlety of interpretation. It seems that, for Jung, the 'star-gods', emanating from the 'fullness' of the Pleroma where there are no opposites, nevertheless partake of paradoxical 'antimonies' as every archetypal potency does when it enters the domain of human existence, and may express themselves as devils or angels according to the sphere of individual life in which their meaning is symbolised in the natal horoscope, and according to the extent of individual consciousness.

Jung's knowledge of his natal horoscope, and the various interpretations of it given to him by other astrologers, would inevitably have coloured his perceptions of the planets – not from the archetypal perspective (all the planetary gods, in both the diagram and the painting of the *Systema*, arise from the same unity), but in his understanding of his own path of development. When the hemispheres and quadrants in which the planetary glyphs appear in the *Systema* diagram are related to those figures in *Liber Novus* who seem to carry overt astrological qualities, it seems appropriate that The Red One, who is Martial, would appear devilish; that the Anchorite, the Scholar, and the Librarian, who are Saturnian, would exhibit a dark and empty intellectual rigidity and emotional dissociation; that Salome, who is lunar, would appear as both the seductive *Luna Satanas* and the redemptive *Mater*

Coelestis; and that Philemon, who is Saturnian, solar, and Mercurial all at once, would appear tricky and versed in the dark arts as well as being a 'Wise Old Man', an individual *Deus Sol*, and a personal embodiment of Phanes, the bringer of light.

The *Systema* and Jung's horoscope

The *Systema* diagram has sixteen *loci* or 'houses' instead of the usual twelve found in traditional horoscopes. The four quadrants of the circle, created by the horizontal and vertical axes, are usually divided into three sectors each, but Jung divided each quadrant into four sectors. Despite this difference – which is absent from the finished painting, in which the sectors have been removed and only the four quadrants remain – the structure of the *Systema* seems to be based on the structure of a horoscope. There are two particular features in the diagram that mirror in a striking fashion two configurations in Jung's birth horoscope, and this is not likely to be coincidental. The *Systema Munditotius* is, according to the title Jung gave it, a cosmological 'system of all worlds', displaying affinities with Gnostic, Orphic, Hermetic, and Neoplatonic cosmological models. But it is also the system of Jung's very personal inner world, presented as a highly individualised interpretation of macrocosmic themes. This expression of timeless, universal components (in the case of the *Systema*, the 'star gods' as archetypal powers) through the highly specific unfolding of a human life (which Jung understood to be reflected in the patterns of the birth horoscope) forms the bedrock of his psychological models for the relationship between the 'objective' psyche – the collective unconscious – and the psyche of the individual.

The first of these striking parallels between the *Systema* diagram and Jung's horoscope is the presence of *Deus Sol*, represented by the astrological glyph for the Sun, at the right side of the horizontal axis of the *Systema* diagram. In *Liber Novus*, the solar giant Izdubar seeks immortality through his pursuit of the Sun setting in the West. Ultimately, he achieves his immortality through being reborn as the Sun itself. This emphasis on the setting Sun as a symbol of eternal life mirrors the placement of the Sun exactly at the Descendant or west point in Jung's natal horoscope, as he was born at sunset. Izdubar's 'Western Land', which, at the beginning of their dialogue, Jung rejects with his rational intellect, seems to correspond to the *Vis Plenum* of the *Systema* diagram. *Deus Sol* placed here in the diagram is not only a mythic representation of an archetypal spiritual renewal that can be found in a number of ancient cosmologies; it is also a specific portrayal of the Sun in Jung's own horoscope, and recreates in the imagery of a cosmological map the entire encounter with Izdubar in *Liber Novus*. The south point of the ecliptic, occupied at the top of the *Systema* painting by the solar Phanes Erikepaios and his accompanying six planetary gods, was viewed by the Neoplatonists as the 'gateway' through which every soul ascends to the spiritual realm. This ancient idea is reflected in the heavenly emphasis of this point in the *Systema*. But Jung seems to have also placed immense value on the west point in the *Systema* diagram, because it reflects *his* soul unfolding through a highly individual journey. Jung left no written interpretations

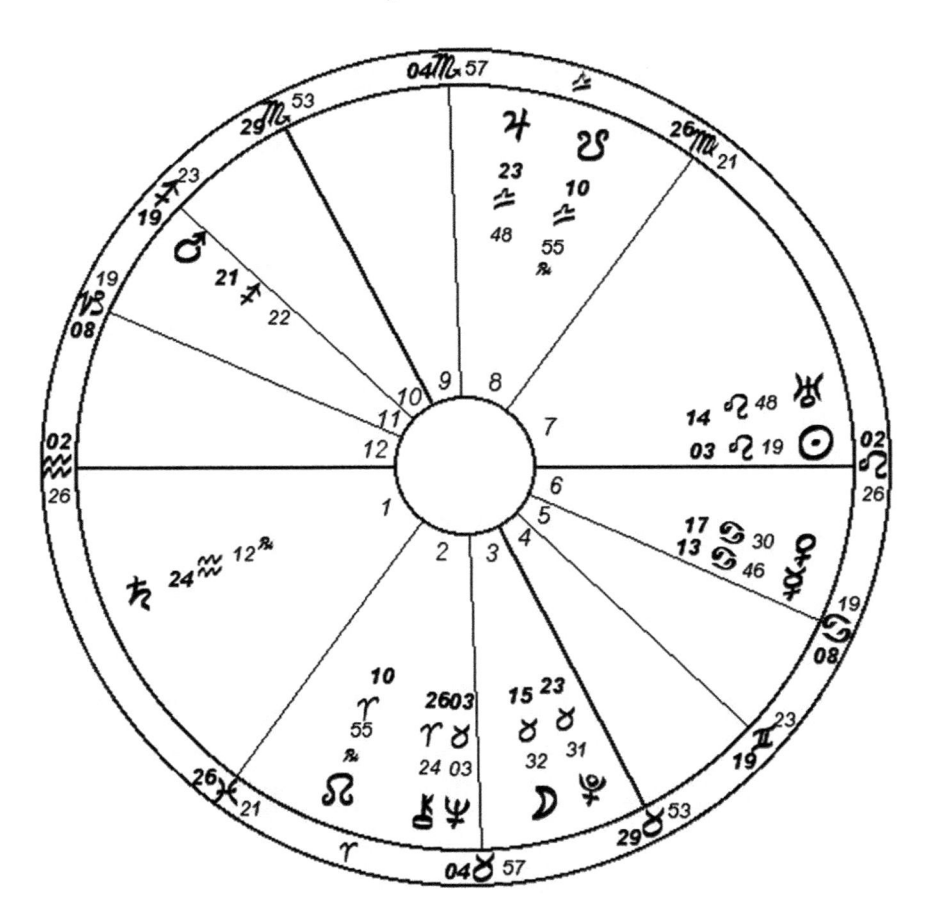

FIGURE 7.9 Horoscope of C.G. Jung

26 July 1875, 7.27 pm SZOT, Kesswil, Switzerland[83]

of his own chart, and it is not possible to know, except through hints and gener-
alisations, how he might have interpreted the placement of his natal Sun. But the
Systema diagram may contribute important insights into his understanding of his
own *Heimarmene*, which he believed was symbolised by the planetary configurations under which he was born.

The *Systema* cosmology focuses on the Sun as both a cosmic divinity and as
the 'divine spark': the Self embedded within the individual human psyche. This is
clear in the diagram from the small, microcosmic solar image at the centre of the
diagram, where all the macrocosmic opposites in all the hemispheres meet and
manifest in a unique way in an individual's 'differentiated' life. In the third sermon
of 'Scrutinies', Philemon informs Jung:

> Our very nature is differentiation. If we are not true to this nature we do
> not differentiate ourselves enough . . . Therefore we die to the same extent
> that we do not differentiate. Hence the creature's essence strives toward dif-
> ferentiation and struggles against primeval, perilous sameness. This is called
> the *principium individuationis*.[85]

In *Liber Novus*, Jung adjures the Serpent that is also his soul: 'Oh holy spirit, grant
me a spark of your eternal light'.[86] The idea of the spark is echoed in a statement by
Poseidonius, a Stoic and Platonic philosopher writing in the first century BCE, that
the human soul is a 'spark', or 'seed' of the 'intellectual fiery breath' of the cosmos.[87]
This fiery spark links *Deus Sol* in the *Systema* with Izdubar's fiery transformation in
Liber Novus. From a solar hero who contains the 'seed' of eternal light, he becomes
the eternal light itself. In the seventh sermon of 'Scrutinies', Philemon describes the
divine world as the macrocosmic form of the innermost divinity within the human
being, declaring:

> Man is a gateway, through which you pass from the outer world of Gods,
> daimons, and souls into the inner world, out of the greater into the smaller
> world . . . At immeasurable distance a lonely star stands in the zenith. This is
> the one God of this one man, this is his world, his Pleroma, his divinity . . .
> This star is the God and the goal of man. This is his lone guiding God, in
> him man goes to his rest, toward him goes the long journey of the soul after
> death, in him everything that man withdraws from the greater world shines
> resplendently. To this one God man shall pray . . . When the greater world
> turns cold, the star shines.[88]

In the second sermon of 'Scrutinies', the identity of this 'lone guiding God' has
already been revealed: 'We call God HELIOS or sun'.[89]

Jung's emphasis in *Liber Novus* on the divine spark within the individual seems
to have provided one of the chief elements in his idea of individuation, which on a
psychological level represents oneness or integration with the inner Self. In terms
of Jung's understanding of astrology, the chief astrological symbol for this inner

spark in the individual is the Sun in the horoscope. One of Alan Leo's great astrological innovations at the beginning of the twentieth century was his emphasis on the natal Sun, not only as the core of individual character, but also, in accord with Theosophical doctrines, as the symbol or vessel of the 'Central Spiritual Sun':[90] the macrocosm incarnating in the microcosmic human being. Leo understood the Sun in the horoscope as 'the vehicle through which the Solar Logos is manifesting': every human soul, he declared, echoing Poseidonius, is 'a Divine Fragment'.[91] This theme is reflected in Leo's interpretation of the solar glyph: the circle (the macrocosm of divinity) with a point at its centre (the microcosmic individual). Leo's mentor, Blavatsky, had in turn acquired many of her ideas about the Sun from the solar-centred pagan monotheism of late antiquity, and drew on such sources as Thomas Taylor's translation of the Emperor Julian's *Oration to the Sovereign Sun* to promulgate the idea, as Blavatsky put it, of the 'invisible' Sun as 'the origin and end of the incorruptible and eternal spirit'.[92] Given Jung's reliance on Leo's books when he began to develop his astrological knowledge, it seems that Leo's perspective, which fills the pages of *Liber Novus* and underpins the cosmology of the *Systema*, was enthusiastically welcomed as the mythic portrayal of a psychological reality.

Many of the discussions of astrological symbols found in the *Collected Works*, such as Jung's descriptions of the zodiacal signs of Leo (in which his natal Sun was placed) and Taurus (in which his natal Moon was placed), may be based, in part, on his understanding of his horoscope. It is difficult to discern which of these interpretations were rooted in his own observations combined with Alan Leo's writings, and which were derived from the models offered by astrological, alchemical, and late antique Hermetic and Neoplatonic texts. The themes Jung wove around the west point of the *Systema* diagram, and his encounter with Izdubar in *Liber Novus*, suggest that he perceived his natal Sun, setting at the west point of the horoscope, as a tremendous and irresistible drive toward discovery of, and entry into, the realm of the numinous, counterbalanced by an equally tremendous and irresistible drive toward the imprisoning darkness of his natal Saturn placed close to, and ruling, the Ascendant or east point of the horoscope.

Alan Leo commented that an emphasis on the west point in the birth horoscope – a factor that was stressed in the chart Van Ophuijsen produced for Jung – brings the individual 'more under the influence of fate':

> You will not stand alone and create your own destiny: for you are fated to always have someone either helping you or advising you. It may seem as though you had less free-will than others . . . but in reality it has a far more important meaning than this, for it means the merging of the Personality into the Individuality, whenever you are ready to realise the value of this surrender.[93]

Jung's preoccupation with astral fate, or *Heimarmene*, seems to be related to a chronic sense that his life was not entirely in his own hands. The 'someone' whom Leo described as helping or advising was often a human catalyst, such as Freud, Emma

Jung, Sabina Spielrein, or Toni Wolff. But sometimes the helpers were those figures whom Jung encountered in his visions, who personified archetypal potencies and whose orchestrator and leader was the figure of Philemon. The 'merging of the Personality into the Individuality', in Leo's Theosophical framework, refers to a union between the ordinary everyday personality and those mental and spiritual aspects of the individual receptive to the spark of divinity that uses the horoscope as its vessel in incarnation.[94] This in turn mirrors Jung's focus on psychological integration as the union of the conscious personality with the Self. Although Jung's concept of the Self was not fully developed until long after he had completed work on *Liber Novus*, a preliminary formulation of the idea appeared in 1916,[95] and Jung had already noted Plotinus' description of the soul's natural movement 'around something interior, around a centre'.[96] Some of the unique astrological features of the *Systema*, and also the idea of a union between ordinary and supraordinary dimensions of the personality, appear to be related directly to Leo's Theosophical cosmology, which was rooted in Blavatsky's borrowings from the Neoplatonists.

The second element in the *Systema* diagram that seems directly related to Jung's horoscope is Saturn, which is placed beside *Luna Satanas* at the east point of the diagram. Saturn in Jung's horoscope also lies near the east point, although it is just below it rather than above it; the planet was about to rise on the eastern horizon when Jung was born, in contrast to the Sun, which was setting in the west. Saturn is thus placed in a position of immense importance in Jung's natal chart, as John Thorburn pointed out in his interpretation. It is not only the 'Master of the House' by virtue of its rulership of the Ascendant, but it also occupies a place close to the Ascendant, in its own sign of Aquarius. All of Jung's many comments on Saturn, including its associations with the alchemical *nigredo* and the *prima materia*, tend to refer to darkness, although not necessarily to evil. The polarity of solar light, with its connotations of meaning, individuation, and immortality, and Saturnian darkness, with its connotations of constriction, suffering, and the limitations of mortality, seem to have dominated Jung's thinking and emotions when he created the *Systema Munditotius*. The struggle repeatedly described in *Liber Novus* as a battle between rational scientific thought and the realm of mystical vision is likewise reflected in this polarity of Saturn and the Sun, placed at opposite sides of Jung's horoscope as well as at opposite sides of the *Systema*.

Saturnian figures are involved in the most painfully restrictive themes in *Liber Novus*: the frightened Scholar who imprisons his Daughter; the dessicated Librarian who denigrates religious feeling; and the crassly insensitive Professor who incarcerates Jung in a psychiatric ward because he is a visionary. Philemon, Jung's inner 'guru' or psychopomp, is not a stereotypical Saturnian gaoler, but he too is frustrating and threatening in characteristic Saturnian fashion because his enigmatic responses to Jung's questions offer no room for the idea of freely given redemption or grace. Everything must be worked for, as Jung declares to him: 'You want your garden to bloom, and for everything to grow *from within itself*'. Yet the painful and restrictive archetypal potency known in astrology as Saturn contains within it, according to Jung's astrological thinking, an eternal spark of individual solar light and meaning, and constitutes Jung's personal daimon, the ruler of his natal horoscope, and the shape and colouring of his task and his fate.

These two important links between the *Systema* and Jung's horoscope suggest that, although the *Systema* diagram is a cosmological map in the ancient tradition and not a duplicate of Jung's horoscope in any literal way, it also reflects a deeply personal perception of horoscopic expression. It seems that Jung considered the two levels of the astrological cosmos – universal (the *Systema*) and personal (the natal horoscope) – as a unity, and they need to be explored together in order to gain insight into the particular ways in which Jung understood his planetary 'gods'. The chief potencies that dominate the planetary journey of *Liber Novus* as well as Jung's horoscope are the Saturnian Philemon, the *oikodespotes* or Master of the House, and Phanes, the 'shining one' who 'brings the Sun', represented in the *Systema* not only as a noetic cosmocrator, but also as Jung's personal *Deus Sol*.[97]

Jung's horoscope and *Aion*

The *Systema* may also provide insights into the ways in which Jung understood his 'task' in the context of the new Aion he believed to be dawning. That this cosmological map is, among other things, an image of the collective psyche of the new Aion is suggested by the presence of Phanes, rather than Jesus, as the governor of the cosmos, and by Abraxas, rather than Satan, as the *Dominus Mundi*. Like Max Heindel, Jung viewed the astrological Aions as a pair of opposing zodiacal constellations rather than as a single constellation,[98] and the great collective shift into a new God-image represented by the incoming Aion was symbolised not only by Aquarius, but also by the Aquarius-Leo polarity. With his natal Sun placed in Sun-ruled Leo – described by Jung in *Liber Novus* as his 'solar nature' – and Aquarius on the Ascendant, ruled by the planet he referred to as 'old Saturnus', Jung apparently perceived his individual character and destiny to be inextricably linked with, and mirrored macrocosmically by, the new religious images and currents that he identified as the manifestations of the new Aion.

In 1925, discussing the vision recorded in *Liber Novus* of his transformation into the crucified lion-headed being, Jung stated that he felt he was being 'put through' an initiation into the ancient mysteries:

> In this deification mystery you make yourself into the vessel, and are a vessel of creation in which the opposites reconcile.[99]

This lion-headed human figure who 'reconciles' the opposites is an image from the Mithraic mysteries, as Jung indicated in *Psychology of the Unconscious*, and he is also Saturn-Kronos, the 'demiurge and highest archon' known to the Gnostics as Ialdabaoth, who has a lion's face.[100] Jung's leontocephalus is an image of the polarity of Aquarius and Leo, the celestial Man and the celestial Lion conjoined and united: a kind of reversed image of the about-to-be-born 'rough beast' in Yeats' own prophetic poem about the changing of the Aions, *The Second Coming*, which has 'a shape with lion body and the head of a man'.[101]

Jung's leontocephalus seems to describe not only the new Aion, but a distillation and reconciliation of the primary zodiacal opposites of Jung's own horoscope. Alan Leo's definitions of Saturn-ruled Aquarius as 'Humanity', and Sun-ruled Leo as 'the Will' that allows 'the inner voice of the mind to speak',[102] together point to the idea that the fate of the collective rests on the shoulders of every individual who is conscious of inner realities. Jung firmly believed that 'if things go wrong in the world, this is because something is wrong with the individual, because something is wrong with me'.[103] Jung's painting of the 'Caster of Holy Water' reproduces this pairing in a different way: the youthful figure pouring water from the jug is Aquarian, but the solar disk behind his head is Leonine, as the Sun is the planetary ruler of Leo. As they are in the figure of Philemon and the paradoxical processes of the alchemical *opus*, the Sun and Saturn are once again conjoined.

It seems that Jung understood himself to be an individual 'vessel' for the polarity of the new Aion, and the work he pursued for his own integration was also work on behalf of a collective that he feared was already beginning to struggle blindly and destructively with the same dilemmas: the rediscovery of the soul; the acknowledgement of good and evil as inner potencies, and the terrible responsibility that comes with that acknowledgement; and the recognition of a central interior Self which alone can integrate the opposites. That Jung took his task very seriously, and felt he had failed in it as he moved toward the close of his life, is reflected in a letter he wrote to Eugene Rolfe in 1960:

> I have failed in my foremost task: to open people's eyes to the fact that man has a soul and there is a buried treasure in the field and that our religion and philosophy are in a lamentable state.[104]

Perceiving oneself as a vessel is not the same as attempting to found a solar cult, as Noll has claimed. Jung appears to have perceived not only himself, but all those individuals with whom he worked and all those who might be influenced by his ideas in the future, as potential vessels who could, through their individual efforts to achieve greater consciousness, help to facilitate the collective transition into an astrological Aion in which humans would be faced with the terrifying challenge of interiorising and integrating good and evil as inherent dimensions of a previously projected duality (the two opposing Piscean fishes). Attempting to define the nature of his psychology to Aniele Jaffé, Jung commented:

> The main interest of my work is not concerned with the treatment of neurosis, but rather with the approach to the numinous . . . The approach to the numinous is the real therapy.[105]

By the time he wrote *Aion*, Jung had managed to move beyond many of his inhibitions about discussing his 'secret knowledge', including the astrological dimensions of it, because he realised that 'it was my duty to communicate these thoughts'.[106] Jung produced *Aion* after he had nearly died after two dangerous heart attacks; and it seems that facing the possibility of his own demise rearranged his priorities, and he was less inclined to worry about whether the world would think ill of him if they discovered his involvement in astrology. *Aion* might even be seen as the closest Jung came to writing a book about astrology, although it is not an astrology of personal horoscopic interpretations. Lance Owens has suggested that *Aion* is the intellectual key to *Liber Novus*. It might also be suggested that *Aion* is the intellectual key to the *Systema Munditotius*, just as *Septem sermones* provides the visionary key to the *Systema*'s cosmology. *Aion* can provide a multitude of insights into how Jung understood his own role in the 'Way of What Is to Come'. Although *Aion* is, on the surface, primarily a psychological analysis of the astrological symbolism of the Piscean Aion and the meaning of the Fishes as a divided god-image, there are a number of references which suggest that the task of integrating the unresolved conflicts left behind by the opposition of the two Fishes lies in the hands of those individuals who are capable of recognising and doing something about it.

Jung did not specifically mention the zodiacal sign of Leo in *Aion*. But he made two revealing observations about the lion itself: it is a symbol of both the archangel Michael, who battles the forces of darkness in 'the shape of a lion',[107] and Christ as the Lion of Judah, the '*bellicose* lamb',[108] pointing to a connection with the solar warrior-hero Jung described extensively in *Psychology of the Unconscious*. He apparently understood his Leonine inner journey as a heroic task, like that of Izdubar. Any interior struggle with the problem of good and evil requires the strength, heart, and courage of the lion, and not simply an arsenal of intellectual theories, or a naively idealistic belief that kindness and good intentions, like the spirit portrayed in the musical *Hair* in the late 1960s, will conquer all. But although Leo the Lion is not mentioned in *Aion* as a specific zodiacal constellation, Jung had a good deal to say about both Aquarius and Saturn, its planetary lord. The collective problem of the union of opposites, in the Aquarian Aion, can be solved 'only by the individual human being'.[109] Thus, by implication, the Leonine dimension of the Aion, like the Aquarian, needs to be constellated within, to generate the necessary courage to carry the burden of individual consciousness that might, in turn, gradually exercise a transformative effect on the collective psyche of which the individual is a part. The paradoxical idea that it is only through the individual that the collective can be redeemed, and only through the collective that the individual can find meaning and the necessary sustenance to pursue the struggle of individuation, is central to Jung's understanding of the Aquarius-Leo polarity. Individuality and individualism are not identical; the former is a mutually fertile marriage of individual and collective, while the latter reflects a rebellion against the collective that secretly masks unconscious identification with it.

Saturn, as a planetary god, was for Jung synonymous with both the *prima materia* and the *lapis philosophorum*, the beginning and end of the alchemical *opus*. As his chart ruler, it seems that Jung believed Saturn's daimon demanded that he, as an individual, undertook the same task as had the alchemists, in search of that indestructible centre that could unite the opposites. Saturn's stone, which Jung painted in *Liber Novus*, is 'opaque and black' yet 'shining like a mirror', signifying 'the polarity and union of opposites'; it is a 'uniting symbol'.[110] Although Jung's only mention of Saturn in relation to his own horoscope appears in his letter to Upton Sinclair, every statement he made about this planet in *Aion* would have held a special personal significance for him. Although Saturn is a *maleficus* in medieval lore, nevertheless in *Aion* Jung highlighted the fact that, in earlier Egyptian texts, it was associated with the Sun-god.[111] His knowledge of his natal horoscope with its Leo-Aquarius polarity, and his interpretation of his chart ruler Saturn as a symbol of the uniting of the opposites, strongly suggest that he viewed the relationship between his natal horoscope and the archetypal dominants of the incoming new Aion as a clear statement of his individual life purpose.

Jung's analysis of the various religious changes and upheavals accompanying the turbulent progress of the developing god-image during the Piscean Aion expresses clearly his conviction that it is through individuals that such new and powerful ideas are first expressed. For example, the year 1239, according to Jung, was 'an epoch noted for its spiritual instability, revolutionary heresies and chiliastic expectations'. One of the most influential figures to announce the coming of a 'new age of the spirit' at this time was Joachim di Fiore (1135–1202), who 'took part in that great movement of the spirit', and who prophesied the imminent advent of the 'age of the Holy Ghost'.[112] Joachim, in Jung's view, was a man upon whom the fire of the 'living spirit' had descended; but Joachim was 'one of many', motivated by 'the urge of the archetype to realize itself'.[113] Among others receptive to the archetypal impetus of the time – roughly just past the midpoint of the Piscean Aion – Jung cited Albertus Magnus (1193–1280), Thomas Aquinas (1225–1274), Roger Bacon (1214–1294), and Meister Eckhart (1260–1327). Jung seems to have believed that he, like these important visionaries of the Piscean era, was similarly motivated by the 'urge of the archetype'; he too had experienced the fire of the living spirit, but in his case it was the spirit of the new Aquarian Aion, imagined in the form of Phanes rather than the Holy Ghost. The cosmology of the *Systema*, rooted in a perception of the astrological Aions as great collective expressions of a particular archetypal potency striving 'to realize itself', is both a map of the psychological dynamics of the new Aquarian epoch, and a representation of the goal that Jung believed himself to be destined to pursue, and as he understood it to be portrayed in his birth horoscope.

Notes

1 Plotinus, Ennead IV:2.1.
2 Jung, CW9i, ¶634.
3 Jung, *MDR*, p. 220. See also Jung, *Liber Novus*, pp. 206 and 364.
4 Jung, *Liber Novus*, p. 364.
5 Jung, *MDR*, p. 222–23. See also Jung, CW9i, p. 355, n. 1. The painting did not appear as the frontispiece to the first English edition of CW9i, published in 1959.
6 Image in Jung, *Liber Novus*, p. 363, © 2007 Foundation of the Works of C.G. Jung, Zürich, used by permission of W.W. Norton & Co., Inc.
7 For the Hereford *Mappa Mundi*, see P.D.A. Harvey, *Mappa Mundi* (London: British Library, 1996); Naomi Reed Kline, *Maps of Medieval Thought* (Woodbridge: Boydell Press, 2001).
8 See Robert Fludd, *Utriusque cosmi maioris scilicet et minoris metaphysica atque technica historia in duo volumina secundum cosmi differentiam diuisa*, 3 volumes (Oppenheim: Theodor de Bry, 1617–618), Vol. 1, p. 7, for the image titled *Integrae Naturae Speculum Artisque Imago*

('The Mirror of the Whole of Nature and the Image of Art'). Jung had an original edition of this work. For more on Fludd, see Joscelyn Godwin, *Robert Fludd* (Grand Rapids, MI: Phanes Press, 1991).

9 Jung, CW9i, ¶¶627–384. See also Jung, 'Mandalas', in Jung, CW9i, ¶¶713–18.

10 Jung, CW9i, ¶¶630 and 634.

11 The letter is not included in *C.G. Jung Letters* but is reproduced in Jung, *Liber Novus*, p. 364.

12 *Black Book* V, p. 169, reproduced in Jung, *Liber Novus*, p. 363.

13 Asheville Jung Center, Asheville, North Carolina, web-based seminar, *Window of the Soul*, 10 May 2012, with Murray Stein and Paul Brutsche.

14 Shamdasani, 'Introduction', in Jung, *Liber Novus*, p. 206.

15 Barry Jeromson, 'The Sources of *'Systema' Munditotius'*, Jung History 2:2 (2007), pp. 20–22.

16 Barry Jeromson, '*'Systema' Munditotius* and *Seven Sermons*', *Jung History* 1:2 (2005/6), pp. 6–10. <www.philemonfoundation.org/resources/jung_history/volume_1_issue_2>.

17 See Jung, *Liber Novus*, p. 364.

18 See Frank Robbins, 'A New Astrological Treatise', *Classical Philology* 22:1 (1927), p. 14. See also the discussion of Michigan Papyrus 149 in Wilhelm Gundel and Hans Georg Gundel, *Astrologumena* (Weisbaden: Steiner, 1966), pp. 25 and 36.

19 Firmicus Maternus, *Matheseos* II:14.

20 Auguste Bouché-Leclercq, *L'astrologie grecque* (Paris: Ernest Leroux, 1899), pp. 279–80. Jung possessed the original edition of this work.

21 Irenaeus, *Adversus haereses*, I:17.1. Jung's edition of Irenaeus was a Greek-to-Latin translation: *Irenaei episcopi lugdunensis contra omnes haereses*, ed. and trans. J.E. Grabe (Oxford, 1702). Jung also possessed a German translation: *Des heiligen Irenäus fünf Bücher gegen die Häresine*, 2 volumes (Munich: Josef Kösel, 1912).

22 For Jung's early references to the quaternity and the Pythagorean *tetraktys*, see Jung, CW6, ¶791 and n. 76. For later references to the quaternity, see, among a great many others, Jung, CW11, ¶¶243–85; Jung, CW12, ¶¶31, 150, 295, 469, 550; Jung, CW9ii, ¶¶188, 304, 406.

23 Jung, CW12, ¶314 and Plate 100.

24 Jung, CW12, ¶313.

25 Jung, CW9ii, ¶410.

26 For the Pleroma in Platonism, see John M. Dillon, 'Pleroma and Gnostic Cosmos', in Richard T. Wallis and Jay Bregman (eds.), *Neoplatonism and Gnosticism* (Albany: SUNY Press, 1992), pp. 99–110. For the Pleroma in Christian sources, see Paul, Colossians 2:9; Elaine Pagels, *The Gnostic Paul* (London: Continuum, 1992), pp. 53–94, 137–40; Paul Carus, *The Pleroma* (Chicago: Open Court, 1909). For the Pleroma in Gnostic literature, see, among others, Jonas, *The Gnostic Religion*, p. 180. For the concept in modern philosophy, see Werner Hamacher, *Pleroma*, trans. Nicholas Walker and Simon Jarvis (Stanford, CA: Stanford University Press, 1998), p. 92.

27 Mead, *Fragments of a Faith Forgotten*, p. 342.

28 Jung, *Liber Novus*, p. 370.

29 Jung, *Liber Novus*, p. 347.

30 For Jung's references to the term in the *Collected Works*, see, among many others, Jung, CW9i, ¶533; Jung, CW9ii, ¶¶75, 80, 120, 344; Jung, CW11, ¶¶620, 629, 675, 733, 748.

31 The term 'Pleroma' is not used in Christian cosmological maps, but its presence is indicated by the divine and angelic realms that lie beyond those of the planets and fixed stars.

32 Although Leo did not use the term, Blavatsky, on whose work Leo depended, discussed the Pleroma in a Gnostic context in her commentary on the first publication of Mead's translation of *Pistis Sophia*; see *Lucifer* 6:33 (1890), pp. 230–39. See also Blavatsky, *The Secret Doctrine*, 2:160, where she refers to it as 'the synthesis or entirety of all the spiritual entities'.

33 Jung, *Liber Novus*, p. 370.

34 'Erikapaios' is also spelled 'Erikapaios'; see Cook, *Zeus*, Vol. 2 Part 2, p. 1327. Jung preferred the latter spelling.

35 The importance in late antiquity of the celestial heptad and the correspondences between the seven planets, the seven vowels of the Greek alphabet, the seven notes of the musical scale, the seven metals, and the seven colours of the spectrum is emphasised in Dieterich, *Abraxas*, p. 47. Jung relied heavily on this work for many elements in the 'Systema' cosmology.

36 See, for example, a gold *aureus* minted during the reign of the emperor Domitian, with a child seated on a celestial globe flanked by seven stars (British Museum RIC209a); a green jasper amulet of Abraxas shown with seven stars, British Museum G575; a haematite amulet of a lion with seven stars, British Museum G239; a bronze amulet of Hekate and Abraxas with seven stars, British Museum G137. See also Nos. 23 and 31 in Campbell Bonner, *Studies in Magical Amulets, Chiefly Graeco-Egyptian* (Ann Arbor: University of Michigan Press, 1950), pp. 326 and 328. On amulets dedicated to a goddess, the Sun as the dominant deity is sometimes replaced by the Moon, shown as a crescent with seven stars; see, for example, a *denarius* of Julia Domna, British Museum RSC173, with the crescent Moon beneath seven stars. Sometimes the rayed head of Helios or Sol is shown on one side of a coin, with the crescent of the Moon and the seven stars on the reverse.

37 Jung, *Psychology of the Unconscious*, p. 542, n. 7.

38 Porphyry, *De antro nympharum*, 11, in Thomas Taylor (trans.), *Select Works of Porphyry* (London: Thomas Rodd, 1823), pp. 186–89.

39 Ambrosius Aurelius Theodosius Macrobius, *In Somnium Scipionis*, in D. Nisard (ed. and trans.), *Macrobe, Varron et Pomponius Méla* (Paris: Dubochet, Le Chevalier, and Ganier, 1883). This Latin-French bilingual edition seems to be the one Jung used. For an English translation, see William Harris Stahl (trans.), *Commentary on the Dream of Scipio by Macrobius* (New York: Columbia University Press, 1952).

40 Jung, *Dream Interpretation, Ancient and Modern*, p. 9.

41 Illustration of a late antique gemstone showing the lion-headed serpent Chnoumis, private collection; illustration from 'The Worship of Priapus' by Richard Payne Knight (London: Dilettanti Society, 1786), © Bridgeman Images.

42 King, *The Gnostics and Their Remains*, Figure 2, p. 41 with description on p. 432, and Plate 15, p. 340 with description on p. 434. The second reference is to a chalcedony amulet in the British Museum Collection inscribed with the image of the lion-headed serpent and the phrase, 'I am Chnoumis, Sun of the Universe'. King refers to both as the 'Agathodaemon Serpent'.

43 King, *The Gnostics and Their Remains*, p. 178. For Jung's many references to the Agathodaimon Serpent, see, among others, Jung, CW5, ¶¶410, 580, 593, and Fig. 37, ¶¶594; Jung, CW9i, ¶¶560; Jung, CW9ii, ¶¶291–93, 366, 385.

44 For this engraving and its similarity to the background of Jung's painting of Izdubar, see Chapter 2.

45 Chnoumis is usually shown with a crown of seven rays, or with a circle of seven stars surrounding him. In the amulet shown above, he has twelve rays, probably representing the twelve zodiacal signs, and seven eggs emerging from his mouth.

46 This description of Eros first appears in Plato's Symposium, where he is described as 'a great daimon': Plato, *Symposium,* 202d.

47 Jung, *Liber Novus*, p. 351.

48 Jung, CW7, ¶¶32–33.

49 For modern scholarly discussions of Eros as a 'great daimon', see, among others, Steven Berg, *Eros and the Intoxications of Enlightenment* (Albany: SUNY Press, 2010), pp. 95–130; Diskin Clay, *Platonic Questions* (University Park: Penn State University Press, 2000), pp. 66–68.

50 Jung, *Psychology of the Unconscious*, p. 494, n. 27. See also Jung, *MDR*, p. 387, where he describes Eros as 'a *kosmogonos*, a creator and father-mother of all consciousness'.

51 For the history of the *menorah*, see Rahel Hakili, *The Menorah, The Ancient Seven-Armed Candelabrum* (Leiden: Brill, 2001), pp. 204–9. For Jung's references to Philo during the period he worked on the diagram of the "Systema", see Jung, *Psychology of the*

Unconscious, pp. 315, 492 n. 8, 537 n. 18, and 550 n. 99. Jung's editions of Philo's works were in Latin: Philo Alexandrinus, *Opera quae supersunt*, ed. Leopold Cohn and Paul Wendland, Vol. 3–6 (Berlin: Walter de Gruyter, 1898–1915), and a rare sixteenth-century edition titled *Philonis Iudaei, scriptoris eloquentissimi, ac philosophi summi, lucubrationes omnes quotquot haberi potuerunt: cuius opera uterque est integritati restitutus* (Basel: Sigmund Gelen, 1561).

52 Philo, *On the Life of Moses*, II:102–105.

53 For the esoteric meaning of the *menorah* in the Jewish Kabbalah and its Christian derivations, see Ilia M. Rodov, *The Torah Ark in Renaissance Poland* (Leiden: Brill, 2013), pp. 185–87; Moshe Idel, 'The Throne and the Seven-Branched Candlestick', *Journal of the Warburg and Courtauld Institutes* 40 (1977), pp. 290–92; Moshe Idel, 'Binah, the Eighth Sefirah', in *In the Light of the Menorah*, Israel Museum Exhibition Catalogue, ed. I. Fishof (Jerusalem, 1999), pp. 142–46.

54 See Daniel Matt, 'Introduction', in *Zohar: The Book of Enlightenment*, ed. Daniel Chanan Matt (Mahwah, NJ: Paulist Press, 1983), p. 36; Eva Frojmovic, *Imagining the Self, Imagining the Other* (Leiden: Brill, 2002), p. 63.

55 Jung, *Liber Novus*, p. 351.

56 In a discussion with his Soul in *Black Book* 6, Jung was asked how many 'lights' he wanted, three or seven; Jung replied that he 'would like seven lights', apparently preferring the astrological heptad to the trinity. See Jung, *Liber Novus*, p. 354, n. 125.

57 For Apollo as 'Lord of Mice', see Andrew Lang, *Custom and Myth* (London: Longmans, Green, 1884), pp. 103–120; Theodorakis, 'Apollo of the Wolf, the Mouse and the Serpent'.

58 Jung, *Liber Novus*, p. 29.

59 Jung, *Liber Novus*, p. 274.

60 *Deus monas* – the 'solitary god' – appears to be a hybrid term combining Latin (*deus* = god) and Greek (*monas* = solitary). The word *monas* was used by John Dee – another author with whom Jung was familiar – to describe a figure he invented in 1564, the 'Monas Hieroglyphica', which combines the planetary glyphs for the Sun, Moon, Mercury, Venus, and the alchemical symbols of the four elements. For Dee's own explanation, see John Dee, *The Hieroglyphic Monad*, trans. C.H. Josten, *Ambix* 12 (1964), pp. 84–221. Jung had an earlier English translation of this work: John Dee, *Monas Hieroglyphica*, trans. J.W. Hamilton-Jones (London: Watkins, 1947).

61 *Apolcaypse of John* (*Revelation*), 4:5.

62 Jung, *Liber Novus*, p. 351.

63 Jung, *Liber Novus*, p. 370, citing *Black Book* 5.

64 Jung, CW14, ¶467–68.

65 Jung, CW13, ¶183.

66 Plato, *Symposium*, 180d–e.

67 Plato, *Timaeus*, 36b.

68 Jung, *Liber Novus*, p. 370.

69 Leo, *How to Judge a Nativity*, pp. 36–37.

70 Leo, *How to Judge a Nativity*, p. 37.

71 Heindel, *Message of the Stars*, pp. 32 and 45.

72 Heindel, *Message of the Stars*, p. 46.

73 See Greene, *Jung's Studies in Astrology*, chapter 2.

74 For Jung's understanding of the unstable receptivity of the trance medium and its relationship with hysteria, see Jung, CW1, ¶¶45–48, 54–60; Jung, CW18, ¶¶697–740, 746–56.

75 See Jung, *MDR*, pp. 215–16, for the bizarre events accompanying the writing of Philemon's 'sermons'.

76 Leo, *The Key to Your Own Nativity*, p. 96.

77 *Freud-Jung Letters*, 255F, p. 422.

78 Leo, *The Key to Your Own Nativity*, p. 137.

79 Emma Jung published two works of her own: *Die Graalslegend in psychologischer Sicht*, co-authored with Marie-Louise von Franz (Zürich: Walter Verlag, 1960), and *Anima and Animus* (New York: Analytical Psychology Club of New York, 1957; originally published separately as *Wirklichkeit der Seele* (Zürich: Psychologische Abhandlungen 4, 1934) and *Die Anima als Naturwesen* (Zürich: Rascher, 1955).

80 According to a personal communication from Gerhard Adler (1904–1988), co-editor of the *Collected Works* and editor of the *C.G. Jung Letters*, who worked with Jung from 1932 until Jung's death in 1961, Toni Wolff was well-versed in astrology and could interpret horoscopes.

81 Jung, *Psychology of the Unconscious*, pp. 99, 105. See Betegh, *The Derveni Papyrus*, Col. 13, where the author states that Orpheus likened the Sun to a phallus.

82 Leo, *The Key to Your Own Nativity*, p. 143.

83 Computer-generated horoscope calculated by Io Edition programme, Time Cycles Research, http:www.timecycles.com.

84 Jung, *Liber Novus*, p. 347.

85 Jung, *Liber Novus*, p. 329.

86 Poseidonius, *The Fragments*, Vol. 1, ed. L. Edelstein and I.G. Kidd (Cambridge: Cambridge University Press, 1972), Frag. 101, p. 104.

87 Jung, *Liber Novus*, p. 349.

88 Jung, *Liber Novus*, p. 349.

89 See Nicholas Campion, *A History of Western Astrology, Vol. 2* (London: Continuum, 2009), p. 232.

90 Leo, *How to Judge a Nativity*, p. 29; Leo, *The Art of Synthesis*, p. 1.

91 Blavatsky, *Isis Unveiled*, I:302. For Blavatsky's acknowledgement of Taylor, see Blavatsky, *Isis Unveiled*, I:284, 288, and II:108–9; Blavatsky, *The Secret Doctrine,* I:425, 453, and II:599. For Taylor's translation of Julian, see *The Emperor Julian's Oration to the Sovereign Sun*, in Thomas Taylor, *Collected Writings on the Gods and the World* (Frome: Prometheus Trust, 1994 [London: Edward Jeffrey, 1793]), pp. 51–76.

92 Leo, *The Key to Your Own Nativity*, pp. 161–62.

93 For Leo's distinction 'Personality' and 'Individuality', see Leo, *Esoteric Astrology*, pp. 58–62.

94 See Jung, 'The Structure of the Unconscious', in Jung, CW7, ¶¶442–521. See also the editors' note in Jung, CW6, ¶183, n. 85.

95 Plotinus, Ennead VI; see Greene, *Jung's Studies in Astrology*, chapter 4.

96 In the view of Neoplatonic writers such as Porphyry, Saturn and the Sun would have been considered the primary significators of Jung's natal horoscope, as both are dignified through placement in their own 'domiciles', both are strengthened by their positions on or near one of the four cardinal points of the horoscope, and both are 'dispositors' that ultimately preside over the signs in which all the other planets are placed.

97 For Heindel's and Jung's proclivity to view signs as a pair of opposites, see Greene, Jung's *Studies in Astrology*, Chapter 6.

98 Jung, *Analytical Psychology*, p. 99. See Shamdasani's n. 211 in Jung, *Liber Novus*, p. 252.

99 Jung, CW9ii, ¶128.

100 William Butler Yeats, *The Second Coming* (1919), in *Collected Poems of William Butler Yeats* (London: Macmillan, 1933), p. 211.

101 Leo, *Esoteric Astrology,* p. 73.

102 Jung, CW10, ¶329.

103 C.G Jung, Letter to Eugene Rolfe, in Eugene Rolf, *Encounter with Jung* (Boston: Sigo Press, 1989), p. 158.

104 Aniela Jaffé, *Was C.G. Jung a Mystic?* (Einsiedeln: Daimon Verlag, 1989), p. 16.

105 Cited in Margaret Ostrowski-Sachs, *From Conversations with C.G. Jung* (Zürich: Juris Druck & Verlag, 1971), p. 68.

106 Jung, CW9ii, ¶128.

107 Jung, CW9ii, ¶167.

108 Jung, CW9ii, ¶142.

109 Jung, CW9ii, ¶¶213 and 216.
110 Jung, CW9ii, 129.
111 Jung, CW9ii, ¶¶140 and 137.
112 Jung, CW9ii, ¶142.

CONCLUSION

θεος εγενου εξ ανθρωπου.
Out of a human, you will become a god.[1]

—Orphic funerary tablet

Man becomes through the *principium individuationis*. He strives for absolute individuality . . . Through this he makes the Pleroma the point that contains the
greatest tension and is itself a shining star, immeasurably small, just as the Pleroma is immeasurably great. The more concentrated the Pleroma becomes, the
stronger the star of the individual becomes. It is surrounded by shining clouds, a
heavenly body in the making, comparable to a small sun. It emits fire. Therefore
it is called: εγω (ειμι) συμπλανος υμιν αστηρ Just like the sun, which is also
such a star, which is a God and grandfather of souls, the star of the individual is
also like the sun, a God and grandfather of souls . . . Whoever does not follow
the *principium individuationis* to its end becomes no God, since he cannot bear
individuality.[2]

—C.G. Jung

Liber Novus and the *Hypnerotomachia*

The meandering pathways of *Liber Novus*, distilled from the *Black Books* in which
Jung initially recorded his inner experiences, portray a journey that bears close
parallels with the ancient mythic narrative of the celestial ascent of the soul. Jung's
direction, however, was not upward toward a *unio mystica* with an ineffable, transcendent godhead, but rather, inward and often down, through a circuitous process
he referred to as individuation, always moving toward a mysterious interior core,
both personal and transpersonal, which he later called the Self. Like Theseus navi-
gating the dark passages of King Minos' labyrinth – a word which Jung himself
used to describe the twists and turns of his chaotic visions[3] – he needed a golden

Ariadne's thread to guide him. During his work on *Liber Novus*, this thread was woven from many fibres. Among these, the astrological symbols and narratives that, in his view, reflected archetypal patterns known in earlier epochs as planetary gods or daimons, comprised a major part. Later in his life, alchemy provided him with another, equally resonant narrative that seemed to present a recognisable map of the journey of individuation. But he never lost his sense of the importance of astrological symbolism, which he viewed as inextricably bound with the alchemical *opus*: 'Alchemy is inconceivable without the influence of her elder sister astrology'.[4]

The late antique world of Neoplatonic, Gnostic, Hermetic, Jewish, Orphic, and Mithraic literature was not the only source from which Jung drew inspiration. Any medieval or Renaissance text describing the archetypal soul-journey, whether planetary or alchemical, was likewise relevant to his understanding of the individuation process. Commenting on the soul-journey described in a late fifteenth-century work called *Hypnerotomachia Poliphili* and attributed to Francesco Colonna, Jung noted that the author had created a psychological document that is 'a perfect example of the course and the symbolism of the individuation process'.[5] One of the most obvious literary parallels for the soul-journey of *Liber Novus* – and for many other artistic works that followed its completion in 1320 – is Dante's *Divina Commedia*. Linda Fierz-David, in her commentary on Colonna's enigmatic work, states that the *Commedia* had provided the basic structure for the *Hypnerotomachia*.[6] Planetary symbolism was endemic to the world-view of Dante's time, and is reflected in the *Commedia* in the specific themes and symbols of the seven spheres of heaven and the seven spheres of hell. Jung had a high regard for the *Commedia* as an example of a 'visionary' artistic work that allows 'a glimpse into the unfathomable abyss of the unborn and of things yet to be'.[7] He also viewed Dante's imaginal guide, the Roman poet Virgil, as a psychopomp similar to his own Philemon. But there is an important difference between this great medieval work and *Liber Novus* that suggests that Jung was thinking more of Colonna than of Dante as he developed and refined his material.

This difference lies largely in Dante's espousal of a strictly Christian religious agenda, portrayed within a strictly Aristotelian cosmology. Fierz-David suggests that, in Dante's vision, 'the world is graded in heights and depths according to a precise and purely medieval hierarchy'.[8] The hierarchy encompasses the seven planetary spheres and the eighth sphere of the fixed stars, beyond which lies the ninth sphere of the *Primum Mobile* or 'Unmoved Mover' of the universe.[9] Although it might seem that Dante's ninth sphere finds a faint echo in the Pleroma of Jung's *Systema* diagram, and the eighth sphere of the fixed stars might appear to parallel the domain of Phanes Erikepaios and his star-gods, there was no place in Dante's Christian vision of Paradise for planetary daimons, nor for an androgynous Orphic-Mithraic primal divinity, especially one with a lion's head. And Jung's Pleroma, unlike Dante's 'Unmoved Mover', is both nothing and everything, as Philemon informs him: a womb and matrix that is one with its emanations, rather than a transcendent creator-god operating the levers of a clockwork universe.

> It is nothingness that is whole and continuous throughout. Only figuratively, therefore, do I speak of creation as part of the Pleroma. Because, actually, the

Pleroma is nowhere divided, since it is nothingness. We are also the whole Pleroma, because, figuratively, the Pleroma is the smallest point in us, merely assumed, not existing, and the boundless firmament about us. But why then do we speak of the Pleroma at all, if it is everything and nothing![10]

In Dante's *Paradiso*, the ancient planetary gods have been transformed into blessed abodes for those saints who embody the traditional virtues of the planets: in Jupiter's sphere, for example, Dante encounters souls conspicuous for their justice during life, and in Saturn's sphere, he meets those who have passed their lives in holy contemplation.[11] Jung never attempted to structure *Liber Novus* in such a deliberate way, or impose a conventional religious world-view on it; nor did he attempt to deny or diffuse the potency and autonomy of the planetary daimons. Instead, he honoured the fluid twists and turns of his visions even through the 'layers' he later applied to clarify the original spontaneous text. And on Jung's soul-journey in *Liber Novus*, no Virgil arrived to lead the way. His only guides through most of his encounters – with the exception of Philemon's teachings in 'Scrutinies', and perhaps the insights and companionship of Toni Wolff – were the precarious grip of his rational consciousness on the visions that at times threatened to overwhelm him, and the containment provided by his talismanic paintings with their *sunthemata*.

Colonna's *Hypnerotomachia* seems to have held a great fascination for Jung during the time he worked on *Liber Novus*, perhaps because it was so impenetrably enigmatic, so strangely similar to his own visions, and so deliciously free of the medieval Christian doctrines in which the *Divina Commedia* is embedded. The culmination of the planetary journey, for Colonna, is not a vision of the radiant sphere of the *Primum Mobile* beyond the realm of the fixed stars, but rather, a *hierosgamos* or sacred marriage that occurs amidst the voluptuous splendours of the Isle of Kithaira, the abode of the goddess Venus. Jung was still unaware of the significance of the alchemical references in the *Hypnerotomachia* when he first read it in a French translation some time before 1922,[12] and he stated many years later that in this work, he had 'sensed, rather than recognized, more and more things I was later to encounter in my study of alchemy'.[13] But he knew that the book was important, and he even questioned whether it had in fact been the first stimulus for his later involvement with alchemical symbolism: 'Indeed, I cannot even say how far it was this book which put me on the track of alchemy'. Like the stages of the alchemical *opus*, and the planetary ascent of the soul in Hermetic, Gnostic, and Neoplatonic texts, Jung compared the *Hypnerotomachia* with the individuation process, and placed it, along with the *Divina Commedia*, Goethe's *Faust*, and the paintings and poetry of William Blake, in that category he called 'the visionary mode of artistic creation'. He also came to view the *Hypnerotomachia*, like other alchemical works of the Renaissance period, as a compensation for the crystallised medieval Christian outlook of the collective psyche.[14] Something similar could be said of *Liber Novus* in relation to the world of northern European Protestantism in the early twentieth century. Evidently Colonna, like Joachim di Fiore, was one those through whom 'the urge of the archetype' was attempting to realise itself against the increasingly oppressive 'Spirit of This Time'. According to Jung, the 'visionary' type of creative work

> derives its existence from the hinterland of man's mind, as if it had emerged from the abyss of prehuman ages, or from a superhuman world of contrasting light and darkness . . . Sublime, pregnant with meaning, yet chilling the blood with its strangeness, it arises from timeless depths: glamorous, daemonic, and grotesque.[15]

The same might apply to *Liber Novus*, in which Jung was still engrossed when he made this statement in 1930.[16]

Poliphilo, the protagonist of the *Hypnerotomachia*, pursues his labyrinthine wanderings 'with fearful wonderment',[17] for, like Jung, he has no guide. The complex structure of the first part of the text, in which Poliphilo's various encounters include not only human and divine beings, but also architectural and natural landscape features such as streams, ruins, and fountains, is echoed in tone, although not in precise content, by many of Jung's descriptions in *Liber Novus*, in which landscape features form part of the symbolic dimensions of each of the characters. Joscelyn Godwin, in his introduction to the only complete English translation of the *Hypnerotomachia*, refers to its 'unapologetic paganism' and suggests that it is like the bible of a 'heretic religion', mixing Christian motifs with the images of pagan antiquity.[18] Jung understood the book, like his own visions, to have both a 'personal and superpersonal character'.[19] It is likely that he saw his own enigmatic work reflected in this obscure Renaissance artefact. His comment on the visionary type of art – that its essence is 'not to be found in the personal idiosyncrasies that creep into it . . . but in its rising above the personal and speaking from the mind and heart of the artist to the mind and heart of mankind' – perhaps describes what he hoped his own efforts would achieve.[20]

Colonna's work is riddled with astrological references that are far more explicit than those in *Liber Novus*; but Italian Renaissance culture in the late fifteenth century was steeped in astrology, and Colonna's planetary encounters needed no disguise to protect him from the ridicule of his colleagues. As Poliphilo begins his dream-journey after a tormented and sleepless night, he describes the dawn sky, in which

> Boastful Orion was ceasing to pursue the seven weeping sisters [the Pleiades] who adorn the shoulder of the Bull [Taurus].[21]

Jung was deeply interested in these astrological references. He interpreted the *hierosgamos* of Poliphilo with his beloved Polia as 'the union with the soul, the latter embodying the world of the gods' – precisely the kind of transformative experience that Iamblichus' theurgy was intended to achieve – and noted later that not only does Poliphilo's *hierosgamos* take place in the month of May, but that the glyph of Taurus itself portrays a *coniunctio*.

> Taurus, the zodiacal sign of May, is the House of Venus. In the Greek–Egyptian zodiac the bull carries the sun-disk, which rests in the sickle moon (the ship of Venus), an image of the coniunctio. The Taurus sign is composed of the sun-disk with the moon's horns: b. Cf. the alchemical parallel in Dee, 'Monas hieroglyphica'.[22]

The opening of the *Hypnerotomachia* refers to Taurus through Poliphilo's sighting in the dawn sky of the Pleiades, a group of seven stars in the constellation of the Bull. It is clear from the beginning of the work that Poliphilo's soul-journey will be ruled by the planetary daimon of Venus, in the same way that Jung's journey in *Liber Novus*, from the very first image onward, will be ruled by 'The Way of What Is to Come': the transition into the Aion of Aquarius, ruled by the planetary daimon of Saturn.

Like Jung, Colonna included a great number of images to illustrate the important encounters of his journey, although they are engravings rather than paintings. Jung used one of these engravings, an image of Venus as 'Mother of All Living', in *Symbols of Transformation*, the revised version of *Psychology of the Unconscious*, although the engraving did not appear in the earlier version of the work because he had not yet encountered the *Hypnerotomachia* when he first wrote it.[23] Some of Colonna's engravings display the same kind of unabashed eroticism as do many alchemical images, such as those of the *Rosarium Philosophorum* which Jung used as an example to illustrate the psychology of the transference.[24] Each of Colonna's engravings also contains specific *sunthemata*. For example, Poliphilo encounters an altar of the goat-god Priapus (a stand-in for Pan) in the realm of Queen Eleuterilida ('child of freedom'), whose palace walls are adorned by the names of the seven planets, and whose throne is placed under the Sun. Colonna's engraving portrays this goat-god carrying a scythe, which, as Fierz-David notes in her commentary, is one of the traditional attributes of Saturn.[25] The juxtaposition of a solar ruler whose name implies freedom or free will with a Saturnian goat-god is strangely echoed in Jung's blendings of solar and Saturnian symbolism in *Liber Novus*.

Colonna's engravings also often include numerological references (usually seven, connoting the seven planets, or four, connoting the four elements, or twelve, connoting the twelve signs of the zodiac) that hint at an astrological journey. The engraving of the plan of the Island of Kithaira, the abode of Venus, is an example of this characteristic type of alchemical-astrological numerology: numerous staircases lead to various gardens, porticoes, and colonnades, and every one of these staircases has seven steps. Like Jung, Colonna peppered his text with names written in the Greek alphabet, and his elaborately designed *schema* of the Isle of Kithaira, like Jung's *Systema*, suggests both cosmological and highly individual dimensions of a single soul-journey. Colonna's labyrinthine passage to the centre does not, however, arrive at a 'central spiritual Sun', nor at the integrated solar Self, a union of Phanes and Abraxas, that lies at the centre of Jung's *Systema* diagram. Instead, it culminates in an erotic *coniunctio* that reflects Venus rather than Saturn as the planetary lord of the journey. It appears that Colonna, like Jung, paid no heed to any traditional planetary order, but described his own intensely individual process of integration in his visionary work. Colonna's birth date is not known, but it seems likely that in his horoscope the 'Master of the House' was in fact a Mistress.

The similarities between *Liber Novus* and the *Hypnerotomachia* do not imply that Jung was trying to model his own work on Colonna's. During the time he worked on *Liber Novus*, Jung had access to many cosmological maps, from medieval *mappae mundi* through Renaissance models of the universe to Tibetan mandalas, and many descriptions of the celestial soul-journey, from ancient versions such as Plato's 'Myth of Er' in the *Republic* to the Theosophical writings of the early twentieth century. It is unlikely that Jung was attempting to mimic Colonna's journey or, for that matter, anyone else's. Apart from the genuine spontaneity of his initial visions, Jung was far too aware of the dangers of attempting to compress the symbols of the imaginal world into a specific intellectual system; rather, he understood his task to be a respectful refining of material emerging directly from the unconscious, without any imposition of an *a priori* structure. The hermeneutics that he applied were meant to clarify rather than codify, and the ideas emerged from the images, rather than the images from the ideas. Amplifying his visions with astrological symbols deepened Jung's understanding, but did not restrict the outpourings of his imagination to a particular preconceived design. But the *Hypnerotomachia*, like the soul-journeys of the Gnostics, Hermeticists, and Neoplatonists, seems to have held an extraordinary significance for Jung, because he believed it mirrored the ancient planetary journey of the soul in a highly personal form, which in turn reflected his own understanding of an archetypal psychological process that was both personal and universal.

Jung's planetary soul-journey

Since Jung, according to his own statements, viewed the natal horoscope as a map of the individual psyche, it is not surprising that he was prepared to work imaginally with the astrological symbols and their accompanying imagery as *sunthemata* in a theurgic process, akin to the alchemical work with the planetary metals, but as interior images rather than projections onto material substances. While spontaneous dream imagery often yielded creative results, the invocation and interpretation of specific archetypal figures through the use of astrological symbols seems to have provided Jung with a direct route into the underlying patterns of the *mundus imaginalis*: that intermediary zone that Iamblichus understood to be the sacred ground where divine and human could meet, and where the intense conflict and suffering that Jung experienced during the period following his break with Freud could be confronted in a way that generated a fruitful dialogue between conscious aspiration and unconscious compulsion. The most important figures of *Liber Novus* are strongly coloured by the astrological associations that are directly relevant to Jung's natal horoscope. And although the goal of his efforts might have been a healing of his own conflicts through an integration of the warring elements of his personality, Jung never ceased to seek a more universally applicable psychological understanding of what he experienced. This understanding, rooted as much in astrology and its 'younger sister' alchemy as in the psychiatric models developing at the time, formed the basis for the body of work that is now known as analytical psychology.

The consistent theme of the planetary soul-journey underpins virtually all of Jung's sources, from the Orphic, Neoplatonic, Hermetic, and Gnostic currents of antiquity, through the alchemical, magical, and Kabbalistic speculations of the Middle Ages, the Renaissance, and the early modern period, to the occult revival of the late nineteenth century and the early years of dynamic psychology, whose left hand was quietly but firmly immersed in the waters of German Romanticism, mesmerism, scrying, spiritualism, ritual magic, and oracular Theosophical pronouncements on the destiny of the soul. In all these sources, the human imagination is valorised as a gateway, and in them Jung believed he had found parallels for his ideas about the nature and teleology of the human psyche. The earlier currents were expressed in religious language, but were understood by Jung to be profoundly psychological in the sense that he utilised the term: they concerned themselves with the 'Spirit of the Depths' and its relationship with the interior dimensions of human life, and with the teleology of the microcosmic human being within the macrocosmic whole of the 'objective psyche'. They were focused on inner experience rather than literal dogma; on transformation and integration rather than sublimation or obedience to a prevailing authority, scientific or religious; and on individual responsibility rather than collective blame or an external and irrevocable fate. The bleak figure of the Tramp in *Liber Novus* emerges as one of Jung's most poignant portrayals of the aridity of a life lived without meaning, devoid of any connection to an inner centre that might provide a sense of participation in a larger, interconnected whole.

In *Liber Novus*, Jung utilised astrological imagery as both a structure to contain the chaotic nature of his visions and a form of hermeneutics that allowed him greater insight into the internal processes that the visions portrayed. He was convinced that all human beings, from time immemorial, have possessed a kind of unconscious knowledge of astrology as an intuitive perception of the qualities of time. Referring to a patient's painting in one of his Tavistock lectures, given in 1935, he noted that, in the painting,

> He also gathers in the stars. That means that the cosmos, his world, is collected into the picture. It is an allusion to the unconscious astrology which is in our bones, though we are unaware of it.[26]

As a self-avowed thinking-intuitive type, Jung was driven by what he called 'a passionate urge toward understanding';[27] it was not enough for him to simply pass through the fire and emerge safely on the other side, with his work, his marriage, and his sanity intact. *Liber Novus* might justifiably be viewed as a work of art, sufficient unto itself. But Jung the scientist was not content merely to have produced it; he needed to understand it. And Jung the prophet was not prepared to hoard his hard-won insights solely for his own benefit; he was convinced that any contribution from an 'individuated' individual, however small, could make a difference to the fate of humanity, which he believed had arrived at a dangerous and terrifying crisis-point as the imminent Aquarian Aion dawned. Ultimately Jung abandoned further work on *Liber Novus* in order to assemble his various insights into a coherent psychological model:

> In the Red Book I tried an aesthetic elaboration of my fantasies, but never finished it. I became aware that I had not yet found the right language, that I still had to translate it into something else. Therefore I gave up this aestheticizing tendency in good time, in favor of a rigorous process of *understanding*.[28]

Understanding, however, did not preclude a continuing exploration of the symbolic world. The mythic journey of the soul, as a portrayal of the individual's inward journey to the Self, was a theme of profound importance to Jung throughout his life, because the Self is the 'principle and archetype of orientation and meaning'.[29] He wrote about the soul-journey as an archetypal narrative of individuation on many occasions, using both the planetary ascent and the alchemical stages of transformation as a means of 'amplifying' this seminal mythic theme. He also understood the Major Arcana of the Tarot to provide a similar symbolic portrayal of the soul's journey, and many of the Tarot images are, like those of alchemy, related to astrological symbolism. Occultists such as Waite assigned planetary gods and zodiacal signs to particular cards, such as Venus to the card of the Empress, the Moon to the card of the High Priestess, and the sign of Aries to the card of the Emperor;[30] and the four elemental 'suits' of the Tarot – cups, pentacles, swords, and wands – owe their traditional interpretations to the four elements of astrology.[31] The images of the Major Arcana inform the figures of *Liber Novus* in ways that allow these two great symbolic systems, astrology and the Tarot, to enhance and enrich each other.

Although Jung later noted the relationship between the 'seven phases of the alchemical process' and the seven planetary spheres, he did not confine his descriptions of the individuation process to a specific number of astrologically significant steps such as seven or twelve.[32] Nor should any interpretation of the images of *Liber Novus* be confined in this way, astrological or otherwise, for these images do not follow a neat planetary order of seven or a zodiacal order of twelve, and they encompass many symbolic references other than astrological symbols. However, the initial and final phases of Jung's journey do seem to correspond closely with the beginning and end of the alchemical *opus*, portrayed at the beginning by the 'psychic suffering' and 'war on a moral plane' of the Saturnian *nigredo*, and culminating in the solar alchemical gold: a direct inner experience which on a spiritual level, according to Jung, reflects the soul's 'faculty of relationship to God', and on a psychological level reflects the 'unified self'.[33] *Liber Novus* does indeed begin with Saturn – not in the guise of the *senex* who appears throughout the work in so many different masks, although he presents himself soon enough in the figure of Elijah – but in 'The Way of What Is to Come': the Saturn-ruled Aion of Aquarius, with which Jung felt his own journey to be inextricably bound, and which he prophesied would initially be a true *nigredo* within the collective psyche as human beings faced the profound and necessary confrontation with the problem of their own evil.

In every human life, Jung believed that there is teleology at work: a meaningful development or movement towards some goal or fulfilled potential that was secretly present from the beginning. The alchemical stages, like the planetary journey, 'could just as well represent the individuation process of a single individual'.[34] It seems that, given the parallels which Jung perceived between his own soul-journey and that of the collective of which he was a part, he hoped that his inner work, undertaken in part from the desperation of attempting to resolve an intolerable inner conflict, might also result in an important contribution to the incipient chaos he feared was descending on the world around him. Jung insisted that it was on the shoulders of the individual that the fate of the collective ultimately rests:

> It is therefore a hopeless undertaking to stake everything on collective recipes and procedures. The bettering of a general ill begins with the individual, and then only when he makes himself and not others responsible. This is naturally only possible in freedom, but not under a rule of force, whether this be exercised by a self-elected tyrant or by one thrown up by the mob.[35]

The astrological world of *Liber Novus* is relevant to anyone seeking to penetrate the mind of one of the great thinkers of modern times. The work is a profoundly personal journey that reveals the most private inner conflicts and imaginings of an extraordinary individual. But Jung believed that all his work – including *Liber Novus*, which, despite his reluctance to see it published in his lifetime, was clearly prepared for the eventuality of others reading it – would be relevant because of that archetypal process of individuation, mirrored in the myth of the planetary journey of the soul. Jung understood this journey to be the potential story of every human life, whether or not it is ever able to be successfully fulfilled; and he also understood it to be the essential conscious choice and task of each individual, if any kind of resolution can be found for the destructive potential of a blind and unconscious collective driven by compulsion and oblivious to the necessity of personal responsibility and genuine conscious choice. As the twenty-first century progresses, whether or not it is indeed the time of entry into the Aquarian Aion as Jung believed it to be, his perceptions seem to be proving entirely prophetic.

Notes

1 Fourth-century BCE Orphic funerary tablet or *lamella* from Thurii. See Alberto Bernabé and Ana Isabel Jiménez San Cristóbal, *Instructions for the Netherworld: The Orphic Gold Tablets* (Leiden: Brill, 2008), p. 81.
2 Jung, *Liber Novus*, p. 370. The Greek phrase, which in English states, 'I am a star, wandering about with you', is from Dieterich, *Eine Mithrasliturgie*, p. 8, line 5; see Jung, *Liber Novus*, p. 370, n. 1.
3 Jung, *MDR*, p. 202.
4 Jung, CW14, ¶222.
5 Jung, CW14, ¶297. The original work is *Hypnerotomachia Poliphili* (Venice: Aldus Manutius, 1499). A truncated English translation appeared in 1592, but the first complete English version was only published four centuries later, translated by Joscelyn Godwin (London: Thames and Hudson, 1999). See also Couliano, *Eros and Magic*, pp. 42–48.

6 Linda Fierz-David, *The Dream of Poliphilo*, trans. Mary Hottinger (New York: Pantheon, 1950; first published in German as *Der Liebestraum des Poliphilo*, Zürich: Rhein Verlag, 1947; repr. Dallas: Spring, 1987), p. 11.

7 Jung, CW15, ¶141. For Jung's numerous references to Dante, see Jung, CW20, 'Dante'.

8 Fierz-David, *The Dream of Poliphilo*, p. 11.

9 For Dante's debt to Aristotle, see Patrick Boyde, *Dante, Philomythes and Philosopher* (Cambridge: Cambridge University Press, 1981), pp. 43–201.

10 Jung, *Liber Novus*, p. 347.

11 Dante, *Paradiso* XVIII–XXI, trans. Laurence Binyon, in Paolo Milano (ed.), *The Portable Dante* (London: Penguin, 1975), pp. 366–546.

12 F. Béroalde de Verville (trans.), *Le Tableau des riches inventions* (Paris: Matthieu Gillemot, 1600).

13 Jung, CW18, ¶1749. This statement was made in Jung's 'Foreword' to Fierz-David, *The Dream of Poliphilo*, a psychological commentary and paraphrase of the *Hypnerotomachia* first published in German by one of Jung's students. Jung wrote his Foreward in 1947, and declared in the opening paragraph that 'it must be twenty-five years' since he had encountered the French translation of the work by Béroulde de Verville. This means he was studying the work by 1922, in the midst of working on *Liber Novus*.

14 Jung, CW15, ¶154.

15 Jung, CW15, ¶141.

16 The original version of this essay, 'Psychology and Literature', was first published as 'Psychology and Poetry', trans. Eugene Jolaws, in *Transition* 19/20 (June 1930), and appeared three years later in a new translation by W.S. Dell and Cary F. Baynes, in Jung, *Modern Man in Search of a Soul* (London: Kegan Paul, Trench, Trubner, 1933).

17 *Hypnerotomachia*, p. 13.

18 *Hypnerotomachia*, p. xviii.

19 Jung, CW18, ¶1750.

20 Jung, CW15, ¶156.

21 *Hypnerotomachia*, p. 11.

22 Jung, CW13, ¶193 n. 104.

23 Jung, CW5, Fig. 1, ¶113. In the text below the image, Jung commented: 'To such a *daimonion* man falls an abject victim unless he can categorically reject its seductive influence at the outset'.

24 Jung, CW16, ¶¶353–539.

25 See Fierz-David, *The Dream of Poliphilo*, pp. 125–28, for her comments on the analogies between Priapus, Pan, and Saturn. For more on Queen Eleuterilida, see Peter Dronke, 'Francesco Colonna's Hyperotomachia and its Sources of Inspiration', in Peter Dronke (ed.), *Souces of Inspiration: Studies in Literary Transformation: 400–1500* (Rome: Edizioni di Storia e Letteratura, 1997), pp. 161–242.

26 Jung, CW18, ¶412.

27 Jung, *MDR*, p. 354.

28 Jung, *MDR*, p. 213.

29 Jung, *MDR*, p. 224.

30 The card of the Empress portrays the astrological glyph of Venus on a heart-shaped shield. The High Priestess has the crescent Moon at her feet. The Emperor's throne bears rams' heads, representing Aries the Ram, ruled by Mars.

31 For historical material on the Tarot, including Waite's images, see Greene, *Magi and Maggidim*, pp. 96–110 and 363–75, and the references given there.

32 Jung, CW13, ¶398.

33 Jung, CW14, ¶494.

34 Jung, CW12, ¶3.

35 Jung, CW9i, ¶618.

BIBLIOGRAPHY

Cited works by C. G. Jung

Collected works

_____, *The Psychogenesis of Mental Disease*, CW3, trans. R.F.C. Hull (London: Routledge & Kegan Paul, 1960)

_____, *Symbols of Transformation*, CW5, trans. R.F.C. Hull (London: Routledge & Kegan Paul, 1956)

_____, *Psychological Types*, CW6, trans. R.F.C. Hull (London: Routledge & Kegan Paul, 1971)

_____, *Two Essays on Analytical Psychology*, CW7, trans. R.F.C. Hull (London: Routledge & Kegan Paul, 1972)

_____, *The Structure and Dynamics of the Psyche*, CW8, trans. R.F.C. Hull (London: Routledge & Kegan Paul, 1960)

_____, *The Archetypes and the Collective Unconscious*, CW9i, trans. R.F.C. Hull (London: Routledge & Kegan Paul, 1959)

_____, *Aion: Researches into the Phenomenology of the Self*, CW9ii, trans. R.F.C. Hull (London: Routledge & Kegan Paul, 1959)

_____, *Civilization in Transition*, CW10, trans. R.F.C. Hull (London: Routledge & Kegan Paul, 1964)

_____, *Psychology and Religion*, CW11, trans. R.F.C. Hull (London: Routledge & Kegan Paul, 1958)

_____, *Psychology and Alchemy*, CW12, trans. R.F.C. Hull (London: Routledge & Kegan Paul, 1953)

_____, *Alchemical Studies*, CW13, trans. R.F.C. Hull (London: Routledge & Kegan Paul, 1967)

_____, *Mysterium Coniunctionis*, CW14, trans. R.F.C. Hull (London: Routledge & Kegan Paul, 1963)

_____, *The Spirit in Man, Art and Literature*, CW15, trans. R.F.C. Hull (London: Routledge & Kegan Paul, 1966)

_____, *The Practice of Psychotherapy*, CW16, trans. R.F.C. Hull (London: Routledge & Kegan Paul, 1954)

_____, *The Development of Personality*, CW17, trans. R.F.C. Hull (London: Routledge & Kegan Paul, 1954)

_____, *The Symbolic Life*, CW18, trans. R.F.C. Hull (London: Routledge & Kegan Paul, 1977)

Other cited works by Jung in English and German

_____, *Psychology of the Unconscious*, trans. Beatrice M. Hinkle (New York: Moffat, Yard & Co., 1916)

_____, *Memories, Dreams, and Reflections*, ed. Aniela Jaffé, trans. Richard and Clara Winston (London: Routledge & Kegan Paul, 1963)

_____, 'The Psychological Aspects of the Kore', in C.G. Jung and C. Kerényi, *Essays on a Science of Mythology: The Myth of the Divine Child and the Mysteries of Eleusis* (Princeton, NJ: Princeton University Press, 1963)

_____, *C.G. Jung Letters*, 2 volumes, ed. Gerhard Adler, trans. R.F.C. Hull (London: Routledge & Kegan Paul, 1973–76)

_____, *The Visions Seminars*, 2 volumes (Zürich: Spring, 1976)

_____, *Septem Sermones ad Mortuos: Written by Basilides in Alexandria, the City Where East and West Meet*, trans. Stephan A. Hoeller, in Stephan A. Hoeller, *The Gnostic Jung and the Seven Sermons to the Dead* (Wheaton, IL: Theosophical Publishing House, 1982), pp. 44–58

_____, *Dream Analysis: Notes of the Seminar Given in 1928–1930 by C.G. Jung*, ed. William C. McGuire (London: Routledge & Kegan Paul, 1984)

_____, 'Preface', in Cornelia Brunner, *Anima as Fate*, trans. Julius Heuscher and Scott May (Dallas, TX: Spring, 1986), pp. ix–xiv

_____, *Visions: Notes of the Seminar Given in 1930–1934 by C.G. Jung*, ed. Claire Douglas, 2 volumes (Princeton, NJ: Princeton University Press, 1997)

_____, *Children's Dreams: Notes from the Seminar Given in 1936–1940*, eds. Lorenz Jung and Maria Meyer-Grass, trans. Ernst Falzeder and Tony Woolfson (Princeton, NJ: Princeton University Press, 2008)

_____, *The Red Book: Liber Novus*, ed. Sonu Shamdasani, trans. Mark Kyburz, John Peck, and Sonu Shamdasani (New York/London: W.W. Norton, 2009)

_____, *Jung on Astrology*, selected and introduced by Keiron le Grice and Safron Rossi (Abingdon: Routledge, 2017)

Jung, C.G. and Sigmund Freud, *The Freud-Jung Letters*, ed. William McGuire, trans. Ralph Manheim and R.F.C. Hull (London: Hogarth Press/Routledge & Kegan Paul, 1977)

Jung, C.G. and Erich Neumann, *Analytical Psychology in Exile: The Correspondence of C.G. Jung and Erich Neumann*, trans. Heather McCartney (Princeton, NJ: Princeton University Press, 2015)

Primary sources

Agrippa, Heinrich Cornelius von Nettesheim, *De occulta philosophia libri tres* (Köln: J. Soter, 1533)

Atwood, Mary Ann, *Hermetic Philosophy and Alchemy: A Suggestive Inquiry into 'The Hermetic Mystery' with a Dissertation on the More Celebrated of the Alchemical Philosophers* (London: Trelawney Saunders, 1850)

Berthelot, Marcelin, *Les origines de l'alchimie* (Paris: G. Steinheil, 1885)

————, *Collection des anciens alchimistes grecs*, 3 volumes (Paris: G. Steinheil, 1887–88)

Besterman, Theodore, *Crystal-Gazing* (London: Rider, 1924)

Bischoff, Oswald Erich, *Die Elemente der Kabbalah*, 2 volumes (Berlin: Hermann Barsdorf, 1913–20)

Blavatsky, H.P., *Isis Unveiled: A Master-Key to the Mysteries of Ancient and Modern Science and Theology*, 2 volumes (London: Theosophical Publishing, 1877)

————, *The Secret Doctrine: The Synthesis of Science, Religion, and Philosophy*, 2 volumes (London: Theosophical Publishing, 1888)

Bloch, Chajim, *Lebenserinnerungen des Kabbalisten Vital* (Vienna: Vernay-Verlag, 1927)

Bouché-Leclercq, Auguste, *L'astrologie grecque* (Paris: Ernest Leroux, 1899)

Cardanus, Jerome, *Commentarium in Ptolemaeum de Astrorum Iudiciis*, in Cardanus, Jerome, *Opera Omnia*, 10 volumes (Lyon, 1663), Vol. 5, pp. 93–368

Carus, Paul, *The Pleroma: An Essay on the Origin of Christianity* (Chicago: Open Court, 1909)

Colonna, Francesco, *Hypnerotomachia Poliphili, ubihumana omnia non nisi somnium esse ostendit, atque obiter plurimascitu sanequamdigna commemorat* (Venice: Aldus Manutius, 1499)

Cory, Isaac Preston, *Ancient Fragments of the Phoenician, Chaldean, Egyptian, Tyrian, Carthaginian, Indian, Persian, and Other Writers; with an Introductory Dissertation; And an Inquiry into the Philosophy and Trinity of the Ancients* (London: Reeves and Turner, 1876)

Cumont, Franz, *Textes et monuments figurés relatifs aux mystères de Mythra* (Brussels: Lamertin, 1896)

————, 'Mithra et l'Orphisme', *Revue de l'histoire des religions* 109 (1934), pp. 64–72

Damascius, *Dubitationes et solutiones de primis principiis in Platonis Parmenidem*, 2 volumes (Paris: Ruelle, 1889)

Eisler, Robert, *Weltenmantel und Himmelszelt: Religionsgeschichtliche Untersuchungen zur Urgeschichte des Antiken Weltbildes*, 2 volumes (Munich: Oskar Beck, 1910)

————, *Orpheus the Fisher: Comparative Studies in Orphic and Early Christian Cult Symbolism* (London: J.M. Watkins, 1921); originally published as a series of articles in *The Quest* 1:1 (1909), 124–139; 1:2 (1910), 306–321; 1:4 (1910), 625–648

Ficino, Marsilio, *De vita triplici*, in Marsilio Ficino, *Opera omnia* (Basel: Heinrich Petri, 1576)

Firmicus Maternus, *Matheseos libri VIII* (Venice: Aldus Manutius, 1501)

Flamel, Nicholas, *Le Livre des figures hiéroglyphiques* (Paris: Veuve Guillemot, 1612)

Fludd, Robert, *Utriusque cosmi maioris scilicet et minoris metaphysica atque technica historia in duo volumina secundum cosmi differentiam diuisa*, 3 volumes (Oppenheim: Theodor de Bry, 1617–1618)

Frobenius, Leo, *Das Zeitalter des Sonnengottes* (Berlin: G. Reimer, 1904)

Heindel, Max, *The Message of the Stars: An Esoteric Exposition of Medical and Natal Astrology Explaining the Arts of Prediction and Diagnosis of Disease* (Oceanside, CA: Rosicrucian Fellowship, 1918)

————, *Ancient and Modern Initiation* (Oceanside, CA: Rosicrucian Fellowship, 1931)

Hollandus, Johann Isaac, *Opus Saturni*, in Basilius Valentinus, *Of Natural and Supernatural Things*, trans. Daniel Cable (London: Moses Pitt, 1670)

Hypnerotomachia Poliphili, ubihumana omnia non nisi somnium esse ostendit, atque obiter plurimascitu sanequamdigna commemorat (Venice: Aldus Manutius, 1499)

Irenaeus, *Irenaei episcopi lugdunensis contra omnes haereses. Libri quinque*, ed. and trans. J.E. Grabe (Oxford, 1702)

————, *Des heilegen Irenäus fünf Bücher gegen die Häresine*, 2 volumes (Munich: Josef Kösel, 1912)

Jensen, Peter, *Das Gilgamesh-Epos in der Weltliteratur* (Strasbourg: Karl Trübner, 1906)

Jeremias, Alfred, *Izdubar-nimrod: Eine altbabylonische Heldensage: Nach den Keilschriftfragmenten Dargestellt* (Leipzig: B.G. Teubner, 1891)

King, Charles William, *The Gnostics and Their Remains: Ancient and Medieval* (London: Bell & Dalby, 1864)

Knorr von Rosenroth, Christian, *Kabbala denudata, seu, Doctrina Hebraeorum transcendentalis et metaphysica atque theologica: opus antiquissimae philosophiae barbaricae . . . in quo, ante ipsam translationem libri . . . cui nomen Sohar tam veteris quam recentis, ejusque tikkunim . . . praemittitur apparatus [pars 1–4]*, 3 volumes (Sulzbach/Frankfurt: Abraham Lichtenthal, 1677–1684)

Leo, Alan, *How to Judge a Nativity, Part One: The Reading of the Horoscope* (London: Modern Astrology, 1899)

————, *How to Judge a Nativity* (London: Modern Astrology, 1908)

————, *Astrology for All* (London: Modern Astrology, 1910)

————, *The Key to Your Own Nativity* (London: Modern Astrology, 1910)

————, *The Art of Synthesis* (London: Modern Astrology Office, 1912)

————, *Esoteric Astrology* (London: Modern Astrology Office, 1913)

————, *Saturn: The Reaper* (London: Modern Astrology Office, 1916)

Lévi, Éliphas, *The Magical Ritual of the Sanctum Regnum*, trans. William Wynn Westcott (private publication, 1896)

Mead, G.R.S. (ed. and trans.), *Pistis Sophia: A Gnostic Miscellany: Being for the Most Part Extracts from the Book of the Saviour, to Which Are Added Excerps from a Cognate Literature* (London: Theosophical Publishing Society, 1896)

———— (ed. and trans.), *Fragments of a Faith Forgotten: Some Short Sketches Among the Gnostics Mainly of the First Two Centuries* (London: Theosophical Publishing Society, 1906)

———— (ed. and trans.), *Thrice-Greatest Hermes: Studies in Hellenistic Theosophy and Gnosis*, 3 volumes (London: Theosophical Publishing Society, 1906)

———— (ed. and trans.), *A Mithraic Ritual* (London: Theosophical Publishing Society, 1907)

———— (ed. and trans.), *The Chaldean Oracles* (London: Theosophical Publishing Society, 1908)

Müller, Ernst, *Der Sohar: Das Heilige Büch der Kabbalah* (Düsseldorf: Diederich, 1932)

Mylius, Johann Daniel, *Philosophia reformata continens libros binos. I. Liber in septem partes divisus est. Pars 1. agit de generatione metallorum in visceribus terrae. 2. tractat principia Artis philosophicae. 3. docet de scientia Divina abbreviata. 4. enarrat 12 grad. Sapientum Philosoph. 5. declarat Amb. in hac Divina scientia. 6. dicit de Recap. Artis Divina Theori. 7. ait de Artis Divinae Recap. Practica. II. Liber continet authoritates philosophorum* (Frankfurt: Jennis, 1622)

Niebelunglied, trans. A. Hatto (London: Penguin, 2004)

Nietzsche, Friedrich, *Die Geburt der Tragödie aus dem Geiste der Musik* (Leipzig: W. Fritzch, 1872)

Papus [Gérard Encausse], *Le Tarot des Bohémiens: Le plus ancient livre du monde* (Paris: Flammarion, 1889)

Paracelsus (Theophrastus von Hohenheim), 1:14.7, *Liber de nymphis, sylphis, pygmaeis et salamandris et de caeteris spiritibus*, in Paracelsus, *Sämtliche Werke*, ed. Karl Sudhoff and Wilhelm Matthiessen (Munich: Oldenbourg, 1933)

————, *Philonis Iudaei, scriptoris eloquentissimi, ac philosophi summi, lucubrationes omnes quotquot haberi potuerunt: cuius opera uterque est integritati restitutus* (Basel: Sigmund Gelen, 1561)

Philo, *Opera quae supersunt*, eds. Leopold Cohn and Paul Wendland, Vol. 3–6 (Berlin: Walter de Gruyter, 1898–1915)

Plutarch, *Lebensbeschreibungen*, trans. Hanns Floerke, 6 volumes (Munich: Georg Müller, 1913)

Rohde, Erwin, *Seelencult und Unsterlichkeitsglaube der Griechen*, 2 volumes (Tübingen: Mohr, 1903)

Roscher, Wilhelm Heinrich, *Ausfürliches Lexikon der griechisches und römisches Muythologie* (Leipzig: B.G. Teubner, 1884–1937)

Ruland, Martin, *Lexicon alchemiae sive Dictionarium alchemisticum* (Frankfurt: Zachariah Palthenus, 1612)

Scholem, Gershom, *Die Geheimnisse der Schöpfung: Ein Kapitel aus dem Sohar* (Berlin: Schocken, 1935)

Schultz, Wolfgang, *Dokumente der Gnosis* (Jena: E. Diederichs, 1910)

Smith, George, 'The Chaldean Account of the Deluge', *Transactions of the Society of Biblical Archaeology* 1–2 (1872), pp. 213–34

Theatrum Chemicum, praecipuos selectorum auctorum tractatus de Chemiae et Lapidis Philosophici Antiquitate, veritate, jure praestantia, et operationibus continens in gratiam verae Chemiae et Medicinae Chemicae Studiosorum (ut qui uberrimam unde optimorum remediorum messem facere poterunt) congestum et in quatuor partes seu volumina digestum (Strasbourg/Oberusel: Lazarus Zetzner, 1602–1661)

Thomas à Kempis, *Das Buchlein von der Nachfolge Christi: Vier Bücher versatzt von Thomas von Kempis und neu übersetzt von Johannes Gortzner* (Leipzig: Karl Tauchnitz, 1832)

Thorburn, John M., *Art and the Unconscious: A Psychological Approach to a Problem of Philosophy* (London: Kegan Paul, Trench, Trubner & Co., 1925)

_____, 'Natus for C.G. Jung', © 2007 Foundation of the Works of C.G. Jung, Zürich

Von Goethe, Johann Wolfgang von Goethe, *Faust: Der Tragödie erster Teil* (Tübingen: J.G. Cotta'schen, 1808)

Waite, A.E., *The Doctrine and Literature of the Kabbalah* (London: Theosophical Publishing Society, 1902)

_____, *The Pictorial Key to the Tarot: Being Fragments of a Secret Tradition under the Veil of Divination* (London: William Rider & Son, 1910)

_____, *The Secret Doctrine of Israel: A Study of the Zohar and Its Connections* (London: William Rider & Son, 1912)

_____, *The Holy Kabbalah: A Study of the Secret Tradition in Israel* (London: Williams & Norgate, 1929)

Translated primary sources

Agrippa, Henry Cornelius, *Three Books of Occult Philosophy (De occulta philosophia)*, ed. Donald Tyson, trans. James Freake (St. Paul, MN: Llewellyn, 1993; first complete English translation, James Freake, London: Gregory Moule, 1651)

Apocryphon of John, trans. Frederik Wisse, in James M. Robinson (ed.), *The Nag Hammadi Library in English* (Leiden: Brill, 1977), pp. 98–116

Aristophanes, *Birds*, in Aristophanes, *The Birds and Other Plays*, trans. Alan H. Sommerstein and David Barrett (London: Penguin, 2003)

Ascension of Moses, in Louis Ginzberg, *The Legends of the Jews*, 2 volumes, trans. Henriette Szold (Philadelphia, PA: Jewish Publication Society of America, 1913)

The Bahir [Sefer ha-Bahir], trans. Aryeh Kaplan (York Beach, ME: Weiser Books, 1989)

Betegh, Gábor (trans.), *The Derveni Papyrus: Cosmology, Theology, and Interpretation* (Cambridge: Cambridge University Press, 2004)

Betz, Hans Dieter (ed. and trans.), *The 'Mithras Liturgy': Text, Translation and Commentary* (Tübingen: Mohr Siebeck, 2003)

Colonna, Francesco, *Hypnerotomachia Poliphili: The Strife of Love in a Dream*, trans. Joscelyn Godwin (London: Thames & Hudson, 2005)

Copenhaver, Brian P. (ed. and trans.), *Hermetica: The Greek Corpus Hermeticum and the Latin Asclepius in a New English Translation* (Cambridge: Cambridge University Press, 1992)

Cumont, Franz, *The Mysteries of Mithra*, trans. Thomas J. McCormack (Chicago, IL: Open Court, 1903)

Damigeron, *De Virtutibus Lapidum: The Virtues of Stones*, trans. Patricia Tahil, ed. Joel Radcliffe (Seattle, WA: Ars Obscura, 1989)

Dan, Joseph (ed. and trans.), *The Heart and the Fountain: An Anthology of Jewish Mystical Experiences* (Oxford: Oxford University Press, 2002)

Dee, John, *Monas Hieroglyphica*, trans. J.W. Hamilton-Jones (London: Watkins, 1947)

_____, *The Hieroglyphic Monad*, trans. C.H. Josten, *Ambix* 12 (1964)

Ficino, Marsilio, *The Book of Life*, trans. Charles Boer (Irving, TX: Spring, 1980)

Firmicus Maternus, Julius, *Ancient Astrology, Theory and Practice: The Mathesis of Firmicus Maternus*, trans. Jean Rhys Bram (Park Ridge, NJ: Noyes Press, 1975)

Herodotus, *Herodotus, Book II: Commmentary 1–98*, ed. and trans. Alan B. Lloyd (Leiden: Brill, 1976)

Hesiod, *Theogony*, in *Hesiod, Vol. 1: Theogony. Works and Days. Testimonia*, trans. Glenn W. Most (Cambridge, MA: Harvard University Press, 2007)

Iamblichus, *De Mysteriis*, trans. Emma C. Clarke, John M. Dillon, and Jackson P. Hershbell (Atlanta, GA: Society of Biblical Literature, 2003)

Maier, Michael, *Atalanta fugiens* (Oppenheim: Johann Theodor de Bry, 1618), trans. Hereward Tilton from British Library MS Sloane 3645, at <www.alchemywebsite.com/atl26-0.html>

Manilius, Marcus, *Astronomica*, trans. G.P. Goold (Cambridge, MA: Harvard University Press, 1977)

Nietzsche, Friedrich, *The Birth of Tragedy: Out of the Spirit of Music*, trans. Shaun Whiteside (London: Penguin, 1993)

Nonnus, *Dionysiaca*, trans. W.H.D. Rouse, 3 volumes (Cambridge, MA: Harvard University Press, 1940)

Origen, *Contra Celsum*, in *The Writings of Origen*, ed. and trans. Frederick Crombie (Edinburgh: Ante-Nicene Christian Library, 1910–11)

————, *Contra Celsum*, trans. Henry Chadwick (Cambridge: Cambridge University Press, 1953)

The Orphic Hymns, trans. Apostolos N. Athanassakis and Benjamin M. Wolkow (Baltimore, MD: Johns Hopkins University Press, 2013)

Pausanias, *Pausanias' Guide to Ancient Greece*, trans. Christian Habicht (Berkeley: University of California Press, 1998)

Peterson, Joseph (ed. and trans.), *The Sixth and Seventh Books of Moses: Or, Moses' Magical Spirit Art Known as the Wonderful Arts of the Old Wise Hebrews, Taken from the Mosaic Books of the Kabbalah and the Talmud, for the Good of Mankind* (Lake Worth, FL: Ibis Press, 2008)

Philo, *On Moses*, in *Philo, Vol. VI: On Abraham. On Joseph. On Moses*, trans. F.H. Colson (Cambridge, MA: Harvard University Press, 1935)

Philostratus, *Apollonius of Tyana*, trans. Christopher P. Jones (Cambridge, MA: Loeb Classical Library, 2006)

Plato, *Laws*, trans. A.E. Taylor, in *The Collected Dialogues of Plato*, ed. Edith Hamilton and Huntington Cairns (Princeton, NJ: Princeton University Press, 1961)

_____, *Phaedrus*, trans. R. Hackforth, in *The Collected Dialogues of Plato*, ed. Edith Hamilton and Huntington Cairns (Princeton, NJ: Princeton University Press, 1961)

————, *Symposium*, trans. Michael Joyce, in *The Collected Dialogues of Plato*, ed. Edith Hamilton and Huntington Cairns (Princeton, NJ: Princeton University Press, 1961)

_____, *Timaeus*, trans. Benjamin Jowett, in *The Collected Dialogues of Plato*, ed. Edith Hamilton and Huntington Cairns (Princeton, NJ: Princeton University Press, 1961)

Pliny the Elder, *The Natural History*, trans. Henry T. Riley (London: H.G. Bohn, 1855)

Plotinus, *The Enneads*, trans. Stephen Mackenna, 6 volumes (London: Medici Society, 1917–30; repr. London: Faber & Faber, 1956)

Plutarch, *The Face Which Appears on the Orb of the Moon*, trans. A.O. Prickard (London: Simpkin & Co., 1911)

Porphyry, *De antro nympharum*, 11, in Thomas Taylor (trans.), *Select Works of Porphyry; Containing His Four Books on Abstinence from Animal Food; His Treatise on The Homeric Cave of the Nymphs; and His Auxiliaries to the Perception of Intelligible Natures* (London: Thomas Rodd, 1823), pp. 186–89.

———, *On the Life of Plotinus and the Arrangement of His Works*, in Mark Edwards (ed. and trans.), *Neoplatonic Saints: The Lives of Plotinus and Proclus by Their Students* (Liverpool: Liverpool University Press 2000), pp. 1–54

Proclus, *The Six Books of Proclus: On the Theology of Plato*, trans. Thomas Taylor (London: A.J. Valpy, 1816)

Ptolemy, *Tetrabiblos*, ed. and trans. F.E. Robbins (Cambridge, MA: Harvard University Press, 1971)

Ruland, Martin, *A Lexicon of Alchemy or Alchemical Dictionary, Containing a Full and Plain Explanation of All Obscure Words, Hermetic Subjects, and Arcane Phrases of Paracelsus*, trans. A.E. Waite (London: privately printed, 1892)

Savedow, Steve (trans.), *Sepher Rezial Hemelach: The Book of the Angel Rezial* (York Beach, ME: Weiser Books, 2001)

Taylor, Thomas (trans.), *Hymns and Initiations* (Frome: Prometheus Trust, 1994)

——— (trans.), *The Hymns of Orpheus: Translated from the Original Greek, with a Preliminary Dissertation on the Life and Theology of Orpheus* (London: T. Payne, 1792)

——— (trans.), *The Emperor Julian's Oration to the Sovereign Sun*, in Thomas Taylor, *Collected Writings on the Gods and the World* (Frome: Prometheus Trust, 1994 [London: Edward Jeffrey, 1793]), pp. 51–76

——— (trans.), *The Mystical Hymns of Orpheus* (London: B. Dobell, 1896)

Thomas à Kempis, *The Imitation of Christ* [*De imitatione Christi*], trans. B. Knott (London: Fount, 1996)

Valens, Vettius, *The Anthology*, trans. Robert Schmidt (Berkeley Springs, WV: Golden Hind Press, 1993–96)

Von Goethe, Johann Wolfgang, *Faust: A Tragedy*, trans. Bayard Taylor (New York: Modern Library, 1950)

Secondary works

Allen, Richard Hinckley, *Star Names: Their Lore and Meaning* (New York: Dover, 1963 [1899])

Anderson, Daniel E., *The Masks of Dionysos: A Commentary on Plato's Symposium* (Albany: SUNY Press, 1993)

Anderson, John P., *Mann's Doctor Faustus: Gestapo Music* (Boca Raton, FL: Universal, 2007)

Assman, Jan, *Moses the Egyptian: The Memory of Egypt in Western Monotheism* (Cambridge, MA: Harvard University Press, 1998)

Bakan, David, *Sigmund Freud and the Jewish Mystical Tradition* (Princeton, NJ: Van Nostrand, 1958; repr. Boston: Beacon Press, 1975)

Bardill, Jonathan, *Constantine, Divine Emperor of the Christian Golden Age* (Cambridge: Cambridge University Press, 2012)

Barrie, Thomas, *The Sacred In-Between: The Mediating Roles of Architecture* (London: Routledge, 2013)

Bauckham, Richard, 'Salome the Sister of Jesus, Salome the Disciple of Jesus, and the Secret Gospel of Mark', *Novum Testamentum* 33:3 (1991), pp. 245–75

Baumann-Jung, Gret, 'Some Reflections on the Horoscope of C.G. Jung', *Quadrant* (Spring 1975), pp. 35–55

Beck, Roger, *Planetary Gods and Planetary Orders in the Mysteries of Mithras* (Leiden: Brill, 1988)

Berg, Steven, *Eros and the Intoxications of Enlightenment: On Plato's Symposium* (Albany: SUNY Press, 2010)

Berger, Pamela, 'Ways of Knowing Through Iconography: The Temple of Solomon and the Dome of the Rock', paper given at Boston College, BOISI Center for Religion and American Public Life, 8 April 2009

Bernabé, Alberto, 'Some Thoughts about the "New" Gold Tablet from Pherae', *Zeitschrift für Papyrologie und Epigraphik* 166 (2008), pp. 53–58

Bernabé, Alberto and Ana Isabel Jiménez San Cristóbal, *Instructions for the Netherworld: The Orphic Gold Tablets* (Leiden: Brill, 2008)

Betz, Hans Dieter (ed. and trans.), *The Greek Magical Papyri in Translation* (Chicago: University of Chicago Press, 1986)

Blakeley, John D., *The Mystical Tower of the Tarot* (London: Watkins, 1974)

Bonner, Campbell, *Studies in Magical Amulets, Chiefly Graeco-Egyptian* (Ann Arbor: University of Michigan Press, 1950)

Breitenberger, Barbara, *Aphrodite and Eros: The Development of Erotic Mythology in Early Greek Poetry and Cult* (London: Routledge, 2013)

British Museum Catalogue of Greek Coins, Central Greece (1963)

Brown, Margery L., 'Hephaestus, Hermes, and Prometheus: Jesters to the Gods', in Vicki K. Janik (ed.), *Fools and Jesters in Literature, Art, and History: A Bio-Bibliographical Sourcebook* (Westport, CT: Greenwood Press, 1998), pp. 237–45

Brown, Norman Oliver, *Hermes the Thief: The Evolution of a Myth* (Madison: University of Wisconsin Press, 1947)

Brumble, H. David, *Classical Myths and Legends in the Middle Ages and Renaissance: A Dictionary of Allegorical Meanings* (London: Routledge, 2013)

Brunner, Cornelia, *Anima as Fate*, trans. Julius Heuscher and Scott May (Dallas, TX: Spring, 1986; first published as *Die Anima als Schicksalsproblem des Mannes* (Zürich: Rascher Verlag, 1963))

Butler, E.M., *The Fortunes of Faust* (Cambridge: Cambridge University Press, 1952)

Calame, Claude, *The Poetics of Eros in Ancient Greece* (Princeton, NJ: Princeton University Press, 1999)

Campion, Nicholas, *A History of Western Astrology, Vol. 2: The Medieval and Modern Worlds* (London: Continuum, 2009)

Cashford, Jules, *The Moon: Myth and Image* (London: Cassell, 2003)

Chaniotis, A., T. Corsten, R.S. Stroud, and R.A. Tybout, 'Pherae. Inscribed gold lamella of an initiate into the cult of Demeter Chthonia, Meter Oreia (and Dionysus?), Late 4th/ Early 3rd cent. BC (55–612)', *Supplementum Epigraphicum Graecum*, Brill Online, 2012, at <http://referenceworks.brillonline.com/entries/supplementum-epigraphicum-grae cum/pherai-inscribed-gold-lamella-of-an-initiate-into-the-cult-of-demeter-chthonia-meter-oreia-and-dionysos-late-4th-early-3rd-cent-b-c-55–612-a55_612>

Clay, Diskin, *Platonic Questions: Dialogues with the Silent Philosopher* (University Park: Penn State University Press, 2000)

Clinton, Esther, 'The Trickster: Various Motifs', in Jane Garry and Hasan El-Shamy (eds.), *Archetypes and Motifs in Folklore and Literature* (Armonk, NY: M.E. Sharpe, 2005), pp. 472–81

Cochrane, Ev, *Martian Metamorphosis: The Planet Mars in Ancient Myth and Religion* (Ames, IA: Aeon Press, 1997)

Colum, Padraic, *The Children of Odin: The Book of Northern Myths* (New York: Macmillan, 1920)

Cook, Arthur Bernard, *Zeus: A Study in Ancient Religion*, 3 volumes (Cambridge: Cambridge University Press, 1925)

Corbin, Henry, *Avicenna and the Visionary Recital* (Princeton, NJ: Princeton University Press, 1960)

———, *The Man of Light in Iranian Sufism* (Green Oaks, IL: Omega, 1994)

Couliano, Ioan P., *Eros and Magic in the Renaissance* (Chicago: University of Chicago Press, 1987)

Croswell, Ken, *Planet Quest: The Epic Discovery of Alien Solar Systems* (New York: Free Press, 1997)

Dan, Joseph, 'Book of Raziel', in *Encyclopaedia Judaica*, 16 volumes (New York: Macmillan, 1971–72),1591–1593.

———, 'Maggid', in *Encyclopaedia Judaica*, 16 volumes (Jerusalem: Keter, 1971), Vol. 11, pp. 698–701

Davies, Owen, *Grimoires: A History of Magic Books* (Oxford: Oxford University Press, 2009)

De Jáuregui, Miguel Herrero, *Orphism and Christianity in Late Antiquity* (Berlin: Walter de Gruyter, 2010)

De Rola, Stanislas Klossowski, *The Golden Game: Alchemical Engravings of the Seventeenth Century* (London: Thames and Hudson, 1988)

Dillon, John M., 'Pleroma and Gnostic Cosmos: A Comparative Study', in Richard T. Wallis and Jay Bregman (eds.), *Neoplatonism and Gnosticism* (Albany: SUNY Press, 1992), pp. 99–110

Drob, Sanford L. 'Towards a Kabbalistic Psychology: C.G. Jung and the Jewish Foundations of Alchemy', *Journal of Jungian Theory and Practice* 5:2 (2003), pp. 77–100

Dronke, Peter, 'Francesco Colonna's Hypnerotomachia and its Sources of Inspiration', in Peter Dronke (ed.), *Sources of Inspiration: Studies in Literary Transformation: 400–1500* (Rome: Edizioni di Storia e Letteratura, 1997), pp. 161–242

Duchesne-Gullemin, Jacques (ed.), *Acta Iranica: Encyclopédie Permanente des Études Iraniennes* (Leiden: Brill, 1978)

Dzielska, Maria, *Apollonius of Tyana in Legend and History* (Rome: L'Erma, 1986)

Edis, Freda, *The God Between: A Study of Astrological Mercury* (London: Penguin, 1996)

Elior, Rachel, 'Mysticism, Magic, and Angelology: The Perception of Angels in Heikhalot Literature', *Jewish Quarterly Review* 1 (1993), pp. 3–53

———, 'The Concept of God in Hekhalot Mysticism', in Joseph Dan (ed.), *Binah: Studies in Jewish History, Thought, and Culture* (New York: Praeger, 1989), Vol. 2, pp. 97–120

Faraone, Christopher, 'Text, Image, and Medium: The Evolution of Graeco-Roman Magical Gemstones', in Chris Entwistle and Noel Adams (eds.), *Gems of Heaven: Recent Research on Engraved Gemstones in Late Antiquity, AD 200–600* (London: British Museum, 2011), pp. 50–61

Fine, Lawrence, *Physician of the Soul, Healer of the Cosmos: Isaac Luria and His Kabbalistic Fellowship* (Stanford, CA: Stanford University Press, 2003)

Fortune, Dion, *The Mystical Qabalah* (London: Ernest Benn, 1935)

———, *Aspects of Occultism* (Wellingborough: Aquarian Press, 1962)

Fowden, Garth, *The Egyptian Hermes: A Historical Approach to the Late Pagan Mind* (Princeton, NJ: Princeton University Press, 1993)

Frojmovic, Eva, *Imagining the Self, Imagining the Other: Visual Representation and Jewish-Christian Dynamics in the Middle Ages and Early Modern Period* (Leiden: Brill, 2002)

Gager, John G., *Moses in Greco-Roman Paganism* (New York: Abingdon Press, 1972)

Gantz, Timothy, *Early Greek Myth: A Guide to Literary and Artistic Sources* (Baltimore, MD: Johns Hopkins University Press, 1993)

George, Andrew R. (ed. and trans.), *The Babylonian Gilgamesh Epic: Critical Edition and Cuneiform Texts*, 2 volumes (Oxford: Oxford University Press, 2003)

Getty, R.J., 'The Astrology of P. Nigidius Figulus (Lucan I, 649–65)', *Classical Quarterly* 45:1–2 (1941), pp. 17–22

Godwin, Joscelyn, *Robert Fludd: Hermetic Philosopher and Surveyor of Two Worlds* (Grand Rapids, MI: Phanes Press, 1991)

Goldenberg, Naomi R., 'A Feminist Critique of Jung', *Signs* 2:2 (1976), pp. 443–49

Gorwyn, Adam and Alan Stern, 'A Chihuahua Is Still a Dog, and Pluto Is Still a Planet', *EarthSky*, 18 February 2010

Graf, Fritz, *Apollo* (London: Routledge, 2009)

Graf, Fritz and Sarah Iles Johnston, *Ritual Texts for the Afterlife: Orpheus and the Bacchic Gold Tablets* (London: Routledge, 2007)

Green, Arthur, 'Shekhinah, the Virgin Mary, and the Song of Songs: Reflections on a Kabbalistic Symbol in Its Historical Context', *AJS Review*, 26:1 (2002), pp. 1–52

Greene, Liz, *Magi and Maggidim: The Kabbalah in British Occultism, 1860–1940* (Lampeter: Sophia Centre Press, 2012)

———, 'The God in the Stone: Gemstone Talismans in Western Magical Traditions', *Culture and Cosmos* 19:1–2 (Autumn–Winter 2015), pp. 47–85

———, *Jung's Studies in Astrology: Prophecy, Magic, and the Cycles of Time* (London: Routledge, 2018)

Gullfoss, Per Henrik, *The Complete Book of Spiritual Astrology* (Woodbury, MN: Llewellyn, 2008)

Gundel, Wilhelm and Hans Georg Gundel, *Astrologumena* (Weisbaden: Steiner, 1966)

Guthrie, W.K.C., *Orpheus and Greek Religion* (London: Methuen, 1952)

Hakili, Rahel, *The Menorah, The Ancient Seven-Armed Candelabrum: Origin, Form, and Significance* (Leiden: Brill, 2001)

Hamacher, Werner, *Pleroma: Reading in Hegel*, trans. Nicholas Walker and Simon Jarvis (Stanford, CA: Stanford University Press, 1998)

Hammer, Olav, *Claiming Knowledge: Strategies of Epistemology from Theosophy to the New Age* (Leiden: Brill, 2004)

Hanegraaff, Wouter J., *New Age Religion and Western Culture: Esotericism in the Mirror of Secular Thought* (Leiden: Brill, 1996)

Harding, Esther, *The Way of All Women: A Psychological Interpretation* (London: Longmans, Green, 1933)

Harkness, Deborah E., 'Shows in the Showstone: A Theater of Alchemy and Apocalypse in the Angel Conversations of John Dee (1527–1698–9)', *Renaissance Quarterly* 49 (1996), pp. 707–37

———, *John Dee's Conversations with Angels: Cabala, Alchemy, and the End of Nature* (Cambridge: Cambridge University Press, 1999)

Harrison, Jane Ellen, *Themis: A Study of the Social Origins of Greek Religion* (Cambridge: Cambridge University Press, 1927)

Harvey, P.D.A., *Mappa Mundi: The Hereford World Map* (London: British Library, 1996)

Hedegård, Gösta, *Liber Iuratus Honorii: A Critical Edition of the Latin Version of the Sworn Book of Honorius* (Stockholm: Almqvist and Wiksell, 2002)

Hijmans, Steven, *Sol: The Sun in the Art and Religions of Rome* (unpublished PhD dissertation, University of Groningen, 2009)

Hobley, Brian, *The Circle of God: An Archaeological and Historical Search for the Nature of the Sacred* (Oxford: Archaeopress, 2015)

Hoeller, Stephan A., *The Gnostic Jung and the Seven Sermons to the Dead* (Theosophical Publishing House, 1982)

Hordern, James, 'Notes on the Orphic Papyrus from Gurob (P. Gurob 1; Pack 2 2464)', *Zeitschrift für Papyrologie und Epigraphik* 129 (2000), pp. 131–40

Hotakainen, Markus, *Mars: From Myth and Mystery to Recent Discoveries* (New York: Springer, 2008)

Idel, Moshe, 'The Throne and the Seven-Branched Candlestick: Pico della Mirandola's Hebrew Source', *Journal of the Warburg and Courtauld Institutes* 40 (1977), pp. 290–92

————, *Hasidism: Between Ecstasy and Magic* (Albany: SUNY Press, 1995)

————, 'Binah, the Eighth Sefirah: The Menorah in Kabbalah', in *In the Light of the Menorah*, Israel Museum Exhibition Catalogue, ed. I Fishof (Jerusalem, 1999), pp. 142–46

————, 'Transmission in Thirteenth-Century Kabbalah', in Yaakov Elmon and Israel Gershoni (eds.), *Transmitting Jewish Traditions: Orality, Textuality, and Cultural Diffusion* (New Haven, CT: Yale University Press, 2000), pp. 138–65

————, *Absorbing Perfections: Kabbalah and Interpretation* (Leiden: Brill, 2002)

————, *Kabbalah and Eros* (New Haven, CT: Yale University Press, 2005)

————, *Saturn's Jews: On the Witches' Sabbat and Sabbateanism* (London: Continuum, 2011)

Jacobs, Louis, 'Uplifting the Sparks in Later Jewish Mysticism', in Arthur Green (ed.), *Jewish Spirituality, Vol. 2: From the Sixteenth Century Revival to the Present* (New York: Crossroad, 1987), pp. 99–126

————, 'The Maggid of Rabbi Moses Hayyim Luzzato', in Louis Jacobs (ed. and trans.), *The Jewish Mystics* (London: Kyle Cathie, 1990), pp. 136–47

Jaffé, Aniela, *C. G. Jung: Word and Image* (Princeton, NJ: Princeton University Press, 1979)

————, *Was C. G. Jung a Mystic? And Other Essays* (Einsiedeln: Daimon Verlag, 1989)

Jastrow, Morris, *The Religion of Babylonia and Assyria* (Boston, MA: Athenaeum Press, 1898)

Jensen, K. Frank, *The Story of the Waite-Smith Tarot* (Melbourne: Association of Tarot Studies, 2006)

Jeromson, Barry, '*Systema Munditotius* and *Seven Sermons*: Symbolic Collaborators in Jung's Confrontation with the Dead', *Jung History* 1:2 (2005/6), pp. 6–10

————, 'The Sources of *Systema Munditotius*: Mandalas, Myths and a Misinterpretation', *Jung History* 2:2 (2007), pp. 20–22

Johnston, Sarah Iles, *Hekate Soteira: A Study of Hekate's Roles in the Chaldean Oracles and Related Literature* (Oxford: Oxford University Press, 2000)

————, 'Introduction: Divining Divination', in Sarah Iles Johnston and Peter T. Struck (eds.), *Mantikê: Studies in Ancient Divination* (Leiden: Brill, 2005), pp. 1–28

Jonas, Hans, *The Gnostic Religion: The Message of the Alien God and the Beginnings of Christianity* (Boston, MA: Beacon Press, 1958)

Jung, Emma, *Anima and Animus: Two Papers* (New York: Analytical Psychology Club of New York, 1957); originally published separately as *Wirklichkeit der Seele* ('On the Nature of the Animus') (Zürich: Psychologische Abhandlungen 4, 1934) and *Die Anima als Naturwesen* ('The Anima as an Elemental Being') (Zürich: Rascher, 1955)

Jung, Emma and Marie-Louise von Franz, *Die Graalslegend in psychologischer Sicht* (Zürich: Walter Verlag, 1960)

Kaldera, Raven, *Pagan Astrology: Spell-Casting, Love Magic, and Shamanic Stargazing* (Rochester, VT: Inner Traditions/Destiny Books, 2009)

Kelley, David H. and Eugene F. Milone, *Exploring Ancient Skies: A Survey of Ancient and Cultural Astronomy* (New York: Springer, 2011)

Kerényi, Karl, *The Gods of the Greeks*, trans. John N. Cameron (London: Thames and Hudson, 1951)

————, 'Kore', in C.G. Jung and Carl Kerényi, *Essays on a Science of Mythology: The Myth of the Divine Child and the Mysteries of Eleusis* (Princeton, NJ: Princeton University Press, 1969), pp. 101–55

Kern, Otto (ed.), *Orphicorum fragmenta* (Berlin: Weidmann, 1922)

Kieckhefer, Richard, 'The Devil's Contemplatives: The *Liber Iuratus*, the *Liber Visionum*, and Christian Appropriation of Jewish Occultism', in Fanger (ed.), *Conjuring Spirits*, pp. 250–265

Kilcher, Andreas, 'The Moses of Sinai and the Moses of Egypt: Moses as Magician in Jewish literature and Western Esotericism', *Aries* 4:2 (2004), pp. 148–70

Kingsley, Peter, *Ancient Philosophy, Mystery, and Magic: Empedocles and Pythagorean Tradition* (Oxford: Clarendon Press, 1995)

Kinsley, David, *The Goddesses' Mirror: Visions of the Divine from East to West* (Albany: SUNY Press, 1989)

Klibansky, Raymond, Erwin Panofsky, and Fritz Saxl, *Saturn and Melancholy: Studies in the History of Natural Philosophy, Religion, and Art* (New York: Basic Books, 1964)

Kline, Naomi Reed, *Maps of Medieval Thought: The Hereford Paradigm* (Woodbridge: Boydell Press, 2001)

Knight, Gareth, *Dion Fortune and the Inner Light* (Loughborough: Thoth, 2000)

Land, M.F., 'Visual Optics: The Shapes of Pupils', *Current Biology*, 16:5 (2006), pp. 167–68

Le Cenci Hamilton, Leonidas (trans.), *Ishtar and Izdubar: The Epic of Babylon* (London: W.H. Allen, 1884)

Lesses, Rebecca Macy, *Ritual Practices to Gain Power: Angels, Incantations, and Revelation in Early Jewish Mysticism* (Harrisburg, PA: Trinity Press, 1998)

Lewy, Hans, *Chaldaean Oracles and Theurgy: Mysticism, Magic, and Platonism in the Later Roman Empire* (Paris: Institut d'Études Augustiniennes, 2011 [1956])

Luck, Georg, *Arcana Mundi: Magic and the Occult in the Greek and Roman Worlds* (Baltimore, MD: Johns Hopkins University Press, 1985)

Macey, Samuel L., *Patriarchs of Time: Dualism in Saturn-Cronus, Father Time, the Watchmaker God, and Father Christmas* (Athens: University of Georgia Press, 2010)

Mann, Thomas, *Doktor Faustus: Das Leben des deutschen Tonsetzers Adrian Leverkühn, erzählt von einem Freunde* (Frankfurt: S. Fischer, 1947)

Marcovich, Miroslav, *Studies in Graeco-Roman Religions and Gnosticism* (Leiden: Brill, 1988)

Mastrocinque, Attilio, 'The Colours of Magical Gems', in Chris Entwistle and Noel Adams (eds.), *Gems of Heaven: Recent Research on Engraved Gemstones in Late Antiquity, AD 200–600* (London: British Museum, 2011), pp. 62–68.

Mather, Matthew, *The Alchemical Mercurius: Esoteric Symbol of Jung's Life and Works* (London: Routledge, 2014)

Mathers, Samuel Liddell MacGregor (ed. and trans.), *Grimoire of Armadel* (posthumously published, London: Routledge & Kegan Paul, 1980; repr. San Francisco, CA: Red Wheel/Weiser, 2001)

Matt, Daniel, 'Introduction', in Daniel Chanan Matt (ed.), *Zohar: The Book of Enlightenment* (Mahwah, NJ: Paulist Press, 1983)

McDemott, Rachel Fell and Jeffrey John Kripal (eds.), *Encountering Kali: In the Margins, at the Center, in the West* (Berkeley: University of California Press, 2003)

Meier, C.A., 'Ancient Incubation and Modern Psychotherapy', in Louise Carus Mahdi, Steven Foster, and Meredith Little (eds.), *Betwixt and Between: Patterns of Masculine and Feminine Initiation* (Peru, IL: Open Court, 1987), pp. 415–27

Michel-von-Dungern, Simone, 'Studies on Magical Amulets in the British Museum', in Chris Entwistle and Noel Adams (eds.), *Gems of Heaven: Recent Research on Engraved Gemstones in Late Antiquity, AD 200–600* (London: British Museum, 2011), pp. 82–83

Mirecki, Paul Allan, 'Basilides', in *The Anchor Bible Dictionary*, Vol. 1, p. 624

Moyer, Ian S., *Egypt and the Limits of Hellenism* (Cambridge: Cambridge University Press, 2011)

Neugebauer, Otto and H.B. van Hoesen, *Greek Horoscopes* (Philadelphia, PA: American Philosophical Society, 1987)

Noll, Richard, *The Jung Cult: Origins of a Charismatic Movement* (Princeton, NJ: Princeton University Press, 1994)

North, John D., *Stonehenge: A New Interpretation of Prehistoric Man and the Cosmos* (New York: Simon and Schuster, 1996)

Ostrowski-Sachs, Margaret, *From Conversations with C.G. Jung* (Zürich: Juris Druck & Verlag, 1971)

Ovid, *The Metamorphoses of Ovid*, trans. Allen Mandelbaum (New York: Harcourt Brace, 1995)

Page, Sophie, *Magic in Medieval Manuscripts* (London: British Library, 2004)

Pagels, Elaine, *The Gnostic Paul: Gnostic Exegesis of the Pauline Letters* (London: Continuum, 1992)

Pavitt, William Thomas and Kate Pavitt, *The Book of Talismans, Amulets and Zodiacal Gems* (London: William Rider & Son, 1922)

Peterson, Gregory R., 'Demarcation and the Scientistic Fallacy', *Zygon* 38:4 (2003), pp. 751–61

Picart, Caroline Joan S., *Thomas Mann and Friedrich Nietzsche: Eroticism, Death, Music, and Laughter* (Amsterdam: Editions Rodopi, 1999)

Picatrix, trans. John Michael Greer and Christopher Warnock (Iowa City, IA: Renaissance Astrology/Adocentyn Press, 2010)

Quispel, Gilles, 'Gnostic Man: The Gospel of Basilides', in *The Mystic Vision: Papers from the Eranos Yearbooks* (Princeton, NJ: Princeton University Press, 1968), pp. 210–46

Radnor, Karen and Eleanor Robson (eds.), *The Oxford Handbook of Cuneiform Culture* (Oxford: Oxford University Press, 2011)

Redner, Harry, *In the Beginning Was the Deed: Reflections on the Passage of Faust* (Berkeley: University of California Press, 1982)

Reichl, Anton, 'Goethes Faust und Agrippa von Nettesheim', *Euphorion* 4 (1897), pp. 287–301

Reiner, Erica and David Pingree, *Babylonian Planetary Omens* (Groningen: Styx, 1998)

Ribi, Alfred, *The Search for Roots: C.G. Jung and the Tradition of Gnosis* (Los Angeles, CA: Gnosis Archive Books, 2013)

Ritter, Helmut and Martin Plessner (eds. and trans.), '*Picatrix': Das Ziel des Weisen von Pseudo-Magriti* (London: Warburg Institute, 1962)

Robbins, Frank, 'A New Astrological Treatise: Michigan Papyrus No. 1', *Classical Philology* 22:1 (1927), p. 14

Rodov, Ilia M., *The Torah Ark in Renaissance Poland: A Jewish Revival of Classical Antiquity* (Leiden: Brill, 2013)

Rolf, Eugene, *Encounter with Jung* (Boston: Sigo Press, 1989)

Rosenfield, John M., *The Dynastic Art of the Kushans* (Berkeley: University of California Press, 1967)

Rossi, Safron, 'Saturn in C.G. Jung's Liber Primus: An Astrological Meditation', *Jung Journal* 9:4 (2015), pp. 38–57

Rowland, Susan, *Jung: A Feminist Revision* (Cambridge: Polity Press, 2002)

Rudhyar, Dane, 'Carl Jung's Birthchart', at www.mindfire.ca/Astrology and The Modern Psyche/Chapter Six - Carl Jung's Birthchart.htm>, originally published in Dane Rudhyar, *Astrology and the Modern Psyche* (Sebastopol, CA: CRCS, 1976)

Russo, Joseph, 'A Jungian Analysis of Homer's Odysseus', in Polly Young-Eisendrath and Terence Dawson (eds.), *The Cambridge Companion to Jung* (Cambridge: Cambridge University Press, 2008), pp. 253–68

Sasportas, Howard, 'The Astrology and Psychology of Aggression', in Liz Greene and Howard Sasportas, *Dynamics of the Unconscious* (York Beach, ME: Samuel Weiser, 1988), pp. 1–74

Schaeffer, B.E., 'Lunar Visibility and the Crucifixion', *Quarterly Journal of the Royal Astronomical Society* 31:1 (1990), pp. 52–67

Schäfer, Peter, *The Hidden and Manifest God: Some Major Themes in Early Jewish Mysticism*, trans. Aubrey Pomerance (Albany: SUNY Press, 1992)

Scholem, Gershom, *Origins of the Kabbalah*, ed. R.J. Zwi Werblowsky, trans. Allan Arkush (Princeton, NJ: Princeton University Press, 1987; originally published in German as *Ursprung und Anfänge der Kabbala*, Berlin: Walter de Gruyter, 1962)

———, *On the Kabbalah and Its Symbolism*, trans. Ralph Mannheim (New York: Schocken Books, 1965)

———, *Kabbalah* (New York: Keter Publishing House, 1974)

———, *On the Mystical Shape of the Godhead: Basic Concepts in the Kabbalah*, trans. Joachim Neugroschel (New York: Schocken Books, 1991)

Schwartz-Salant, Nathan, *The Mystery of Human Relationship: Alchemy and the Transformation of the Self* (London: Routledge, 2003)

Secret, François, 'Sur quelques traductions du Sefer Raziel', *REJ* 128 (1969), pp. 223–45

Segal, Robert A. (ed.), *The Gnostic Jung* (Princeton, NJ: Princeton University Press, 1992)

Seznec, Jean, *The Survival of the Pagan Gods: The Mythological Tradition and Its Place in Renaissance Humanism and Art*, trans. Barbara F. Sessions (New York: Pantheon, 1953)

Shamdasani, Sonu, 'Introduction', in C.G. Jung, *The Red Book: Liber Novus*, ed. Sonu Shamdasani, trans. Mark Kyburz, John Peck, and Sonu Shamdasani (New York/London: W.W. Norton, 2009)

———, 'Who Is Jung's Philemon? Unpublished Letter to Alice', *Jung History* 2:2 (2011), <www.philemonfoundation.org/resources/jung_history/volume_2_issue_2>

———, *C.G. Jung: A Biography in Books* (New York: W.W. Norton, 2012)

Sharman-Burke, Juliet, *Understanding the Tarot: A Personal Teaching Guide* (London: Eddison/Sadd, 1998)

Shaw, Gregory, *Theurgy and the Soul: The Neoplatonism of Iamblichus* (University Park: Penn State University Press, 1995)

Smith, H.S. and H.M. Stewart, 'The Gurob Shrine Papyrus', *Journal of Egyptian Archaeology* 70 (1984), pp. 54–64

Smith, Robert C., *The Wounded Jung: Effects of Jung's Relationships on His Life and Work* (Evanston, IL: Northwestern University Press, 1997)

Sperling, Harry and Maurice Simon (trans.), *The Zohar*, 5 volumes (London: Soncino Press, 1931–34)

Spring, Elizabeth, 'Obama's Astrological Chart; Jung's Astrological Chart' (12 November 2008), at <http://northnodeastrology.blogspot.co.uk/2008/11/obamas-astrological-chart-jungs.html>

Stein, Diane, *The Women's Book of Healing* (New York: Random House, 2011)

Stein, Murray, 'Critical Notice: *The Red Book*', *Journal of Analytical Psychology* 55 (2010), pp. 423–25

———, 'What Is *The Red Book* for Analytical Psychology?', *Journal of Analytical Psychology* 56 (2011), pp. 590–606

Stein, Murray and Paul Brutsche, *Window of the Soul: The Red Book Images of Carl Jung*, Asheville Jung Center, Asheville, North Carolina, web-based seminar (10 May 2012)

Stenring, Knut (trans.), *The Book of Formation (Sepher Yetzirah) by Rabbi Akiba ben Joseph* (New York: Ktav Publishing House, 1923)

Stern, Allen and Jaqueline Mitton, *Pluto and Charon: Ice Worlds on the Ragged Edge of the Solar System* (New York: John Wiley and Sons, 1998)

Swartz, Michael D., *Scholastic Magic: Ritual and Revelation in Early Jewish Mysticism* (Princeton, NJ: Princeton University Press, 1996)

Theodorakis, Michael G., 'Apollo of the Wolf, the Mouse and the Serpent', *Kronos* 9:3 (1984), pp. 12–19

Tick, Edward, *The Practice of Dream Healing: Bringing Ancient Greek Mysteries Into Modern Medicine* (Wheaton, IL: Theosophical Publishing House, 2001)

Torijano, Pablo A., *Solomon the Esoteric King: From King to Magus, Development of a Tradition* (Leiden: Brill, 2002)

Trachtenberg, Joshua, *The Devil and the Jews: The Medieval Conception of the Jew and Its Relation to Modern Antisemitism* (New Haven, CT: Yale University Press, 1943)

_____, *The Origins of the Mithraic Mysteries: Cosmology and Salvation in the Ancient World* (Oxford: Oxford University Press, 1991)

Ulansey, David, 'Mithras and the Hypercosmic Sun', in John R. Hinnells (ed.), *Studies in Mithraism* (Rome: L'Erma' di Brettschneider, 1994), pp. 257–64

Van den Broek, Roelof, 'The Creation of Adam's Psychic Body in the *Apocryphon of John*', in Roelof Van den Broek and M.J. Vermaseren (eds.), *Studies in Gnosticism and Hellenistic Religions* (Leiden: Brill, 1981), pp. 38–57

Van der Laan, J.M., *Seeking Meaning for Goethe's Faust* (London: Continuum, 2007)

Von Franz, Marie-Louise, *The Feminine in Fairy Tales* (Putnam, CT: Spring, 1972)

Von Glinski, Marie Louise, *Simile and Identity in Ovid's Metamorphosis* (Cambridge: Cambridge University Press, 2012)

Walker, C.B.F., *Cuneiform* (Berkeley: University of California Press, 1987)

Wehr, Demaris S., *Jung and Feminism: Liberating Archetypes* (Boston, MA: Beacon Press, 1989)

Wehr, Gerhard, *An Illustrated Biography of Jung*, trans. M. Kohn (Boston: Shambhala, 1989)

Werblowsky, R.J. Zvi, *Joseph Karo: Lawyer and Mystic* (Philadelphia, PA: Jewish Publication Society of America/Oxford University Press, 1977)

West, M.L., *The Orphic Poems* (Oxford: Oxford University Press, 1983)

White, Gavin, *Babylonian Star-Lore: An Illustrated Guide to the Star-Lore and Constellations of Ancient Babylonia* (London: Solaria, 2008)

Wili, Walter, 'The Orphic Mysteries and the Greek Spirit', in Joseph Campbell (ed.), *The Mysteries: Papers from the Eranos Yearbooks* (Princeton, NJ: Princeton University Press, 1955), pp. 64–92

Wolfson, Elliot R., *Through a Speculum That Shines: Vision and Imagination in Medieval Jewish Mysticism* (Princeton, NJ: Princeton University Press, 1997)

_____, 'Beyond the Spoken Word: Oral Tradition and Written Transmission in Medieval Jewish Mysticism', in Yaakov Elmon and Israel Gershoni (eds.), *Transmitting Jewish Traditions: Orality, Textuality, and Cultural Diffusion* (New Haven, CT: Yale University Press, 2000), pp. 167–224

Wroth, Warwick William, 'A Statue of the Youthful Asklepios: Telesphoros at Dionysopolis', *Journal of Hellenic Studies* 3 (1882), pp. 283–300

Yates, Frances A., *The Occult Philosophy in the Elizabethan Age* (London: Routledge & Kegan Paul, 1979)

Zambelli, Paola, *White Magic, Black Magic in the European Renaissance: From Ficino, Pico, Della Porta to Trithemius, Agrippa, Bruno* (Leiden: Brill, 2007)

Websites

http://faculty.indwes.edu/bcupp/solarsys/Names.htm
http://gemstonemeanings.us/black-onyx-meaning/
http://lucite.org/lucite/archive/abdiel/liber_juratus.pdf

http://marygreer.wordpress.com/2008/04/18/carl-jung-on-the-major-arcana/
http:planetarynames.wr.usgs.gov
www.celtnet.org.uk/gods_c/cocidius.html
www.jewelinfo4u.com/Black_Onyx.aspx#sthash.LfzMTVsO.dpbs
www.jewelrynotes.com/heres-what-you-should-know-about-onyx/
www.tairis.co.uk/index.php?option=com_content&view=article&id=125:the-dagda-part-1
&catid=45:gods&Itemid=8

INDEX

Page numbers in italic indicate a figure on the corresponding page.

9781138289161